I COULD

DIE AT ANY

MOMENT

I Could Die at Any Moment is published under Catharsis, a sectionalized division under Di Angelo Publications, Inc.

CATHARSIS

Catharsis is an imprint of Di Angelo Publications.

Di Angelo Publications
4209 Santa Monica Blvd, #200
Los Angeles, California

Library of Congress
I Could Die at Any Moment
ISBN: 978-1-955690-59-1
Paperback

Words: Greg Hill
Cover Design: Savina Mayeur
Interior Design: Kimberly James
Editors: Matt Samet, Willy Rowberry

Downloadable via www.dapbooks.shop and other e-book retailers.

For educational, business, and bulk orders, contact distribution@diangelopublications.com.

1. Biography & Autobiography --- Adventurers & Explorers
2. Sports & Recreation --- Extreme Sports
3. Sports & Recreation --- Mountaineering

I COULD DIE AT ANY MOMENT

GREG HILL

DAP BOOKS

DI ANGELO PUBLICATIONS

Contents

INTRODUCTION

A couple of deep breaths . . . in . . . out . . . in . . . out . . .

I need to start, but I am fearful of the repercussions of putting pen to paper. Giving this idea form makes it a reality — this notion that you, my children, my family, my friends, will be reading this book once I'm gone. I certainly hope that my death will occur once I'm old and that it will be of natural causes, but the harsh truth is that this probably won't be the case. When you push as hard as I do, adventuring in the mountains, death is an ever-present specter.

Since you are reading this, I should start with, "I am sorry — absolutely heart-stoppingly sorry." I know that you must be mad, hurt, and wondering why I'm gone. There are no words I can say that will comfort you . . . but I'll try to explain.

By nature, I am an adventurer, a risk-taker, and a lover of life on the edge. I can say that this is who I am and will forever be; this is built into my unchangeable DNA.

I worry that if I die on some adventure, whether skiing a steep face, climbing a narrow ridge, or searching for the next thrill, you will never really understand why I couldn't stop. I fear that you will never "get" why I needed to live the way I have. This story is my way of sharing the great life I have led, and hopefully, it will clarify why

I could choose no other path but this one. I have witnessed what happens when a massive avalanche sweeps down a Himalayan peak, catching thirty people off guard, sleeping in their tents. I listened to their frantic screams echoing in the darkness as they searched for their friends and lost tentmates. I watched as some of their souls left their bodies lying in the snow at 20,000 feet on some pointless objective in the mountains. I have been filled with overconfidence and made huge decision-making errors — I once looked over my shoulder and spied an avalanche chasing me down an alpine slope, eventually swallowing me. My mouth filled with snow as I tumbled downhill over and over for thousands of feet, wondering if these were my last moments and whether it had all been worth it. And yet, and yet, and yet, I go back to the mountains — time and time again.

Most likely, I have worried you endlessly over the years, like when you received calls from me after my body was broken in the mountains of Pakistan or when I rushed to make a satellite call after the disaster on the Himalayan giant Manaslu, before the media splashed the garish details all over the internet. Yet I also hope that my buoyant energy after an endurance marathon in the mountains or my excitement after an adventure has inspired you to live the life you yearn for, for yourself.

In some ways, it is easier to be vulnerable and write this believing that I won't be around when you read it. Our society props up successes and shuns failures, but so much can be learned from failure — from either making the "wrong" decision but surviving or from making the "right" decision and trying your very hardest, but still failing to meet the goal. This much I have learned in the mountains.

Like any lifelong adventurer (I'm forty-seven as I write these words), I have made thousands of great decisions and some poor ones. Many of those bad decisions still turned out well, but a couple came close to ending me. You might be surprised that I am 100 percent okay with that. It's not that I want to die — no fucking way! On the contrary, I want to live as long as possible. Life is so incredible — especially on the edge!

There is something call the Mountaineer's Pact, but maybe it should more generally be the Adventurer's Pact. This pact is the complete — and necessary — acceptance that the dangers and unknown factors that lurk in the wild could lead to injury and death. We all like to think that we're invincible, and that accidents only happen to others, not ourselves. And we tend to believe that we will make all the right decisions. But this is pure ignorance: avalanches do not recognize experience, and tumbling rocks don't go around people who make only the right choices. Miscalculations happen. Accidents happen. Death happens.

Looking into the eyes of some of my fellow climbers as they perished on Manaslu in 2012, I wondered if they knew the risks or understood the realities of adventure. Had they made the pact, or had they blissfully, obliviously set off up this hazardous Nepalese mountain, assuming the guides would keep them safe?

On the other hand offsetting this harsh reality are those countless perfect moments: the priceless seconds of watching pink morning light illuminate the summits, spying shadows as they play across pristine snowy slopes, and those incredibly calm moments sitting on a summit with all the challenges of the climb behind you. There is so much given to the adventurer, immeasurable rewards for being willing to challenge oneself, to take risks and push into the unknown.

The lessons I have learned have forged me into who I am. The confidence I gained getting good at rock climbing in my teens solidified my character and helped me overcome my insecurities. Being adventurous taught me the wonder of the world. To savor life. To challenge my fears and see where I'd end up.

Right now, fear is my biggest tormentor — not in the mountains, but as I sit at my desk, trying to find the right words to tell this story. This isn't about pushing my body higher and further than I ever have. This isn't about having a calm mind as I ski down a mountainside rimmed with cliffs. It's not about trying to stay relaxed as I walk a ridge that falls away thousands of feet on either side. Writing this book is scarier than all of that — I want this to be my honest legacy. What stories or insights can I give my kids that will empower them to lead a better life than my own? Which of my failures should I focus on? What happens if my story is, well, boring?

Okay, a few more breaths, in through the nose and out through the mouth. In . . . out . . . in . . . out . . . Breath by breath, step by step, this is how we accomplish our goals and how we create our stories.

CHAPTER ONE

THE HERO SYNDROME

*"Happiness for me is found in breathing hard and living life
as loud as possible. I need and crave intense moments. All
other thoughts and worries become secondary when I have to
concentrate fully on the challenge at hand."*
— *Excerpt from letters to my family*

December 19, 1975: The power had gone out earlier in the night, and the clear skies let the night air cool to -40 degrees. Still, Deane Hill lay comfortable in the warm bath at our home in the remote wilderness of Quebec, near the town of Sutton in the Canadian Appalachians

The contractions were coming faster now, a pressure on her lower abdomen that increased with each volley. She let my father, Derek Hill, know that I was ready to come out, and he drove off to get the neighbor to watch over my older brother, Graham (five); and my twin sisters, Natalie and Christy (three). Recalls my mother, "I can distinctly remember the sound of the frozen tires on the road, a hard, whirring sound as the hard rubber strained to grip the icy surface. Thirty minutes later, I was ushered into the hospital and, like . . . boom . . . I gave birth."

I was born jaundiced and a little sickly looking, but otherwise a healthy baby, weighing around seven pounds.

My parents were high school sweethearts who started dating at fourteen years of age. My dad, who was always very driven, got his pilot's license at sixteen, and at eighteen became Air Canada's youngest commercial pilot. My mom also worked in aviation, as a stewardess for an executive airline. Graham was born when my parents were twenty-one; he was quickly followed by Natalie and Christy the following year. Four years later, I came along, the baby of the bunch.

By the time I was three, my parents' relationship was falling apart; they soon divorced, and my father began seeing a woman named Betsy, who would later become my stepmother. Betsy and her two young sons, Jeremy and Adrian, moved in with us when I was five. Betsy was a long-haired, bell-bottom-wearing, smiley preschool teacher. Jeremy at eight years old was stout in a slightly tubby way, and he towered threateningly over me, whereas Adrian was just three months older and felt like someone I would become friends with.

Now I found myself the youngest in a family of six kids, though I spent half my time at my mom's, where it was just us four kids plus her. Being the youngest in such a large family changes a person in strange ways. We were always on the go, and little me would get lost in the chaos; I started to internalize my feelings and not share much, because it seemed like no one would care anyway — not for a lack of empathy, but for a lack of time and energy.

This is pure conjecture, but I believe I started to do wild things to be noticed — to feel important. Every time I entered a room, I would say, "Hi," even if I had just left a few minutes before. Then I realized that if I climbed to the top of a tree and hung off a branch, people would notice me even more. If they noticed me, that meant I was one step closer to being accepted. Being accepted felt very important — my need to be a part of something was growing.

Sutton, Québec, was an ideal place to grow up: both of my parents' houses were surrounded by deciduous forests, and our neighbors were well out of sight. My dad's place was an amazing log home that he and my mom had built together, deconstructing two 100-year-old og barns in Ontario and transporting the lumber to Sutton, then rebuilding it like a Lego set. Out front, they dug a large pond that was stream-fed and built a barn for some horses. We had a few Canadian geese and a golden retriever. It really was an idyllic eastern Canadian property — the perfect place for all of us kids to run wild, even if my older siblings were always pulling pranks on me.

One day, when I was six, we kids were all out in the barn doing chores, when Graham picked up a dried piece of horse poo. He looked at all of us and pretended to take a big bite.

"Hmmm, it's actually pretty good! Greg, you should try some," Graham said.

The dung had a perfect bite-sized piece missing.

"Okay," I said. I wanted nothing more than the approval of my older siblings. They all looked down at me, waiting.

"C'mon, Greg," someone said.

"Yeah, do it, Greg," said someone else.

I picked up the dung and took a solid bite. It was dry and crunchy, with a seedy, slightly nutty taste.

Through my full mouth, I said, "You're right — it's not bad!" But my siblings couldn't contain themselves and burst out laughing. They'd tricked me once again! I spit out everything in my mouth and reddened with shame. What was it about me that made me so unworthy, I wondered. And what would I need to do to get my siblings to love and accept me? Self-doubt was always amplifying the fears in my head.

I have always been a lover, wanting and searching for love. I was an anxious little boy in kindergarten, and this discomfort permeated my body and expressed itself as warts, lots of warts, like a few on my toes, a few on my feet, and some on my knees, elbows, and hands. At one point, I counted fifty-one warts — imagine that. Not only were the warts unsightly, but they made me visibly very different from the other kids. To pound a nail deeper into my shame, there was a rule that we had to hold hands while we walked between classes. I distinctly remember hearing, "I don't want to hold hands with Greg — he has warts all over them! That's gross!" Though it was an uncomfortable time, one girl in my class, Marie-Claude, would accept me, warts and all. We held hands between classes then became a "couple" for the next three years, sneaking little kisses behind the snowbank, with me giving her gifts each Valentine's Day.

After we tried all sorts of wart remedies, including having a doctor freeze them off, my mom brought me to Mr. Miltimore, a local farmer. While I sat in his barn, Mr. Miltimore held my hands and looked at them from all sorts of angles. Finally, he spat on his own hand and rubbed it into my warts. That was possibly why they disappeared; I like to think Mr. Miltimore's kindness had finally helped me feel less anxious.

One way I've sought acceptance over the years is by becoming proficient at something to the point where people recognize that I am good. More importantly, where I feel good enough. The power of knowing you have skill at something builds self-confidence and personal happiness. By "good," I suppose I mean better than average, and as shitty as that sounds, comparing myself to others has helped me determine where I am and where I need to get to. I don't really need to be the best — just one of the better ones. People applauding for me is them expressing their acceptance of me.

Approval has always been a drug for me, validating my worth. In class, when the teachers would ask a question, I always enjoyed being quicker than most and trying to say the right answer. Getting it right would make me feel worthwhile; getting it wrong would redden me with shame.

It's amazing how quickly one can swing from happy moments to deep despair. My anxious thoughts were like that: I would feel great, laughing with my friends over some joke, and then I would say something that my inner Greg would immediately latch onto and worry about. Feeling stupid, I would then doubt everything. Thoughts are lightning quick and can swing my mind so rapidly.

In third grade, I entered my first running race, a three-mile fun run near Cowansville, Quebec. I had never really raced apart from the smaller ones we did in gym class, and the excitement I felt at the starting line was unforgettable. I was so energized that I ran way too fast at the beginning, trying to keep up with the older, bigger kids. Eventually, the lack of oxygen made me slow down, but I continued to dig deep and to push myself.

A voice appeared in my head.

"Come on, Greg, you've got this!" urged the voice. "Slow a bit and recover. Drive those knees. See that person — wear them down; catch up to them. Doesn't passing them feel good?"

Between breaths, the deep and powerful voice urged me on: Come on . . . come on . . .

This voice, which I've since come to dub my "inner coach," began his lifelong career that day, being as supportive and as mean as he needed to. I desperately wanted to do well in this footrace so that everyone could see that I was worth paying attention to. I breathed hard, accessed all my reserves of strength, and pushed myself right to the end, crossing the finish line red-faced, breathless, and drenched in sweat. Thrilled with my third-place finish in the elementary-school category, I staggered to the side of the parking lot and threw up in the bushes.

We were an outdoorsy family in general, but we really shined as a skiing family. Sutton had an incredible ski hill, conveniently named Mount Sutton. Though small compared to the mountains I graduated to later, the hill had its challenges: steep little shots, glades to ski through, and seven chairlifts to keep you constantly thrilled. I was immediately hooked on skiing, that unbridled feeling of sliding down snow, like the thrilling moments you get tobogganing, but with total control. I began to crave that intimate interaction between gravity, speed, and terrain, interpreted through my body as I attempted to flow over the snow, maximizing the feeling of falling. Skiing was a sport full of wonder.

I started ski racing at age ten and would go skiing all day Saturdays and Sundays. It was my first real departure from having a parent around all the time, and it was always fun, even though I wasn't particularly good at it. Better yet, cute girls from Montreal regularly spent their weekends skiing at Mount-Sutton, a big allure for preteen me.

Skiing for me has always captured the feeling of freedom. It's as close to flying as we can get (ignoring BASE jumping and wingsuit flying!). You can go as fast as your courage allows, letting the fresh, cold air flow by your face and into your lungs, supercharging your breathing. It's intoxicating to court tremendous speed yet remain in control on steep, snowy slopes, letting the skis slide faster and faster. Your senses are tuned into the metal edges, feeling them track through the snow, bending through the turns, snapping back up and propelling you into the next turn. Exhilarated from the run, you join your friends and ride back up, chatting about where to go next. Then you follow each other, whooping and hollering, hitting jumps and flying alongside each other through the air. Skiing creates camaraderie; you build an amazing connection with the friends whom you spend days with on chairlifts, on the slopes, and in the lodge.

There is also a feeling of letting go while remaining present, with no social insecurities or pressing life issues weighing you down. On my skis, I couldn't get mad at myself for saying something wrong or for misjudging a social scene. It's about paying attention to the moment, to your skis sliding on the snow, and staying alert for the upcoming pitches. With focused attention, you make decisions on where to turn, jump, slide, or stop. If you are not 100 percent present, you might crash.

This feeling of freedom is intoxicating, so much so that I would often skip school and go skiing with my parents on powder days. Those days of riding up Chair Four at Sutton, eating nuts and dried fruit and skiing with my mom are imprinted in my memory. I also loved chasing my dad down the glades, his boots touching each other as he parallel-turned elegantly in front of me. Honestly, the feeling of skiing is so closely linked with skipping school that, to this day when I ski, I feel like I'm playing hooky.

Dealing with older brothers, I quickly learned to be agile and adaptive. Jeremy was a classic stepbrother, cutting me zero slack and picking on me and his younger brother, Adrian, to show his dominance. There was a time he nailed me in the face with a roundhouse kick, his random shoulder punches, and his throwing darts at us as we ran away from him. Yet, Jeremy also taught me to anticipate things and run fast when all else fails, skills that would come in handy later in the mountains.

For years, I assumed we were poor people living in the countryside, but I later realized that we were very privileged — in fact, pretty much the definition of white privilege, with all the comforts and amazing opportunities.

My dad has always been supportive of me and my siblings, but he's also a very driven man; he likes being busy, endlessly working and rarely relaxing. Typically, he will wear a pair of ripped jeans and a straw hat on his head, his skin deeply bronzed from being outside. His strong and gnarled hands are always working on something. He imposed a serious work ethic on all his children, ensuring we worked for everything we got — we were deserving if we earned it. If we stacked wood all day, we earned a beer. And at ten years old, a beer s a big deal — a big deal because it takes all week to finish it. If we wanted a mountain bike, it wasn't free; we had to save up half the cost and then my dad would pay for the other half. These were constants, whether he was buying and developing land (when he wasn't flying planes), building houses, selling them, making money, or being frugal with what he had. I have embraced many of his qualities, save frugality. My father was also constantly dreaming up his next scheme, buying his next sailboat or developing his next piece of property. He instilled in me the idea that we can work hard and achieve our dreams, and we can learn and build things that are initially beyond us by applying hard work and dedication.

One of the more pivotal things he ever did was reading "The Lord of the Rings" to us children. When I was five, every night that

I was sleeping at his house, my dad would read to us from J. R. R. Tolkien's books. As a young dreamer, I was transported along on Frodo's epic journey. Our father's voice would carry us to Middle Earth and the challenges the tiny Hobbits faced. Their lives seemed so much more meaningful than the life of an average human, as they fought through peril after peril. The relationships between the characters, their unconditional acceptance of each other — this connection was what I yearned for.

I remember heading out into the woods behind our house, looking for my own quests and dragons to slay. Building my own weapons from branches in the forest, I would wander around fighting fictitious beasts, flinging nun-chucks at trees and building forts to protect against enemies. Thus began my search for my inner hero's journey in my book of my life. It was my first immersion in the hero syndrome, which the psychologist Carl Jung described as "a phenomenon affecting people who seek heroism or recognition, usually by creating a desperate situation which they can resolve."

Desperate situations . . . there would be a lot of those in the decades that followed. I have probably always been a mama's boy, but the label was solidified as I watched her deal with being a single mom trying to make ends meet. As her youngest, I was the one that needed her the most, and I always felt that she needed me, too. I grew up in two very different families: my mom's vegetarian house and my dad's a meat-eating one. My dad's home was wealthier, with luxuries like computers, while the other was supported by a single working mom with lesser financial means.

My mom raised us with compassion and patience. Her way was calm, and I especially wanted to be a good son for her. She worked as a real estate agent, and despite her limited finances she showed me that first and foremost, it's your attitude that dictates your life — and attitude is something we can all control.

While penning this memoir, I wanted to include all sorts of stories that show how my character developed, my narcissism making me believe that these childhood stories would be interesting to readers. It was an idyllic life — sometimes turbulent, with the divorce and me wanting to keep everyone happy, but overall my younger life was great. We really are the sum of all the people we meet melded with the life we have lived and seen through the lens of who we are. I do know I was influenced by my stepfather, Bob, who was a part of my life from age five to fourteen, his influence being mostly about soul-searching and finding the true you. Belief in myself would in fact become very important to me.

Chapter Two

THE REALITIES OF RISK

*"Any wisdom that I would like to give you in life can be learned
through my adventures."*
— Excerpt from letters to my family

In the fall of 1987, my stepmother, Betsy, gave birth to a blonde baby girl named Jesse. At age eleven, I was perfectly positioned to help out, and I grew fond of my new little sister. it's a fondness that has only grown over the years.

My dad has always had big dreams, one of which was owning a sailboat and perhaps sailing it around the world. He had grown up sailing on the Saint Lawrence River near Montreal and always dreamed of more. In 1988, when I was in eighth grade, he bought a forty-eight-foot sailboat named Nid Ami in the British Virgin Islands; the plan was to fly down to pick the boat up and then sail back up along the Eastern Seaboard. My sister Natalie and I would join Dad, as well as Betsy, Jesse, and Betsy's friend Lorraine. As we sailed, we stopped to visit perfect sandy beaches, to snorkel amongst incredible corals, and to eat delectable street food on the islands.

Eventually, we began a five-day crossing from the British Virgin Islands to the Bahamas. It was my first open-water crossing. I was excited as I watched the islands disappear from view, and was mesmerized by the vast emptiness of the Caribbean. Then, the boredom crept in; for days, there was nothing to do except read fantasy novels and nothing to see except huge, rolling waves, flying fish, and enormous starry skies. There was only the rhythmic tranquility of the boat slicing through the water, moved by the winds. After five days, we reached San Salvador Island, which local lore pegged as the first place Christopher Columbus had landed in the New World. Here, we brought Natalie to shore and put her in a taxi to the local airport, as she needed to fly home to work. I was envious; I was bored with inactivity and ready to leave. It was a classic case of adolescent angst, living what would be a dream for most people and yet too privileged to realize what a gift this was, all the while wanting to do something else.

With Natalie gone, I was more listless than ever, so I sought ways to entertain myself. One afternoon, as I lay on the deck reading, I found myself staring up at the mast, which stood about thirty-five feet tall. At the twenty-five-foot mark, horizontal metal bars spread the support wires away from the mast. I had already climbed up several times and loved the feeling of being up in the crow's nest, taking in the commanding views across the open ocean. I imagined standing on these spreaders, holding onto the wires, and then leaping into the sea from the perch — a thirty-foot jump! This seemed way more entertaining than the book I was reading, and I began to give the idea serious consideration. I had jumped off bigger cliffs before, though the logistics here were trickier. I would need to hold onto the wires and push off and away from the mast with my feet to clear the deck, or else risk splatting into it from twenty-five feet. Each time I pictured myself making the jump, my heart sped up and I'd get a surge of adrenaline — a delicious drip.

"Hey, Dad, do you think I could jump from the spreaders into the water?" I asked my father, who was wiping a nearby hatch with a soapy sponge.

"Why not? Let's do it!" he said. One of dad's summertime activities has always been jumping off cliffs; he still does it even now, in his seventies. So naturally, this proposition interested him. A need for adrenaline has run in our family for generations. My dad's father was a daring officer in World War II, where he bravely led the charge into flying bullets. Dad, too, has always had a need for challenge, from his days competing in motorcycle trials, to sailing ice boats on the frozen rivers, to skiing endless runs at Mount Sutton.

My father and I climbed the ladder to the spreaders, with me in front, working slowly up the rungs. I was surprised by how much the small waves made the mast sway. What was tiny and inconsequential down on the deck grew in amplitude with each foot we climbed higher. By the top, my heart was pounding loudly in my ears. The drip of adrenaline was almost nonstop.

Standing up on the spreaders, I caught my breath and assessed the jump. Now that I was planning on going for it, the ocean looked much farther away, its surface an unforgiving blue-green plateau broken only by the wavelets. Up this high, the mast swayed five feet side to side, the six-inch waves amplified by the twenty-five-foot climb.

"Dad, you first," I said, my voice dry with fear.

"It was your idea, Greg," he said matter-of-factly. He did have a point.

I eked my way out slowly to the end of the spreaders, with Betsy and Lorraine gathering below to watch, suddenly looking like miniature versions of themselves. I tried to slow my heartbeat and focus on the jump, estimating my timing, trying to sync up my launch with the rocking of the boat. There was a fifteen-second pause between each wave, but then the mast's change in the direction was sudden. I would wait until it was leaning out so that the jump would be almost straight down to the sea. The mast tipped away from and then swayed back toward me. I readied myself to jump.

I took a couple of deep, calming breaths.

"Come on, Greg," I urged myself. "You can do this." I anchored my toes in for a good push-off just as the mast tipped my way. Looking straight into the water, I pushed off and jumped. Just then, the mast moved away from me, and I got zero leverage for my jump. Instead of looking at a nice, splash-down landing in the sea, I was looking straight at the white fiberglass surface of the deck. Suspended momentarily in midair, I could not decide what to do; fear and doubt coursed through my body. I needed to either commit to the jump fully and hope I didn't smash into the deck or find a way to extricate myself. Self-preservation kicked in.

I reached back desperately for the guywires, but there was

nothing but woven metal strands to grab — really nothing for my fingers to lock on to — and I started to fall. I struggled my hardest to hold the guywires with my left hand, with the goal of guiding my hand down toward the spreaders, where I hoped I could stop my fall by grabbing the aluminum bar. That slipped through my fingers, too. I realized then that I couldn't stop my fall, but could only guide it with my left hand on the guywires and try to land upright.

Twenty-five feet later, I crashed onto the deck, taking the impact with my feet and legs. As I straightened back up, I looked just ten inches to the left, to the gaping maw of the kitchen hatch. Had I landed there, I would have plummeted through the hole and likely sheared my arms off at the shoulders. Betsy ran over to check on me.

"Are you okay?" she asked.

I assessed my numbed body; I was walking, moving, and talking. Somehow, I had gotten away unscathed.

Stumbling toward her, I said, "I'm okay."

But then my eyes darted to my left hand, the one with which I'd grabbed the guywires. It had rammed into the V where the wires came together through the spreader. My palm was red with blood where the skin had been worn off, and my first three fingers had a deep, bloody groove in them. And my pinky was . . . missing, just a white shard of bone left sticking out of my hand, the skin peeled back to reveal the first knuckle.

"Holy fuck, goddam, what the fuck!" I cried. For the first time ever, I'd sworn loudly and uncontrollably in front of my parents. "I tore my goddamn finger off!!!"

My dad looked down from the mast, then sprinted down the ladder to my side. Fortunately, Lorraine was a nurse, and she reacted quickly by getting the first-aid kit, wrapping my hand to stop the bleeding, and giving me Tylenol to deal with the pain.

After the initial shock, I was surprisingly calm and clear. I watched my dad climb back up to retrieve my finger, which had lodged tightly in the V of the wires. The tiny digit, or what was left of it, was placed in a bag with ice. I remember looking at it, feeling detached — emotionally as well as physically. It was a tiny upper pinky finger with two long and twisted tendons sticking out of it, a former part of me that now looked like it belonged to nobody.

On shore on San Salvador Island there was only a small infirmary, which took us an hour to reach. I remember lying on the sheet in the white-walled room, crying uncontrollably. I was overcome with how close I had been to dying and how my inability to fully commit to the jump had made me fail. I was not invincible after all. The satisfying taste of adrenaline had become like delicious nectar to a hummingbird. I knew I was going to walk the line of adventure the rest of my life, so how could I remember the message here and commit completely to my endeavors in the future?

Had I really understood the dangers and had I been willing to accept this outcome? The idea of the Adventurer's Pact started to percolate in my head. These thrills, these wild activities, have a flip side, and I had to be ready to accept it.

Eventually, we realized that the best course of action would be to fly to Miami to get quality medical attention and possibly reattach my finger. Betsy and I flew there together in a four-seater Beaver, dodging massive Caribbean thunderstorms, with me still in a state of shock, while my dad and Lorraine stayed behind with the boat.

Within hours, I had countless doctors coming in to see me; in much better spirits now, I almost gleefully recounted my story, showing off the finger in the bag. It was determined that there were two options: Option one was to reattach the finger, but since my tendons had been torn out of my forearm, I would be unable to move it. Option two was to cut the bone shorter and reattach the skin over this nub. It seemed pointless to have a finger that did not move, so I chose the latter.

After March break ended, I returned to school, a novelty amongst the 2,000 or so kids at Massey-Vanier High School; no one else had jumped from a mast and ripped their finger off. My hand was bandaged, and my arm was in a sling for the first week. I felt like a hero returning battle-scarred from some epic quest; I enjoyed the notoriety, repeatedly telling my story to the kids who stopped me in the hall. Soon, however, the reality of having a hand that didn't look normal set in. With the sling off and no bandage, you could very clearly see that there was no finger but instead a small bench, and then the palm rolled over and down to my wrist. Initially, a large scar was scabbed up and showed where the doctors had stitched the skin.

I didn't know how long it would take to accept my amputation, and I worried that I would forever be self-conscious of my less-than-perfect hand. I struggled with the consequences of my actions. So many "if only's" ran through my head. Perhaps if I had studied the risks a little more and then had fully committed once I jumped. Or perhaps if I'd pushed less horizontally off the mast and instead propelled myself upward and outward. In the end, these were just pointless mental gymnastics. Really, I had no one to blame but myself. I had to learn acceptance.

I was hard on myself and on my new look, a situation only worsened by the girls who passed me in the hallways, pointed, and said, "Look at your freaky hand." I soon learned to hide it by keeping my left hand in my pocket or always out of view. There are not a lot of issues that arise from not having a pinky; it's hard to form a perfect cup and drink water, but other than that, it is really a cosmetic thing — though a very obvious cosmetic thing. Whenever I met new people, I would have to tell them the story, and it grew tiresome. And the words of those girls have echoed in my insecurities forever.

I knew that I wanted to find the perfect partner, the love of my life. And I was suddenly less than perfect. Whenever I held a girl's hand from then on, I could feel the imperfect stump and the grossness the girls had talked about. I didn't want to be gross; I wanted to be an ideal partner for someone, their perfect complement. Instead, I was a nine-fingered freak. It's amazing how hard we can be on ourselves — the deep self-recrimination, the deep feelings of disgust we can harbor for ourselves. Fortunately, my deep sense of optimism and wonder at all that life has to offer have kept me positive in all aspects of my life, and allowed me to accept this scar of failure.

Chapter Three

BOARDING SCHOOL

"We have one chance here, and [we'd] best make it the best effort possible. It's your only night on stage. Be who you want to be."
— Excerpt from letters to my family

I often wonder how differently things would have gone for me had I not been sent to boarding school. In eighth grade, I was at Massey-Vanier, a rural high school with 2,000 students. Weighing in at eighty pounds, I was the smallest boy in my grade, and often found myself lost in the sea of students. Being small, I desired to prove myself, and I threw myself into wrestling. I was fast and strong for my size, and managed to win many of my matches, to the point that I came second in Quebec and could have gone to Nationals. Being congratulated by people would fill my chest up with pride, and I felt accepted. Knowing that I was good helped me feel better about myself, as did knowing I could defend myself in a fight if that ever happened.

However, my dad wanted more for us kids, so began to send us all off, one by one, to Bishop's College School, a private boarding school in Sherbrooke, Quebec. Graham had gone there for a year, the girls and Jeremy for a few more, and Adrian and I started in ninth grade. I managed to secure a math scholarship, which helped bring the tuition down, but it was still up to $10,000 for a year of boarding. Meanwhile, Graham, being ahead of me, had excelled and set a bar of high expectations for us Hill boys. I had a lot to live up to. I knew this was a chance few have, and that I was one of the lucky ones.

Boarding school is precisely that — you stay and board at school. On day one, as my mother drove away, leaving me on campus, I felt so self-conscious, knowing this was not my comfort zone. Everyone looked so composed and rich, their jewelry gleaming and white teeth grinning. I felt like I didn't deserve to be there. My mangled left hand stayed hidden in my pocket. My anxiety manifested as sarcasm, and I often found myself at odds with the older students who would pick on me and with the teachers who would penalize me with early-morning running laps around campus for my sharp tongue. I have always chosen sexual innuendo as my forte — any time I can interject something funny and sexual, all the better. It's a safer topic in that you rarely offend people; maybe you make them blush, but not much more than that.

Tenth grade was a year of growth for me. I was finally getting bigger and stronger, and felt much better in my own skin. I didn't have to be sarcastic and defensive all the time, and I could let people in more and be a better friend to those around me. My insecurities and self-questioning remained, though I could now keep them at a low mental murmur. Our group started to define itself. What a host of characters it was! It turned out that the rich preppies were all nice people once I took the time to get to know them. Soon I even had a new best friend, Oliver, who'd been in my dorm house in ninth grade but whom I'd been too much of an ass to befriend. Almost like a mentor, Oliver helped me be confident in the crazy side of my personality and encouraged me to let it shine. He was always up for anything — running around the campus naked, climbing on top of buildings, jumping off bridges, scurrying through underground tunnels. Whatever it was, he was game. Life was for living and letting your flow take over. Oliver clued me into the fact that it doesn't matter what others think; what was more important was what I thought about myself. Sure, to be a positive person at all time, you actually have to ignore certain realities, so I consciously chose to be a little naïve. But to this day, this positivity has been my superpower.

Around this time, I also started climbing on the school's indoor wall, a thirty-foot-tall installation with features built out of wood, housed in the school's newly built gymnasium. Walls like this were very rare in the 1990s, so we were very lucky. Having spent so much time climbing trees and scrambling around as a kid, I quickly adapted to this fun new sport. Right away, I was hooked by the physical challenge and the strength and balance climbing required.

The wall had multicolored holds screwed onto it, with specific routes marked with strips of colored tape by our outdoor teacher, Mr. Mortimer. Each route required you to unlock a specific sequence of moves, all while maintaining the body tension to hold yourself into the wall, keeping your hips parallel with the vertical plane. The level of focus necessary to complete the more challenging climbs completely silenced my inner anxiety. It's hard to worry about social acceptance when your fingers are pinching chopstick-sized grips and your feet are pressing down between two matchstick-sized gray footholds, keeping you precariously perched on the wall.

As I learned and progressed, I grew to love the myopic focus climbing cultivated. Though strength was important, quiet and controlled flow was even more so. I was initially good at climbing, but there were certain routes I couldn't do, that I failed at for weeks and months. My strength-to-weight ratio was good: at 145 pounds and with no body fat, the climbs with large holds were easy for me, even on very overhanging walls. Yet if the climb required me to stand on holds the size of matches and balance my way up, I would often fail. Nonetheless, I was mesmerized by the intricacies of balancing my weight on these technical climbs, tensioned between holds, while looking up to study the sequences above. Eventual success brought such a flood of endorphins that I was hooked. The balance of challenge and reward was so gratifying. Soon enough, I was one of the best in our school, which drastically helped my self-confidence. Finally, I had found something that none of my siblings had done at Bishop's College, and I was good at it.

Oliver and I took to climbing like flies to shit; we would be at the wall every Sunday at 7:30 a.m. In 1994, we travelled to the village of Okotoks, in the foothills of the Rockies, to complete in

Junior Nationals. I was climbing well and was tied for first place, until the last climb when I strayed off route and didn't make it far at all, falling into tenth place. Oliver stayed strong and placed sixth. These were the moments when I started to identify myself as a climber.

The same teacher — Mr. Mortimer — who introduced us to climbing also instilled in us a love for adventure. He would take us camping and hiking, planting a seed in me that germinated into a lifelong passion for the outdoors. One freezing winter night in the woods on campus, spent huddled deep in our sleeping bags struggling to stay warm, Mr. Mortimer showed us how to be self-reliant. He shared winter-camping tips like which clothing to wear, how to set the tent platform up in the snow, and how sleeping with a hot water bottle not only keeps you warm but gives you water to start cooking with the next morning. He also demonstrated that one must accept certain hardships if one wants to do extraordinary things.

Around this time, I was also growing muscles — which felt amazing since for most of my life I had been the smallest in our family. I felt like I was closer and closer to being able to defend myself from Jeremy. Looking at the veins on my forearms, or flexing my biceps in the mirror, increased my self-worth. Small, weak, little Greggy was growing bigger and stronger.

Nothing could stop me as I grew into manhood.

Oliver and started to do wild and foolish acts, looking for ways to challenge our strong, new bodies. Things to test our balance, to test our strength. We climbed bridges and buildings, followed dry, dusty culverts under roads, and ran around campus naked. We were young, free, and wild, looking for the next dose of adrenaline. Like any addiction, it started slowly, but soon the feeling of fear triggered such a rush of chemicals that I began to develop a constant need. I savored every drop my body created.

My senior year at Bishop's College, instead of going to party in New Orleans for Mardi Gras, which the rest of our friend group was doing, Oliver and I flew to San Francisco, from where we'd take a bus to Yosemite Valley to climb for a week. But first we needed to take the subway from the airport to the bus station. I was a complete country bumpkin, so I trusted Oliver's city sense. He lived in the somewhat rural town of Hudson, but his family also had a small apartment in Montreal, which meant he had spent far more time in the city than I had. While we waited for the subway car, we watched as a commuter played the shell game with a busker on the platform. I watched the pea get hidden in the middle of the three caps. The commuter wagered $20 that he knew where it was. He pointed to the rightmost cap, and voila . . . it wasn't there.

The busker turned to me and Oliver and asked if we knew where the pea was — and challenged us to wager $60 each. We were both confident it was in the middle. I was also strong from climbing, running cross-country, working out, and playing rugby back at school, so I didn't expect to have any issues if something went awry. At that point in my life, I also naively trusted everyone. No one had taken advantage of me . . . yet. Oliver and I handed over our money to the busker, who, just as the subway car was rolling in, pulled up the middle cap to reveal . . . nothing. We'd been scammed! Or more to the point, we had allowed ourselves to be scammed. The man quickly picked up his stuff, jumped on the subway, and zinged away with our cash. We now had little money left for the trip, which cut deeply into our meal budget.

For the next seven days in Yosemite, we ate a lot of peanut butter and bread, plus ramen noodles, boxes of mac and cheese, and other cheap food. The magnitude of Yosemite scared us; El Capitan towered three thousand feet above the valley floor and was so beyond our scope of climbing knowledge that it seemed impossible. But, of course, it was only impossible at our current skill level. We began learning how to climb traditionally — placing our own removable protection as we went — and did many unconventional, scary things. Our first trad climb was a beautiful, arching crack that split the gray granite. Rated a moderate 5.7, it should have been easy for us — we easily climbed four grades higher at the gym.

Oliver went first, as the lead climber, and began slotting nuts — small metal chocks — in the crack. He put in his first three pieces in over the course of the first forty-five feet; by then, the crack had arched quite a bit. This caused his rope to pull upward on his wedged nuts, which it turns out were not so wedged at all. I watched fearfully as a l three pieces lifted up and out, sliding down the rope to where I was belaying. There he was, fifty-plus feet up the smooth gray granite, balanced and looking good — but with zero protection. Luckily, Oliver was so focused on the climbing up that he didn't know what had happened. I continued to belay, not telling him, worrying it might freak him out and cause him to lose his composure and fall.

This total lack of knowledge was evident in all our climbing. We went sport climbing — clipping bolts fixed in the rock — and I found myself flipped upside down by my rope, with a large rope burn on my inner thigh, having made the rookie mistake of getting the rope behind my leg. Yosemite absolutely schooled us, but we also got unquestionably inspired by the potential of climbing.

Chapter Four

AUSTRALIA: YOUNG-ADULTHOOD SEARCHINGS

"I did understand, though, that life could be what you wanted. You could manifest a great reality. Simply wake up every day excited that life was good, and it would be good. This is one very simple reality of life: you decide who you are."
— Excerpt from letters to my family

After high school, I was accepted into a few universities but deferred them for a year. Instead, I signed up for an exchange program, through Bishop's College, at the Billanook College near Melbourne, Australia. Here, I would assist teachers in outdoor education and theatre which had been a deep passion of mine throughout my time at Bishop's College, where I'd acted in many school plays. I needed to earn money for my upcoming trip, so my stepbrother Jeremy invited Oliver and me to work in the Alberta oilfields with him. He promised that I would make more money than I ever had — mainly due to overtime pay.

We would work in seismic, which is a research stage in the oilfields. Essentially, Oliver and I would lay out kilometers of cables, with little sensors attached to them, forming a massive grid overlaying the earth. The oil company would then either set off a detonation or vibrate the earth with large machines, and the grid of sensors would read the vibrations to determine if oil reserves were below ground. It was a simple job that required no education and no specific skills, other than the ability to withstand whatever Mother Nature threw at you out on those unprotected plains, be it snow, sleet, rain, heat, or wind.

When we arrived at the hotel in Medicine Hat, smack dab in the middle of Alberta, I was just a green, sheltered, private-school kid, totally unprepared for the type of person I was about to spend all day, every day, with. The typical oilfield "lifers" were uneducated, hard-living men who worked for two months straight. They would then take their hard-earned cash and blow most of it on alcohol, drugs, and hookers, returning a week later to earn it all back again. This was not the white privilege I was used to, and I hid my sheltered background — and my big hopes and dreams — earning my coworkers' trust and respect by working hard, including an epic sixty-one-day stint of fourteen-hour workdays. I quickly learned that most of these guys were great people. It was simply that life had never handed them opportunities. They were never taught to dream big, so they didn't. Oh, we laughed and smoked weed and had fun together, but there was always an unwritten rule: to hide our true selves. After six months of hard work, I had saved up $5,000 and I was off to Australia.

My role as an assistant teacher at Billanook College was pretty simple — to help with the outdoor-education programs and some drama classes. One of my tasks was to lead the schoolkids on outings into the Australian Outback. Here, I started forming my future guiding career and developing a deep passion for the outdoors.

One evening, during an overnight backpacking trip with the kids, I was sitting outside my tent, writing in my journal, when I witnessed a spectacular moonrise. Sitting immersed in total blackness, I watched as the moonlight crept across the valley below me, moving up the hill to our campsite. In a surreal twist, a flock of emus was grazing down in the valley, and I could see their shadows lengthening on the fields in the unfiltered white light. The beauty of the moment pierced my soul. I knew then, as much as I've ever known, that the fulfillment I was seeking lay in the outdoors; nature, in its simplicity, stark reality, and unassailable truth, would be my lifelong teacher.

I only wrote in my journals during my twenties, and the Australian journal I kept was my first. Looking back at it, I can see that I was already searching for some deeper meaning in life, trying to imagine a path that would make me happy. A sample entry from that journal:

"Lately, I have read the books The Alchemist and The Diary of a Magus by Paul Coelho, and also The Celestine Prophecy by James Redfield. Anyhow, what these books are mainly about is a quest for the deep meaning of life. A lot of people think that life is all about getting a job, a spouse, children and then aging gracefully with a good retirement fund, but in reality, there must be more . . ."

Another journal entry from that time stands out, also because I wrote it in red pen, which I must have done deliberately as a message to future me. In my journal, I'd written a Q & A for myself:

Q: What do I want in life?

A: To constantly be happy; everything material is irrelevant when you are smiling. To travel to places I cannot pronounce, see sights that most people could never imagine. I want to do things that everyone wants to do but are too scared [to do because of] rejection and failure. I want to be lying on my deathbed, content with how I have lived my life. Period. And [I want] friends to do all these things with.

Q: And now the universal adult question — what do you want to be when you grow up?

A: I don't want to be someone who works with numbers or any irrelevant merchandise. I need a job that leaves me satisfied at the end of the day. I think that helping people, making them better, would be quite satisfying. Perhaps it would be impossible, but I would like to be not completely trapped by red tape. I would like to be in charge.

Marriage: Oh yeah . . . I am hopelessly romantic. I want to be completely in love and married to an incredible woman. To have two or more wild little kids running around and creating chaos in our lives.

Q: What makes me happy?

A: Hanging with good friends. Having no immediate worries. Hanging out in nature. A big chocolate milk. A good scratch. A telephone call to my mom. Success. Just being alive and having choices. Putting on my climbing shoes. Feeling the wind whipping at my face as I fly down the ski slopes. Not feeling that I have to impress anyone. Trying new things. Adrenaline in my veins. A comfy bed.

Chapter Five
UNIVERSITY YEAR ONE

"The typical life that is laid out for us is easy and could be boring. But if you choose to be unique, to live differently, you can experience an incredible life. To be truly great."
— Excerpt from letters to my family

The struggle for who I wanted to become was real. Maybe, I thought, I could follow the standard path, throwing myself into my studies at Dalhousie University in Halifax, Nova Scotia, and working hard toward an educational goal. Perhaps I could become a chiropractor or a kinesiologist.

Before heading off to university, I reached out to Graham and asked him for some sage older-brother advice to set me on a successful path. Graham had earned an architecture degree in college, after which he moved to Seattle and with our cousin Tisha started a company that built web pages. This was back during the Dot-Com Boom, and Graham and Tisha found themselves making web pages for Microsoft, with their business, Sitewerks, quickly booming.

Graham told me two things:

If you are talking to someone you don't want to talk to, simply give them the finger, say, "Shut up," and walk away.

Try to make the right decisions and always be yourself.

Armed with those pearls of wisdom from Graham, I ventured forth into university.

The first week was complete debauchery, with some frosh-week stuff that I mostly skipped. I didn't want to be a jerk to my dorm mates, but I had travelled the world and felt slightly above all that juvenile hazing bullshit. However, I did participate in the final initiation: I drank some gross drink, kissed a codfish, and shouted some inane chant. My initial feeling was one of overwhelm, of feeling like an outsider in every situation at this giant school or while trying to blend in with the large groups at parties and at bars. But gradually, as I made friends and settled in, I began to feel more confident.

I continued to struggle against the shackles of mainstream life. To compensate, I smoked weed frequently and yearned for something different. I studied biology — or at least tried to — so that the doors would be open if I ever really wanted to pursue my education, a prospect that seemed ever more doubtful. The school, meanwhile, had a small climbing wall in the back of the gymnasium, and I continued to push and develop that skill. I probably spent more hours climbing than I did studying. The climbing wall was my haven, where a small tribe of people accepted me without question — folks like the quiet and quirky British Steve, who showed me how to climb silently, and the wilder Collin, who pushed me to work on my upward flow. The wall was tiny, but its short and steep angles let us test ourselves and push each other. On a small plaque, there was a quote: "It's great to have an end to journey toward, but in the end it's the journey that counts." It was sage advice that I'd never forget. I put this philosophy into practice on the wall more than once, sometimes spending months to master the harder climbs — the ones with technical movement and tiny holds. The physical strength climbing gave me was incredible, and my confidence continued to grow. I even entered and did well in a few local climbing competitions, regularly placing in the top three, which boosted my ego and sense of self-worth and confidence.

Although confident on the rock, I still lacked confidence in who I was. This was only worsened by the psychedelic experimentation I did with my friends some Monday nights when, as a group, we would wander through the giant spruce trees that towered over the town's ocean-side park, hanging out in the forest high and wild on psilocybin mushrooms. The mushrooms sent me on a trip of insecurity; it was always an intense bout of self-doubt, coming at me in waves. I would not be secure enough to speak, my inner dialogue so consumed with worry about everything. I couldn't seem to say anything that was cool or interesting, so I mostly just stayed mute. The only person I felt comfortable around was Oliver, my friend from Bishop's College, and I was grateful that he and I were both attending universities in Halifax.

Oliver and I continued to be a wild duo, buildering — climbing buildings — all around the Dalhousie and the King's College campuses, usually late at night. Normal life felt a little boring so we would go out when it was dark and urge each other up these buildings. Barely illuminated by streetlamps, we would climb the corners of these 200-year-old buildings. Often the sandstone had great holds on it, and the joints between the rock blocks often provided great edges, with shadows cast by the streetlights revealing the best footholds. Often we would find ourselves perched fifty feet up, wondering how we were getting down! Or we'd hang off metal girders seventy feet up, dangling our feet over the void, utterly confident that we wouldn't succumb to the inevitable death that awaited if our grip failed — which, we reasoned, it wouldn't because we were young, strong, and well-trained.

One evening on one of these excursions, fifteen feet up the student-union building, Oliver grabbed onto a window, which swung open to reveal a coffee shop. As an entirely spontaneous person, he looked inside and spotted donuts out on the counter. Oliver slipped inside and grabbed the treats, but a third friend with us, Steve, wasn't having any of this and ran away, leaving me — the loyal friend — to wait for Oliver.

Within moments, the cops arrived, careering around the corner in their car, lights flashing. Someone must have alerted them while we were climbing the other buildings. They promptly arrested me, and then pointed their spotlight into the coffee shop, to illuminate Oliver hiding behind the counter. I watched his face crumple with remorse and regret as the light panned across him. Calling with a megaphone, they urged him to come out with his hands up. Oliver passed a bag of donuts out the window and climbed out sheepishly, and then he and I spent a long night in jail for our folly, listening to the drunks ranting in the cell next door, vowing never to fuck up this badly again.

Meanwhile, I continued struggling to focus on my studies. I knew that the most stable path forward was one in which I earned a degree, but I could not take school seriously. The idea that we had to memorize all the names in the periodic table, Latin names, kingdom, family genus, and species, was preposterous to me when, really, we could just look the information up in a book whenever we needed to. Maybe if the style of education were more focused on problem-solving, I would have been more engaged, but I had too much energy and wanted to roam. I struggled with the rules of man, these ideas we had created that then became norms we all had to follow.

Over the winter break that freshman year, I had a chance to go backcountry skiing in British Columbia with my mother and my stepfather, Don, who was turning fifty and wanted to celebrate. He dreamed of heli-skiing, in which a helicopter drops you off at the top of an untracked run, down which a qualified guide then leads you safely through the deepest, lightest powder of your life. However, when Don looked into heli-skiing, he realized that it was too pricey, and he looked into alternatives. He stumbled upon a backcountry skiing lodge in the middle of the mountains, near the town of Revelstoke, British Columbia, which I'd never heard of but which would become so central to my life in the years to come. The cost for the week was around $1,500, and Don offered to pay half if I wanted to join. I had no idea what backcountry skiing was about, but all this powder sounded too dreamy to pass up. I looked at my bank draft and figured I could swing it somehow.

Honestly, I wasn't killing it at school, and still didn't know what to do with my life or my future. I did, however, know that I couldn't pass up this opportunity regardless of my grades. When my dad heard about our upcoming trip, he sent me this strongly worded letter (which I promptly ignored):

> We are from different generations, and you are showing it in ways that are difficult for me to understand. On the one hand, you want money for school; on the other, you are going off on a skiing expedition that I can't afford. I just start to wonder how on Earth this outlook can compete with Asian, European, Indian kids who work and scrape to get high marks and scholarships and come out on top with determination, compassion, and understanding. You have been given all of the chances and opportunities in life, but how hard are you really trying? . . . I would hope to see hard work, respect for what you are being offered, and maybe a little indulgence on behalf of your demanding and realistic father. [With your education,] you have the chance not one person in

1,000 has, and I'd like to see you use it. Everyone can be ordinary.

Graham and I met in Vancouver over the break and hitchhiked up to Revelstoke, a town deep in the Columbia Mountains about a six-hour drive east of Vancouver. The Columbia Mountains are a smaller range than the Rockies but get substantially more snow. The town was magical, with rows of 100-year-old houses hemmed in by deep snowbanks that dwarfed the cars, and streetlights backlighting the snow-covered maple trees. It felt like a magical winter wonderland, and was unlike any place I had ever visited.

The next morning, we — me, Graham, Don, my stepbrother Ian, my mom, and some other friends from Sutton, Bill, Brian, and Sophie Nunnelley — took a helicopter ride into the range to our ski lodge, which lay high at the head of Carnes Creek, a deep, forested valley north of Revelstoke. I loved the perspective outside the window, looking down into the treetops with my face glued to the window. My eyes followed streams up ravines, meandered through these giant forests, searching for animals and their tracks in the snow. A fifteen-minute ride brought us to perfect red chalets at treeline, up on a ridge with massive mountains as a backdrop. The mountains were not composed of sheer rock walls, but instead had gentler, snow-covered flanks. Years ago, we had traveled to Europe and driven around the Alps, so this wasn't my first time in big mountains, but these were different There was untracked snow in every direction, a nearly unbroken sea of white — and everything looked skiable. Wilder yet were the alleyways between the chalets, where snow tunnels had been carved into the deep snowpack to facilitate human passage.

As the helicopter lowered toward the landing pad, a massive cloud of snow blew up into the frigid alpine air. I jumped out and huddled where we were told to. Once the helicopter had flown away, leaving us and our luggage, I stood up and looked around. The tunnels I had spotted were seven-foot-deep corridors of snow. I couldn't believe it — what was this place?

When we walked into the lodge, a smaller, energetic man came up and introduced himself as our guide, Ruedi Beglinger. His tanned face and the crow's feet around his intense eyes spoke of a life spent outdoors. His hands, slightly curled and incredibly strong, looked like talons ready to tear down mountains. He spoke with a thick Swiss-German accent. First, he went through all the house rules and then sized us up with our gear.

"So, none of you have ever ski-toured?" he asked. "Prepare to be introduced to the best form of mountain travel. If you listen to my directions and learn from me, we can have the best week of skiing you will ever experience."

Continuing, the passion for skiing infusing his voice, Ruedi said, "It has been snowing heavily since November, and there is a fresh 60 centimeters of new snow waiting for us. If you think you have skied before, you will realize that this is unlike any skiing you have done — this is the best of the best."

Ruedi explained the touring skis. They looked exactly like

regular downhill skis, except their bindings could either lock into place and act like regular bindings for making turns downhill, or they could unlock to pivot on a hinge near the toe, freeing your heel for uphill and flatland travel as with cross-country skis. Then he brought out the skins. These would help us grip our way up the mountain in something Ruedi called the "skin track." Imagine a cowhide cut to fit the underside of the ski perfectly — that's a climbing skin. The hair of the skin naturally glides one way; if forced the other way, the hairs prevent the ski from sliding back down.

"Upon reaching the top," Ruedi told us, "you simply pull the skin off, switch the binding, and it's powder-skiing time!"

Next, Ruedi brought us outside and showed us how to use our avalanche beacons, small electronic boxes that could both send and receive signals on a specific frequency. Beep . . . beep . . . a little switch allowed us to change our beacons from "send" mode to "receive," picking up signals from the other beacons in case anyone was covered by an avalanche.

Then, through more science (it felt like magic), you could locate how far and in which direction the beacon was from you, tuning into that signal and listening attentively as the sounds changed and increased in volume as you got closer and the signal grew more intense. Finally, you could locate the beacon, or scarily enough, your friends, buried under the snow. Ruedi has us all practice locating buried beacons; even though he was our guide and responsible for our safety, we also needed these skills and would have to respond were there an avalanche. I remember thinking, *Holy shit, this is real.*

"Once you locate the beacon within the smallest distance — usually 1.5 to 2 meters," explained Ruedi, "you then need to probe the snow for the victim."

The probes were similar to tent poles, with six fourteen-inch-long aluminum pieces, all attached with a cord and that, when pulled together, formed an eight-foot pole. We'd carry these probes in our bags in sections, ready to whip out at a moment's notice. It seemed like a tricky thing, deciding whether your probe had hit someone, but Ruedi said poking a person would feel softer than poking a rock. You would probe in a systematic way, covering the ground with intention.

The final step was shoveling the victim out, and for that we would each carry a small, flat-bladed avalanche shovel on our pack. Ruedi explained how avalanche debris could harden quickly, like cement — giant frozen snowballs molded together — making rescue extremely challenging. I could only dream about how scary it would be to be buried alive in an avalanche, or to witness it happen to a friend or loved one. And then to have to respond and rescue them.

At 7:00 a.m. the following day, we gathered outside the lodge, dressed and ready to experience backcountry skiing for our first time. The day would begin with skinning up, following Ruedi as

he laid a skin track up into the mountains. We switched on our beacons, checked each other to make sure they were on, and set out on a gradua incline. The skins were incredible; all I needed to do was slide my left sk forward and stand on it, and then the hairs would grab the srow and stop me from sliding backward. Then, standing on that left foot, I would slide the right ski forward and stand on it, and then repeat . . . over and over.

For two hours, Ruedi set a winding skin track for us up toward the 2,476-meter Woolsey Peak. The day was quiet and calm, and while my body grew accustomed to the motion my eyes roved the terrain. I knew nothing of the hazards, but I could see all sorts of interesting peaks across the range.

Ruedi stopped to give me a pointer: "Greg, you will be faster if you don't lift your ski as much. Slide it forwards; don't walk it."

Taking his sage advice, I watched him effortlessly set the track through the deep, light snow. Soon we were on top of Woolsey Peak a mismatched group of Quebecois, very far from home.

Ruedi gave us clear cirections on where to go and what to do for the descent, then he slid off the peak and was immediately lost in a cloud of snow, making effortless turns in the foot-plus of fluffy powder. I could just spot his head bouncing up and down as he floated down the slope. He looked so elegant, and in total control. Some twenty turns later, Ruedi stopped and waved us down one at a time.

Since this trip was for Don's birthday, we let him go first, followed by my mom. Their initial turns were a little tentative, yet both had some rhythm by the end. Graham snuck in third, and then my turn was finally up. By this point, I had skied thousands of days, including many in Whistler, the massive ski resort in British Columbia, but also back east. However, this backcountry powder was well beyond my expectations. Once I let gravity take over, I was floating through light, fluffy clouds, powder hitting me in the face on every turn and then bouncing me back up so I could breathe, holler with joy, and repeat. I'd never experienced such elation on skis in my life. There was an incredible lightness, a feeling of falling, a feeling of freedom.

That week, I was filled with awe most days — everything was so beautiful, so surreal, it boggled the mind. The idea that our reality could be all about navigating this wild terrain was incomprehensible. Backcountry skiing was amazing. I was always second to the top of any ascent, following close behind Ruedi in his skin tracks. I couldn't help but admire how confidently he led us through hazardous terrain, picking the safest lines, keeping all of us out of harm's way. The pressure of guiding us must have been enormous, and it was only through years of experience and layers upon layers of understanding that Ruedi could predict the weather, avoid avalanches, navigate glaciers, and keep us all safe. I had nothing but respect for him. At night in the lodge, he showed us photos of adventures he'd been on, of first descents down slopes so steep and exposed they boggled the mind. Ruedi told us that, when he was young, his father didn't want him to climb and had confiscated his climbing gear. Still, Ruedi had found a way to sneak away into his beloved Alps, eventually becoming a mountain guide, a job I assumed I would never be qualified to do.

Chapter Six
FOREST FOR THE TREES

"In whatever road you take, make sure to challenge yourself;
nothing evolves without being tested."
— Excerpt from letters to my family

During the summer between freshman and sophomore year, Oliver and I applied for jobs as tree planters for Roots Forestry, an outfit based out of the remote northern city of Prince George, British Columbia. It would turn out to be one of the most challenging yet rewarding jobs of my life. The lessons it taught me about toughness and perseverance have echoed in everything I have done since.

As someone who always liked to be immediately good at something and never shied away from hard work, I was ready — I wanted to crush it, despite not knowing the first thing about tree planting. The most amazing thing about planting is that you get paid per tree, so if you work hard, you are rewarded. The price was usually $0.10 or more per tree, and if you were quick and efficient, you could, I'd heard, earn $300 to $500 a day.

The way it worked was relatively simple: Forestry companies were allotted vast tracts of land and were under contract to manage these areas. They logged specific amounts every year, and then they had to reforest these blocks in the wake of the logging. No two blocks were alike; some were small, measuring one mile by one mile, and some were much larger. The landscape varied, the only constant being that the logging had left a giant scar where there used to be forest. The areas were rarely left clear, and had fallen logs — some small enough to step over, others so large you had to crawl under them or walk around them entirely — and broken tree debris everywhere. The terrain could be free of debris and as easy to walk on as a beach, or it could be a mishmash of overlaid trees and limbs like giant pick-up sticks.

As a long-haired newbie planter, to me this was all foreign ground; I just knew that I wanted to work hard and make as much as money possible. I thought I would be an asset to my new boss, Jeff, but in retrospect, I should probably call him up and apologize for my early days on the job.

On paper, tree planting seemed simple enough: The green seedlings arrived in boxes, typically 200 to 300 per box, each tree roughly half a foot tall with a few inches of roots protruding below. The roots were shaped into a plug of dirt you needed to place carefully in the soil — after clearing away any organic debris — using your foot to worry a small shovel back and forth to create the hole. After the tree was in, you replaced the soil, holding the spruce, pine, larch, cedar, or whatever while you compacted the earth around the root ball to get the tree standing proud. Each planter carried the seedlings in white canvas bags suspended from their waist; Jeff suggested that we carry an hour's worth of seedlings in the bags — however many trees we thought that would be.

Each planter is given their own piece of the block, and it is up to them how they reforest it. The more efficient your strategy, the more time spent planting, which equated to earning more money. But, Jeff told us, the planting needed to be at a particular density — an average of eight feet between seedlings. And the trees needed to be properly planted in good soil, with straight roots, leading to a straight seedling. Those were the only caveats.

That first day, Jeff suggested that I load 200 seedlings into my bags, 100 on each s de. He then hoisted my bags on his hips and demonstrated the technique. With his small, athletic frame he sprang into action, pacing out his steps, surveying the terrain, grabbing each tree with his right hand and sliding it rapidly into the ground. He smoothly planted ten trees in one continuous action.

"That's how it's done, Greg," said Jeff. "The trees need to be spaced eight feet apart. And look like proud seedlings."

I then followed Jeff's example so that I could draw each tree out smoothly. Although we each carried three bags, it was easier to be balanced and only load the side ones, keeping the back one for my Walkman ard maybe some water.

Woah, awkward! The twenty-five pounds of weight hanging off each hip wobbled me in every direction. I hitched the bags up higher, cinched the wa st belt, and took my first tentative steps as a tree planter. I plowed my shovel into the ground, punching and pulling the blade back and forth in the soil. Finally, I had a hole big enough to slide in the tree roots. The first tree I grabbed turned out to be three trees, and I paused to put the other two seedlings back in the bag. I'm wasting precious time, I thought, bending down to plant the seedling, my back groaning in protest.

I took two steps and tried again. This time, I stood hard on my shovel, pushing it deep into the ground. Worrying it around, I got my hole open and grabbed my tree. The little green pine seedling came into my hand easily, and I bent over and pushed it into the soil, making sure the roots were straight.

This time I tried to push the earth snugly and compactly with my foot, but it didn't quite work, so I forced some around with my hand and tried to make the tree look straight. Time was ticking, and I had only planted two trees. I stood up and tried to remember which direction I was headed in. I stumbled to the left and heard trees falling out of my bag, turning to see two pine seedlings lying on the dark dirt. More time wasted by going back to pick them up.

Two steps, and I repeated the process. Tree after tree, I forced the holes open, pushed the trees in, and tried to get faster.

I was only getting paid $0.12 a tree. In other words, the 200 trees I carried would only be worth $24. I wondered how long it would take to get them all into the ground. There was no fluidity to my actions — they had not yet become habitual — so I staggered around and pushed the trees into the earth seemingly at random.

Breathing hard, I picked up the pace, occasionally watching as the veterans fluidly planted their trees, like sewing machines stitching up the soil with seedlings. Some were almost running the whole time. I picked up my pace and jogged the two steps between trees, which often made me forget my planting path. This meant I had to stop, refocus, and try again; I was wasting so much time without planting anything. In the end, instead of planting my 200 seedlings in an hour, I spent three hours at the task, and my frustration was building. I couldn't understand why this seemingly simple job was proving so difficult.

My second round of planting went quicker; I wasn't getting lost as much. Each time I came back up from planting a tree, I didn't feel disoriented; I could remember which direction I'd been heading in. The action of grabbing a tree and planting it had begun to feel more intuitive.

Later in the day, Jeff came to check on my density. He put his shovel in the ground and attached a thirteen-foot cord to it, spinning this around to count how many trees lay within the circle. Hoping for seven or eight trees, he only got five. Damn! But then on another area of my ground, he got nine. I was so inconsistent! I had to rework my piece.

I wandered my piece for the rest of the afternoon, filling in the empty zones and thinning the overly dense ones. The drone of the mosquitos vibrated throughout my defeated soul. I needed to be patient, to breathe and relax — and to accept that I'd be making barely any money during the steep learning curve of these initial few days.

I worked my butt off on day two, and hitting the density was easier because a machine had gone through and mounded up the soil for my trees. I simply needed to plant a tree in the top of each mound and move onwards. Tree after tree went into the ground, and I breathed heavily, nearly sprinting from seedling to seedling, planting my first 200 trees in only an hour and a half — twice as fast as day one. I was going to hit one thousand trees on only my second day, earning $120 for my efforts!

I ate quickly at each bag-up (the time during which you're back at the trucks, refilling your bags with trees), and then ran back to the piece and resumed my furious pace.

Four hundred trees by 11:00 a.m., on par for over 1,000: Go . . . go . . . come on . . . push it . . . go . . . !

Then Jeff stopped me. I knew my density was good because it had been predetermined by the mounding machine; I wondered what was up.

"Greg, I hate to tell you this, but you are going to have to rework your piece," said Jeff. "Two out of every eight trees have bent roots, which means the trees won't grow properly. I know you want to make money, but you have to get your tree quality first."

Holding back tears, I started reworking my piece. It was true, though — I had crammed the tree roots in quickly, forcing them into the ground. Damn! It should have been quality before quantity. I passed my afternoon lost in unpleasant, self-deprecating thoughts, the kind that had plagued me all my life, going back to when I was a little boy lost in the shuffle at my parents' chaotic homes. All I have ever wanted was to be accepted and valued, and here I was once again, a failure.

I would get better at planting; I just needed to calm down and learn first, to take this struggle, accept it, accept myself where

I was at, and work hard at improving my planting technique. And this much I did over the next few weeks, even as my hands callused and bl stered f om the toil and the rain came down in torrential sheets, cloaking the hills in mist, soaking us to the bone, and turning the ground into an ever-more-perilous slip-and-slide.

Once the spring rainy season was over, the bugs came out — bugs unlike anything I'd ever seen. From the small, bulldog-like black flies that burrowed into your clothing and bit into your flesh, to the thousands of mosquitos that never quit, following you around like rabid dogs, howling for blood, to the deer flies diving in for larger chunks of flesh.

Typically, we would all camp out near a lake, a gypsy-esque encampment where more than a hundred of us would be sleeping in our tents, vans, cars, retired school buses, and campers. The drone of mosquitos was almost a constant. The only peaceful, bug-free moments were inside the tent that Oliver and I shared. There were virtually no moments without bugs.

I had a recurring dream that began that first year of planting trees and that ran until I had gained more skills and confidence. I would find myself out on the block, working as hard as possible but getting nowhere. In my peripheral vision, I could see the others working away like automatons, but for me it was like I was prying up floorboards, struggling to put just one tree in the ground. Why was this task so simple for them but so out of reach for me?

The elusive 2,000 trees in a day was a benchmark against

which every planter measured himself. To plant that many your first season was a feather in your cap, or proof of your potential as a tree-planter. Oliver and I had gotten close a few times, but we were only able to make it happen two months into our stint, after we'd both had a lot of practice, each earning a green Roots Reforestation T-shirt and $240 for our efforts.

The connection that forms between individuals who are suffering together is very strong. Our crews became a tight-knit family, and we learned to depend on each other as well as to be dependable. Every night off, we would let loose and howl at the moon, get wasted, smoke pot, eat mushrooms, and periodically run naked through the forest. It was a time of crushing monotony but also of wildness and freedom, a time I would never trade for anything.

Climbing magazine had recently featured the perfect granite of the Stawamus Chief, a monolith rising above the Howe Sound in Squamish, British Columbia, and so Oliver and I headed there for some rock climbing once the planting season was over. We followed perfect cracks on a route called Rock On, linking it into Squamish Buttress to finish, for a ten-pitch adventure. Fueled by enthusiasm, we fought our way up this grippy granite. Neither of us had perfected our crack climbing, and our knuckles and fingertips were raw from the struggle.

False confidence has always led me into interesting situations, and the route's final, crux pitch was pure evidence of that. Taking the lead. I found myself stemmed between two rock ribs, grasping at a crack, teetering in place. I precariously spun my hips into the corner and pushed with them, allowing me to have both feet on the opposite granite rib. Pressured in like this, I felt secure. I spotted an old piton and clipped a quickdraw to it, reassured to finally have some gear, fifteen feet above my last piece. I inched upward, and then I couldn't move any more — something was pulling me down. Scrambling to keep my shit together, I yelled down to Oliver, "Ollie, I'm clipped to the quickdraw! I can't move up and I'm so wedged in here that I can't downclimb either!"

"Be calm, Greg. You'll sort it out!" he called back.

Shit, shit, shit! I thought, then: Come on, Greg, get yourself out of this!

Every nerve and muscle was focused on keeping me from falling out of this wedge, and now I was clipped to the wall. The drips of adrenaline ran quickly.

Calmness overcame me as I surveyed my situation. Strengthened by fear and self-preservation, I eked my way back downward to introduce some slack between me and the piton, unclipped the draw, and then managed to finish the climb, screaming with exhilaration as I hit the finishing jugs.

"Dude, that was the biggest multi-pitch climb we have ever done! Yeeeeeeoooocoooo!"

Oliver said after seconding the pitch, when we were both up

top.

"It's so incredible knowing we can do this shit! That was mega!" I said.

At that point, not only did we have an attraction to rock climbing, but also one to dope. In fact, our attraction to dope was so strong that we'd had to create a contract to not smoke for two months after planting. It read: This 3rd of June 1996, we, the undersigned, are making a solemn promise to no longer partake in the purchasing of dope, aka Mary Jane, hash, etc. We shall go on a dope-free binge of two months. This period commences immediately after this monster joint and ends 61 days later. Signed, Oliver Drake and Greg Hill.

Sitting on top of the Chief, we pulled the monster joint from our backpack; it was like an enormous cigar. We pulled out the contract, reread it, lit the joint, and got absolutely wrecked — so stoned that it took us longer to walk down off the Chief than it had to climb the technical pitches to its summit.

Oliver and I returned to the tree-planting gig the summer after our sophomore year as well. Yes, the work was grueling, but we now had the mechanics down and it was a great way to earn cash for adventuring. Plus, the hardships and suffering created tight friendships. Bitching and commiserating bonds people. We needed to rely on each other every day.

That year, I applied some mental rigor in figuring out how to speed up my planting. Each morning on the way to the block in the van, I would start visualizing my plan for the day. Then, I would wrap my fingers in duct tape while focusing on my target number, armoring my digits and imprinting the desired number in my mind.

The second the van dropped me off, I would load my bags up with trees and set off, working my piece efficiently, continually optimizing the method. If frustration ever welled up, I would scream at the world and let the tension out, pause briefly to accept, and then continue planting. Tree after tree, I ignored the bugs, worked my way through whatever the terrain was, dealt with the weather, and kept my eyes on the goal. On a typical day, we would be dropped off by 8:00 a.m. and work until 4:00 or 5:00 p.m., usually around nine hours on the block with a singular focus the whole time. My mind loved the math; once the day started and I knew how many trees I could plant in thirty minutes, I would multiply that number by eighteen: my goal for the day. If I planted eleven trees that first half hour, then two thousand was possible for the day, as long as I kept myself fed and hydrated, and regulated my moods.

During those long, repetitive days, my inner coach started to find his voice. This "coach" was a total hardass; he learned how far he could push me and what to say to keep me pressing past any perceived limitations. He would insult me; he would compare me to others. No one was as hard on me as he was. "Come on, you pussy, let's keep pushing," he'd tell me. "Fuck, I don't care if you're tired and dehydrated; you said you wanted to make $300, so keep going. No one is stopping you but yourself. Breathe hard, keep pushing, stay calm, and focus . . . come on . . . push it." Positivity was his strength, yet he had to launch an insult every once in a while, too.

So much shit could be thrown at you in a day: hostile terrain, rocky soil, crazy bugs, stinging nettles, underground wasp nests, a tangled forest of logs, rain, bears. With all these variables in play, I began to understand that the success of my days depended less on how shitty all these things were than on my attitude toward them. Every shitty day could be that much better if I consciously chose positive thoughts. Many a day would I wake up, snuggled in the one dry, bug-free place, and just want to stay there, knowing the day was going to be brutal. But then a few deep, calming breaths would pull a smile onto my face, and I'd head out to make the day a positive one.

That year, we ha twenty consecutive days of torrential rain. Each night, I would stuff my boots with newspaper and try to dry everything sufficiently for the next morning. Then I would go to sleep to the sound of the rain hammering my tent, steeling myself to wake up the next morning and head back into that dreadful weather to plant. You would savor every moment in the trucks, hypnotized by the back-and-forth of the windshield wipers, mentally steeling yourself for the day. You knew the first few moments were going to be great — rain hood up, everything as dry as it was going to be — and then thirty minutes later that first drip of water would roll down your back. Two hours in and you were soaked to the bone. If there was no wind, you were grateful; if there was, you were cold. As I worked, savoring the few precious moments when the sun came out and painted the bucolic landscape n godlike rays, I let my mind wander, daydreaming about how I'd spend the money I was saving. I didn't plan on going back to school the following year, but instead traveling around the States and perhaps heading to South America to climb in the Andes.

Endless travel options looped through my thoughts as I got increasingly better at planting. By the end of the season, I was usually among the top three planters on my crew. I was never as fast at the fastest guys, but I was motivated and consistent, which let me rack up big numbers. Well, except for that one shitty day out of every fifteen or so, when my inner coach couldn't figure out the right things to say and my motivation dwindled.

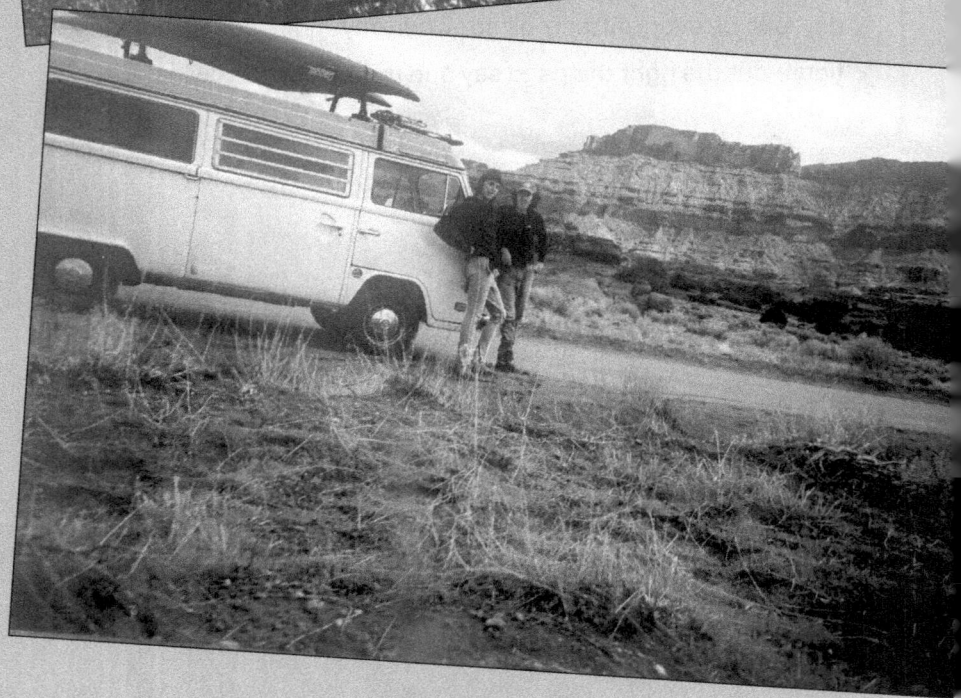

Chapter Seven

ADVENTURE YEAR ONE

"I have lived a life unlike many before me. I have experienced so very much that if I pass away early, it's because I have lived too much. It's true: I have had an amazing life, so much fun, such a wild ride. I do not want it to end and will fight as hard as possible, and never give up."
— Excerpt from letters to my family

At the end of this second planting season, in 1997, my planting friend Chris invited me to visit his mother, who read my astrology charts. She needed the exact date, time, and location of my birth, which she then plugged into a "natal chart." Apparently, I had something akin to "crossed planets," which she said was very rare. This placement created tension between the four archetypal planets and needed an outlet, which went a long way toward explaining my thirst for adventure. Then, as I watched her read my transits — or travelling stars — a sudden, shadowy expression crossed her face. Something ominous seemed to emerge, but she never verbally conveyed it to me.

While I'd been living my life, my brother Graham had grown his company exponentially. The internet was exploding, and Sitewerks was riding the wave of website creation. He and our cousin Tisha had an ideal partnership that made their company blossom, with Tisha the strategist, and Graham the people person.

Graham invited me down to Seattle to see his office of almost 150 employees. He said he would pay for me to be guided up Mount Rainier, the 14,411-foot stratovolcano that towers over the Washington skyline. It felt like a great opportunity, this chance to learn from a guide and broaden my mountain-travel knowledge. Rainier has giant glaciers cascading down every side, with huge blue seracs and yawning crevasses everywhere. It is a breathtaking mountain, hanging ethereally above the city of Seattle and easily visible 100 miles away on clear days. It was by far the largest mountain I had ever considered climbing.

The climb itself had no real technical sections, no rock cliffs or wild ice features; it was mostly a strenuous walk that meandered around the yawning crevasses, with some steep pitches of frozen snow and ice here and there. The challenge was more about dealing with the altitude and its effects. At 10,000 feet at the overnight hut at Camp Muir, my head started to ache and doubt crept in. I wanted to be an asset to my team of five fellow climbers and our guide, yet here I was with a headache, worried that I would be the weak link in the group the next day during our summit push. If I still felt sick in the morning, I would have to tell the group to go on without me.

I sat there watching the sun set on the ring of Pacific Northwest volcanoes, all tantalizing in their beauty. Mounts Adams, Saint Helens, and Hood all glowed orange with the setting sun, looking like peaks from an alien planet or a fantasy novel.

I felt better the next morning, and we climbed to 12,300 feet, where, unfortunately, we had to turn around because of a large avalanche that had cascaded down. Walking up to the debris field was terrifying — the snow deposit was 7 feet deep and 600 feet wide. It appeared to have run from quite far up the slope, a stark reminder of the mountains' fearsome and capricious power.

Rainier was just the start for me. While planting, I had dreamed of going to Aconcagua with Steve, my friend and fellow climber from Dalhousie University. Sitting at 22,873 feet, Aconcagua is the highest mountain in the Americas and has some non-technical routes to the summit. Our plan was to go in November 1997, when it would be late spring in South America — prime climbing season. To save money, I lived out of a white 1978 Volkswagen van, posting up in a parking lot in Whistler, working construction, and continuing to hone my climbing skills by reading books and getting out on rock and in the mountains. I even started free soloing — rock climbing without a rope — when I couldn't find a partner, savoring the freedom of movement it afforded.

For me, climbing was a metaphor for life; I understood that I needed to move slowly and deliberately toward my goals. I needed to have a destination, so that the route in front of me became clear as I went.

As training for Aconcagua, I began climbing in the Coast Mountains on my days off from work. It was a good break from the construction, where one co-worker, a deeply unhappy man, would say, "What are you — an idiot?" any time I didn't know how to do something, which was often given that so many of these tasks were new to me. One day, I found a partner at the climbing gym, and we headed up to climb the 9,000-foot Mount Matier, which is typically a two-day excursion.

The more I climbed, the more I was finding that my tree-planting work ethos — moving quickly, digging deep, staying positive, and having quick breaks every hour — translated well to mountain climbing. So it was also on Mount Matier, on which we ended up blitzing Slalok Mountain, Mount Spetch, and Matier in a single push. Late in the day, we boot-packed our way up the snowy west face at sunset, following the sun onto snowfields lit orange and pink as shadow crept up below us, pushing hard to stay in the light all the way to the summit. Elated, exhausted, and euphoric from such a fantastic day, we walked down the mountain and across a glacier, lit up by a newly risen moon. I wanted every day of my life to be just like this one.

That November, Steve and I met up at the Toronto airport to fly to Santiago, Chile, and then ride the bus to Mendoza, our launching point for Aconcagua. Neither Steve nor I had much high-elevation experience, but we followed the acclimatization advice outlined in books. The main gist was to climb high during the day and sleep lower at night. However, just like on Mount Rainier, I found myself plagued by headaches the higher I climbed, and I even threw up a few times. Steve also had troubles acclimatizing and couldn't get past 18,000 feet, so I ended up higher and alone. Crawling into my tent solo on a windswept piece of desolation on a barren plateau at 19,600 feet, I wrote in my journal, "I rarely discuss death, but it can quickly become a reality. So if I die tonight while I sleep or tomorrow while I climb, I love everyone. It would be a peaceful death, but I will fight it to the end. I love you all Mom, Dad, Betsy, Nat, Graham, Adrian, Jerm, Jessie, Ian, Don, all my friends. It would be a pity to die never having loved."

I had made my pact and was willing to die peacefully if anything went wrong. Already, I knew that the rewards were worth the risk.

Excited, I awoke at midnight, ate some oatmeal, and walked off into the moonlight, which brightly lit the path in front of me in the thin air. The trail forked, and I took the one less traveled . . . which was an absolute mistake, as it faded into a scree field where, hour after hour, I plodded on, rarely moving more than seven steps up the endless scree without needing to sit down to rest. Five and a half hours into my march, I reached the base of the final pinnacle at 21,600 feet, just over a thousand vertical feet shy of the summit. I sat down to eat while the sun rose behind Aconcagua, casting a massive pyramidal shadow over the mountains in front of me. I sat transfixed by the beauty of this moment, but at the same time I knew I didn't have it in me to continue to the summit

I had an internal dialogue with myself: "Greg, you are alone, on the highest mountain you have ever been on, and there is supposedly a dead body somewhere higher up. Do you want to add your body to this grave?"

I was alone, in totally unfamiliar territory, with hazards I may not even have understood, and I was filled with concern. I wanted

Steve there to bounce ideas off and make educated decisions, but he was thousands of feet below.

I thought back on the struggles I had just gone through, in which every uphill step had resulted in sliding backwards half a step in the scree, my heart hammered in my ears, and I gasped to catch my breath between slamming heartbeats, my sad little circle of light illuminating my labors all the while. I didn't know if any of this was worth it. For what gains was I struggling? Why had I chosen this mountain? For simple ego reasons, I realized — "Let's climb the highest mountain we can" — to brag back home that I had conquered the highest mountain in the Americas.

It was then that it hit me that I didn't have enough knowledge of myself and of the risks ahead to justify continuing. Pressing on simply for ego reasons wasn't enough, nor would it have been safe. Feet sliding on the shale, I finally stumbled upon the actual trail, and instead of turning right toward the summit, I pivoted left and ran downhill.

Back from Aconcagua, I didn't stay down for long. I had four months until tree-planting season, so I hit the road with my friend Carl, from Dalhousie, kayaking and climbing our way around the States. He was a better kayaker than me, while I was the better climber, so we would each help the other improve at these sports while we traveled. Our days were filled with time on the rock and on the rivers, our mornings and nights filled with tea, cards, and conversation.

One night we were in the middle of Arizona, well off the beaten track, looking for a campsite to park my VW van in. We stopped to chat with a white-haired, red-eyed, wild-looking older man while we rolled through the ponderosa pines, and he kindly directed us to a vacant spot. That night, as Carl and I sat around the fire drinking vinegary Carlo Rossi red wine and playing cribbage, the man strolled into our camp.

"Mind if I join you?" he asked.

Initially, I was upset that someone would interrupt our casual evening of card playing and wine drinking. But I also knew that it paid to be hospitable to fellow campers, and wondered if perhaps this man had something to teach us.

"Sure, why not? I'm Greg, and this is Carl," I said.

"Nice to meet you. I'm Gus," he said, then eying the license plates on my car, added "What are you Canadian boys up to way down here in Arizona?"

"Climbing and kayaking our way around your awesome countryside," I said, taking a slug off the bottle then passing it to Gus.

Thus started a long night of drinking and stories, with Gus rolling out his life lore, which became more interesting once he started talking about his time as a combat veteran in Vietnam, the stories getting gorier and more insane the deeper we tucked into the bottle. So many of his friends had been shot and killed right in front of him while he, and others, had randomly, miraculously, survived.

"Gus, how do you think you did it?" I asked. "What made you the lucky one while the others weren't?"

Gus jerked drunkenly to his feet, stared at me across the fire, his eyes piercing, and then said, "I never gave up, and if I can tell you something, it's to never give up, never give up . . . never give up." And with that, he stumbled off into the night, leaving us to ponder his wisdom.

I moved to Canmore, Alberta, in November 1998 to gain experience ice climbing and become a better mountain climber. At this point, school was well in my rearview mirror, and I had no plans of ever finishing up my degree, much to my father's chagrin. The mountains were going to be my classroom. Through my stepbrother Jeremy, who lived in Canmore, I got a job at Sunshine Village, a ski resort just outside town. Jeremy invited me to live with him, but I wanted to walk my own path and not be in his shadow — I probably still had some residual fears of his childhood tormenting. Instead, I shared a house with a bunch of men who also worked at Sunshine, stretching my wages of $6.50 an hour to make ends meet in this expensive mountain town, but in all truth blowing way more money than I should have on pot and ice-climbing gear, knowing I could always fall back on my dad or brother to borrow money. I cursed myself for my mediocrity and for not living up to my potential, yet I felt powerless to get out of this psychological rut and just smoked away my problems.

A look through my journals from that period reveals that I had so much yearning and desire, yet also the knowledge that I was not yet ready to actualize my potential. My dilemma was probably best summed up by a quote I'd jotted down from Winnie the Pooh: "How can you get very far if you don't know who you are?"

Working at Sunshine Village on the trail crew helped me rekindle my love for skiing. We worked tightly with ski patrol, and I took the time to learn as much as I could about snow science from them, especially while we worked on Delirium Dive, an alpine area that had been newly opened to the public. Funnily enough, one of the ski patrollers was also named Greg Hill, and he'd been at Sunshine for years. To avoid confusion on the radio, I became "Lefty," since I was missing my left pinky finger.

One weekend, we had a ski-patrol-versus-trail-crew hockey game. I'd never really cared for hockey, though as a kid I had liked skating around on the pond on my dad's property with my siblings. Still, I threw myself into the match, so as not to disappoint my teammates. The game grew more and more heated as it progressed. At one point, I went after the puck with gusto, the blades of my skates cutting and pushing off the ice, my competitive spirit urging me on, when out of my peripheral version I saw the other Greg Hill skating toward the puck too. Having no skills, I barreled right into him, hitting his chin with my head and knocking him onto the ice.

Stunned by the blow, I stood there shakily.

"Jesus, what the hell, Lefty?" he said as I helped him back up.

"Greg, I am so sorry. That was completely accidental," I said, and then helped him skate off the ice and get a bandage for the cut above his eye.

There are many stories in our lives, so why would I tell this hockey anecdote? To me, it captures our innate desire to be individuals. I was not really competitive with Greg, but the idea of two Greg Hills crashing into each other felt illustrative of my desire to be recognized as unique. I didn't want to physically dominate him — that was an accident — I just wanted to be the best Greg Hill I could be, in character, in respect to others, in humility.

My main goal while living in Canmore was to further my ice climbing, and so on days off from work I'd venture out to the local ice. It was an incredible medium to climb on — water, slowly dripping down a rock face, that that had frozen into otherworldly blue pillars like the drippings off a candle. It seemed so improbable that we humans had devised a way to climb these trickles of solid water safely, using crampons on our boots and specialized axes with jagged picks in our hands to puncture the ice, protecting against falls with hollow, tube-like screws you ratcheted deep into the frozen waterfall. The first time I ice climbed I could see the allure. I was strong from rock climbing and thrilled by how solid the "holds" felt from the moment I swung my first tool into the ice and heard it thwack, and then followed up with two nice kicks of my crampon teeth. Often the climbs were up the deep, dark ass-cracks of the mountains — clefts, gullies, and massive fissures raked by spindrift — because that is where it was cold and where the best ice formed, though these routes were often claustrophobia-inducing until you were standing on top, back in the daylight again. The places it took me were so rocky and steep, in these precarious mountain positions.

I was also invited along on a wild ski-mountaineering day that will be forever etched into my mind. This was my second day of ski touring in years, and my friend Rico brought me along for one of his crazy ideas. We were a crew of three, plus a small black dog named Whiskey. Rico was a talented and inspiring skier, whom I had watched effortlessly flow down through a forest, making tight turns around the trees. Also on this trip was Don, aka Kramer, an incredibly experienced ski patroller whom I was excited to learn from.

We set a nice, flowy skin track up through six inches of powder snow, winding up a rocky ridge where the coniferous trees shrunk in size as we passed from the treeline into the alpine. It was properly cold, and the skies were clear, but the winds were blasting across the alpine. Rico, as the leader of the group, stopped us on the ridge and skinned around the wind-blasted corner to have a look, a massive snow plume engulfing him as he went. Then he was out of sight, and immediately I grew worried.

I waited a few seconds, and then hollered, "Hey oh . . . hey yo . . ." the wind whipping my words out of my mouth.

After a waiting an anxious beat, we heard back a faint, "It's all good."

As I slid along Rico's track, the wind blowing me around the corner and around the ridge, the line opened up below me. The slope we were on poured down the mountain side, the cliffs tightening it into a chute that crashed to the valley below. Rico stood there grinning, with Whisky beside him.

"I will ski down first, to those cliffs on the right," Rico said. "Then we ski one at a time. When you ski, follow my tracks so that your slough goes the way I want it to."

Then: "Hee-hee, here we go."

I watched as Rico dropped in with a giggle, arcing beautiful turns towards the choke of the line, his snow slough trending left and staying away from him as he milked the right hand side. I had never skied a line anything like this, and my heart was hammering. Kramer skied up to me and quickly followed Rico's turns into the abyss.

Life-or-death decisions were being made here, and I felt that familiar drip of adrenaline creep in. If we fucked up, we would most likely die, rocketing into the cliff walls at lethal speeds. I didn't know enough to make any educated decisions and so leaned on the team's experience. Was I ready to accept the risks? Was I ready to die for this excitement?

Hells yeah, I was.

I followed their turns, imitating them perfectly, learning how they pushed the snow and aimed it away from where they skied, never letting the slough get above them. Each time I jumped, I could feel the yawning void below, the rocks and cliffs sticking up, waiting to kill me. Whisky, fearless, plowed down after me. The fantastic snow continued into the couloir for a bit, and I followed the team's lead.

"Hee-hee," giggled Rico again, as excited as a schoolboy.

Then: "It looks like we may have to jump this little cliff!" I heard him hit the ground with an ummmfff.

I skied down to the edge, sliding sideways slowly to stay in control. The snow ramp I was on ended in a ten-foot cliff above these weird larger snowballs — the couloir was packed with the iceberg-lettuce-sized snowballs, like those ball pits in bouncy castles, as far down as I could see. Kramer looked over at me, grinning with excitement.

"I have never seen anything like this! It's crazy," Kramer said as he jumped/slid down the ice and into the snowballs. "Just jump down a little lower than I did."

With no other option, I stabilized myself and leapt off both feet. The ten feet sped by and I crashed into the balls. They were hard but they also dispersed the energy of my crash, and I was fine.

"We gotta get out of here as quick as we can. We don't have time to mess around. Those strong winds are changing the conditions overhead, and could easily drop the cornice on us," Kramer said. He started jump-turning down the balls, his turns as awkward as I had ever seen him ski. I followed closely, the snowballs tripping me up a little as I jumped and landed. These turns were nothing like the top turns; in fact, they sucked! I was scared and I moved quickly, never looking back, keeping my focus on just getting safely down the chute.

It was tense as we skied down, though eventually we reached the end of the balls and got back on better snow. The tension of the last forty-five minutes was like a dam bursting as I skied out safely at the bottom. Shaking with relief, we all high-fived at the bottom. We had survived.

The excitement level of ski mountaineering was unlike anything I had felt before—the prelude of excitement, the buildup as you hiked up the mountainside, the tension of the unknown heightening every nerve. Then the complete commitment into uncertainty. The consequences were so real, the moments so intoxicating, the drip of adrenaline so tasty.

I knew I needed more.

On New Year's Eve 1999, I was walking home with Jay, a friend from work. Uncut moonlight bathed the Rundle Massif, a multi-peaked sharp rock ridge high above Canmore, its snow fields glowing with an intensity that made them float surreally above us. The wind, meanwhile, blasted snow off the ridges, spinning the snowflakes into massive, airborne waves, like giant white flags waving off the mountaintops.

"That's why . . . That's why!" Jay shouted, and I knew that he was right. I knew that I'd need mountains in my life forever.

PHOTO CREDIT: MYLES BERNEY

Chapter Eight
SEEKING A SENSEI: 1999/2000

"Always be open and curious."
— Excerpt from letters to my family

In 1999, I was recovering from a shoulder injury, having dislocated my left shoulder by shockloading it while trying too hard on the small crimps of a 5.12c at Nordic Rock, a cliff near Whistler. Without climbing, I'd found myself adrift, wondering just who I was. I needed that feeling of being tested. Of teetering on the edge of risk, body flushed with adrenaline, all focus entirely in the moment. Fingers clinging desperately onto sharp holds, breath calmed and focused. Intentional. I needed the compliments from my partners, the communion between us. The connectedness.

Missing that outlet (at that point I'd been climbing for seven years), I instead threw myself wholeheartedly into backcountry skiing, moving back to Whistler to pursue my passion. I found that ski touring had a great blend of challenge and rewards, very similar to rock climbing. My need for fear would be sated with the ever-present hazards found in the backcountry. In the mountains, there were myriad dangers to contend with, so there also needed to be constant vigilance, if not fear. A slow drip of adrenaline, all day — the perfect drug.

To distract myself from the monotony of skinning up, I began running math games in my head, inspired by all my years of tree planting. I would see how much vertical we were climbing per hour and then add that up to see what we could achieve that day, much like I'd used my rate of trees planted per minute to predict my daily tree-planting total.

One day while out ski touring in the Whistler backcountry, our group ended up doing around 5,500 vertical feet of touring — a huge, exhausting day. During the last hour of that tour, when I knew with certainty that we would climb 5,500 feet, I wondered what that would add up to if I did that every day for a calendar year. The math added up to be close to two million feet, a mind-boggling number. With the upcoming turn of the millennium, I really liked the synchronicity (or magic) of hiking 2,000,000 feet in the year 2000. So, I started to dream up an idea.

However, if I was going to do all this backcountry skiing, I also needed to absorb as much information from experienced mountain guides as I could, and so I signed up for an avalanche course to be held on Rogers Pass. I drove to Revelstoke in a two-wheel-drive Ford van with studded tires and a bed in the back to sleep in. In town, taking in the trees laden with new snow, I felt like I had come home. It was surreal being back in this magical, wintry town. It had been four years since that first incredible backcountry trip, when my mind was opened to the endless possibilities in the mountains.

In the days prior to the course, while out ski touring, I schussed down a slope with the lightest snow billowing over my shoulders; it felt like I was falling s owly through clouds, and I hooted and hollered with unbridled joy. It was a freedom unlike any I'd known: no self-doubt, no self-criticism, no life pressures, just a pure state of being present.

My cousin Magee lived in Revelstoke with a buddy, Frank, so I ended up staying with them the nights before my course. To celebrate the twenty-third birthday their roommate, Shane, we went on a fantastic ski tour in Rogers Pass, up Grizzly Shoulder. The pass is halfway between Calgary and Vancouver, where the Trans-Canada Highway climbs to 4,354 feet to slice through the rugged Selkirk Mountains. The Selkirks get an annual average of twenty feet of fallen snow that typically builds into a six-plus-foot base. And it's perhaps the best snow on Earth for skiing — light and consistently good. For all this good, there has to be a bad, and that is the long history of avalanches in the Selkirk Mountains. Statistically, the interior ranges are responsible for 50 percent of the avalanche fatalities in Canada. In 1910, for example, sixty-two train workers were killed on the pass in two consecutive avalanches that swept the railway, Canada's largest avalanche disaster. And in 1991, nine skiers were killed in a large avalanche while heli-skiing, which is still the largest guided avalanche fatality in BC.

On the way up, Shane and I bonded about our mountain dreams and desires. Standing at six-foot-two, he looked like a long-limbed, barrel-chested surfer, so full of life. absolutely loving the adventure of every day.

"See that couloir up there, Greg?" he asked me. "That's the French Poodle on Grizzly Mountain. You can easily go up the ridge to the left of it and access the line from behind. It's one of the best lines in Rogers Pass. When you carve your first turn, the 1,500 feet of the couloir drops away, untracked and just waiting."

I looked past his finger at a sinuous line of snow splitting two little summits. It almost didn't look skiable to me, but Shane ensured me that it was.

His yearning for more mountain knowledge was almost palpable. Shane recounted how he'd been learning from my first-ever ski guide, Ruedi Beglinger, praising Ruedi's mountain sense and exacting Swiss methodology, and saying he planned to become the best assistant guide Ruedi had ever had. By working with Ruedi, Shane said, he hoped to deepen his own mountain sense as well.

Mountain sense, in Shane's mind, was a combination of all the mountain knowledge gained from every mountain sensei you'd ever met — things like tricks of the trade, snow-science thoughts, ways of using terrain, and so on. All of these layers of knowledge came together to form a book of your own mountain sense, which would inevitably serve as your own guide through the hills.

"You know, to live a life of immortality, you must first live a life worth remembering," Shane concluded. I could see that his need for freedom — the wild kind you can only find in the mountains — was much like my own. As we continued skinning up, he pointed out other lines he wanted to ski and divulged more about the layout and lore of Rogers Pass.

During the avalanche course, we took an in-depth look at how the snow falls, as well as at the different processes like faceting, in which prolonged cold weather sucks the moisture out of the snow and creates more angular surfaces, or the reverse process in which warm temperatures round out the snow crystals and they bond better to each other. In my head, I imagined the rounder shapes gluing the snowpack together, while the angular ones slid easily across each other. The avalanche dynamic involves a complex relationship between temperatures, moisture, snow, wind, and sun, and it takes a lifetime to understand well. And, in the end, avalanches do not recognize experts anyway.

As part of our course, we watched films showcasing the raw power of avalanches. The filmmakers had placed small cameras in boxes, putting these in known avalanche chutes. Then they triggered the slopes above with explosives and filmed the avalanches. The footage showed great walls of snow billowing and thundering down mountainsides, a sight that you could almost call mesmerizing were it not so deadly. With the carefully placed cameras, the clouds would roar right over us, the viewers. You felt as if you were standing there and getting engulfed by the lethal wall of wind and snow.

After seven days of constant snowfall, the morning of December 7 dawned cloudless and cold, a deep-blue winter sky framing the jagged ridgelines of Rogers Pass. We — all eight of us avalanche students plus our two instructors — started skinning up the NRC Gully, a large avalanche path that slides down toward the highway off the peak of West MacDonald. Being in such a big group, it took us a while to get going, and there was a group already well above us. West MacDonald looks like it was designed for skiing — nature had sculpted perfect ski runs, running 4,000 feet directly from the ridgeline to the valley. As we all looked up, our instructor pointed out the other group's skin track above.

"What do you guys think of that skin track up there? Are they making the right choices?" he asked.

"The safest thing we can do is go up the most mature timber and find the least exposed route, minimizing the amount of snow sitting above us."

Given the new meter of snow that had fallen over the previous week, it seemed like the group above was pushing their safety limits and exposing themselves to very large avalanche slopes. When an avalanche starts, it flows down the fall line, almost exactly like water. So, avalanches almost always follow the flow of the land and use the same tracks over and over. On West MacDonald, the 4,000-foot perfect runs were in fact 4,000-foot perfect avalanche paths as well. Lining these paths were lots of big trees that were more than 100 years old, which meant there was also lots of safe terrain, if you stayed in or near the trees. Yet this group was zigzagging up the open slopes, far from the safety of the trees and other protective terrain. This would have been fine with safe conditions, but the week of snow and lots of unknowns in terms of wind effects and cohesion between the layers had greatly increased the risk.

"Historically, more avalanche accidents happen on the first sunny day after a period of storms," the instructor said. "Psychologically, people get caught up in the excitement of the day and push into larger and more complex terrain than they should."

Our group took a different route, skinning 1,200 feet up through mature timber, winding amongst the ancient and towering spruce trees. We hiked a little into the avalanche path, just enough to make space to dig our pits while minimizing our exposure to the mountain above.

For the next thirty minutes, we were heads down, engrossed in the snow, digging away and analyzing the layers, cutting out self-supporting blocks to see how they slid atop the storm layers, and peppering our instructor with question after question. We were starting to notice that the new interface was not bonding well with the lower layers of snow, trending toward dangerous instability.

Suddenly, someone yelled, "AAAAvalanche — AAAAAAvalanche coming! Get out of the way!"

Thousands of feet above, a giant white cloud was swelling and careering down toward us, just like in the avalanche films — except this time, we weren't watching it on a screen. The cloud grew in strength and noise as it approached, sounding like a herd of bison rumbling across a plane or like a 747 taking off, when the whine of the turbines is far away at first and slowly builds till you cannot even hear your thoughts as the jet flies overhead.

Mesmerized by the slide's power and beauty, I stood

transfixed for what felt like ages, then I finally tore my eyes away and sprinted into the forest. As I hit the protection of the timber, the cloud blew by, going at least 60 mph and leaving a deafening silence in its wake. The instructors started calling names, and we realized we were all accounted for. Even our snow pits were okay, dusted under inches of blown snow but otherwise not hit by the heart of the slide, which lay in a massive smear about 200 feet away in the middle of the slope. Downslope, we could see trees poking through the snow, some broken from the blast, others bent completely over.

"Okay, we know that there was a group above us. Likely they triggered it and could have been swept down the entire mountainside," said our instructor, with a practiced calm. "Let's split up and take half the group up the mountain, and the other half can start looking with their beacons downslope."

Some of us skinned upwards, while the rest of us skied down, both groups crisscrossing the avalanche debris with our beacons turned on to receive. For 1,200 scary feet, we searched for a signal from a buried beacon. Listening attentively to our beacons, worried that my slamming heartbeats would mask the sounds, I zigzagged downhill from the forest till I met up with another student in the middle. I scanned swiftly with my beacon, hoping yet not wanting to find any sounds. For twenty heart-stopping minutes, we traversed the debris, finding no beacons.

With no beacons pinging below, this meant the skiers had to be above us — and sure enough, all five of them were soon located. A couple of hours later, a helicopter flew in to assist with the rescue. I volunteered to fly up in the chopper and take a toboggan down to one of the victims. It was wild to witness the size of the slide from the air; it was a mile wide and had run more than a half-mile down the mountainside. At the bottom, strewn across the flats, the debris had piled deeply enough to bury a train. I spied the crown by following the trench of destruction up past where we dug our pits, higher up the mountainside to where a crisp, four-foot-tall wall crowned the slope, crossing gully after gully. The amount of snow involved was impossible to fathom.

Somehow the five people in the group above us had been kept near the top of the mountain, where they had been syphoned up by the trees, saving them from thousands more feet of tumbling but exposing them to impacts against the tree trunks. The helicopter hovered by the slope while we unloaded the toboggan and set up to ski down to a victim. It was my first time skiing with a toboggan, and the sled kept bumping me from behind, though it was manageable. I skied down to a female victim who had already been visited by one of the first rescuers flown up onto the mountain. I knew that she was okay, with a hurt back and a twisted knee but no other significant injuries. While I was helping wrap her up in the toboggan, I overheard chatter on the radio. One of the victims was "code black," meaning dead, while the remaining three were badly banged up and needed to be flown to the waiting ambulances as quickly as possible.

As I talked to the injured girl, I began to realize that I knew some of her crew — and that it included Frank and Shane. Watching them skinning high above us in the morning, I had had no way of knowing that they were my friends, and now one of them — I didn't know who — was code black! I felt my gut roil with panic.

This fucking Adventurer's Pact is harsh. For all the great times, it can turn so quickly. More than once I've had to ask myself, "Is it really all worth it?"

I stayed around to help the mountain-rescue team, watching as the rescuers picked off the toboggan with a long line and flew away into the setting sun. Then I grabbed as much gear as I could and enjoyed some final powder turns for myself and all those who hadn't that day or who never would again.

I met up with the rest of the rescuers at the bottom and got a much more detailed debriefing. Shane, who was the most experienced and fit in the group of five, had been skinning out ahead, setting the track for everyone to follow; it was he who'd triggered the avalanche. The sliding snow swept Shane into the trees and kept moving him downslope, where he'd been killed by multiple impacts. Meanwhile, my other buddy Frank, who was much farther down the slope, got pulled through many small trees and had both of his arms and legs broken, but he'd survived — so far. The other three skiers had, somehow, sustained much lesser injuries.

I had problems digesting the fact that Shane, with whom I had skied a fantastic day just a few days earlier and partied with for his birthday, was dead — at age twenty-three — with so many years ahead of him and such a big thirst for life. His favorite saying had been "To live a life of immortality, you must first live a life worth remembering." That day on West MacDonald, Shane's natural exuberance and love of adventure had clouded his mind to the risks, and he'd paid the ultimate price. In the mountains, the consequences of one's mistakes are very immediate and very real.

Meanwhile, Frank, who'd been airlifted to a hospital, had sustained injuries so severe that the doctors later told him he might never walk again. Frank — my talented athlete friend, who could throw backflips off cliffs and float his snowboard effortlessly down steep, snow-laden mountains — might never snowboard or even walk again. How fucking real was that? And was it worth it? Was I still willing to risk it? At least I was single, with no dependents and no partner to leave behind if I died in the alpine.

After the dreadful avalanche, I needed to find a mentor, and fast. I needed some wisdom to balance the puppyish enthusiasm I was feeling for being in the mountains.

That winter, of 1999/2000, I joined the Employment Insurance (EI) Ski Team. In this "exclusive club," you work all summer, saving money at some well-paying job, then, unable to find comparably paid work during the winter, go on the government dole, collecting EI, which pays out during the winter until you can start working again. Initially, I felt guilty about using the system, but I wanted to gain as much mountain experience as possible, and this was the best way.

On almost any given day in the winter, you could find me out in the mountains, skinning around, often solo since I didn't know anyone else in Whistler who was into ski-touring. Skiing solo, within the limits of my knowledge, made me seek out the easiest and safest ways up mountains. I always searched for the ridge or the ramp that had the least overhead exposure, and I made sure there were no large slopes or cornices looming over my ascent. I sifted through all the learnings from my course and from the ski patrollers at Sunshine Village, and made as the best, most educated decisions I could. In this much larger and more dangerous playing field — large mountains with all sorts of inherent hazards — there was so much to pay attention to compared to relatively tame rock climbing. I was so engaged and I had direction, which helped with my uncertainty in this new arena. That winter, I lived with twelve Australians in a six-bedroom apartment, and at the end of our wild days in the hills, we would all recount our adventures, jokingly saying, "Sponsors are happy," if we'd had a particularly good day out.

I was so hooked on ski mountaineering that I went hard almost every day. The adrenaline drip was so tasty. The more I went out, the more familiar the closest terrain became, fostering a growing confidence that had me pushing further and further.

There was one particular mountain that had me hooked: Decker Mountain, a nearly 8,000-foot peak above town. It had three beautiful and steep couloirs, each one a thread of snow weaving down the broken cliff bands of the north face. These lines were as rowdy and scary looking as any I'd attempted. One day, I came out after eight inches of light powder had fallen; the protected skin track was fairly effortless, without the wind having blown across to bond the snowflakes. The snow here was perfect. However, as I skied into one of the couloirs, I noted that the southwest winds had blown across the tops and loaded them up with more snow. Instead of individual snowflakes, the flakes had bonded into a soft, flexible, Styrofoam-like consistency. As my skis cut horizontally through this, all the snow beneath suddenly peeled away. I hung on desperately with my edges, watching as the snow billowed and crashed 1,000 feet to the valley.

Breathing in and out, I calmed myself. It had been very close, though I must confess that the rest of my turns down Decker that day felt just a little more awesome, with my senses sharpened by the dump of adrenaline. However, at the bottom, the guilt set in and I began to feel badly about almost dying — and I questioned the Adventurer's Pact. I could have easily died tumbling down the rocky couloir, pulled to my untimely death by the snow. My death would have been self-centered, affecting everyone else more than me, leaving them to grieve my loss.

With the risks laid so bare, I started to develop an 80/20 rule in my mind: 80 percent of my being could be embrace the moments and feel the amazingness of the adventure. But 20 percent had to always be looking around, questioning, calculating, and forecasting. No matter how good the conversation with friends was, and no matter how perfect the skiing was, this inspector always has to be analyzing clues and searching for solutions and escape plans.

My ski experience was growing daily, pushing me into bigger and bigger lines. The weather had been consistent for days, with no real avalanche hazard, when one day out ski touring off Blackcomb Peak I ran into Ryan Oakden, a locally famous skier. We chatted briefly and then he said, "Dude, see that line over there — the one that starts above those cliffs and then stays above them the whole way to the valley?"

I looked across and spotted the line, a perfect snow ramp fifteen-to-twenty feet wide that started off the ridge and stayed above the cliff line as it cascaded down. It was diagonal so that your right turns would send snow flowing over the 400-foot cliffs below.

"I've daydreamed about the possibility of skiing that line — is it actually skied?" I asked. "It would be terrifying to watch your slough fall off the cliffs below you!"

"It does get skied, but very rarely. I don't know how to get over there, but I know I can ski it," Ryan quipped.

"I've been all over that ridge and know how to get us there," I said. "If I get us there, will you ski it first?"

Ryan and I skinned and hiked our way over to the line, taking just over an hour. I stood on the ridge and looked down. The line was so committing — steep, savage, exposed, and with no room for error unless you wanted to follow your slough off the massive cliffs. By skiing it, I was accepting all consequences. There were no half measures — if shit went wrong, you died.

It was that simple. The line was complete madness. However, all the math made sense; there'd been little change in the snowpack for weeks, ard I had been skiing a variety of smaller, less committing lines like this and nothing had moved. If there was a day, this was it.

I breathed slowly to calm my nerves, and then said, "Ryan, I won't be able to see you after the second turn, so please ski carefully and don't let your left-turns slough catch you. And then ski way out into the valley where I should be able to see you . . ."

Ryan clipped into his yellow 200-centimer skis and pointed them down the line. He charged into it like the fearsome ski competitor that he was. The first turn was powder and light, while the second sent a massive plume of snow behind him. Then he was out of sight, and all I could see was the trail of his slough flowing off the c iffs into the unknown. For untold, fearful seconds, I waited to find out if he'd made it. Finally, a holler sounded out of the valley and then I saw Ryan straightening out in the basin below.

"Am I okay with the consequences? Am I willing to I die today?" I remember thinking. My cells were buoyed by adrenaline, my thoughts clearer than ever, my blood flowing rapidly through my system, my senses tingling with desire. As I stood there pondering, the answer came to me: Fuck yes, I am.

I slid off into the abyss, my first turn tentative, my second spraying up a wave of snow that I watched tumble off the cliffs. I slid right and quickly pulled in a tight left turn, not letting the snow catch me, then I laid into another right-handed turn. The snow sprayed over the edge of the precipice and the valley looked impossibly distant below, but all was well. I was in my groove. I'd wanted this.

Finally, the exit appeared and all my fears and doubts exploded in the exhilaration of success. I had just skied what I'd thought was an impossible line, and done it with style — I will never forget this feeling. It was all so exhilarating. But I still needed guidance; I was a swordsman with huge potential and no real mountain skill. I needed a mountain sensei to teach me more.

During my avalanche course, I met a fellow student, Scott Newsome, who directed me toward the Canadian Ski Guide Association (CSGA). In April of 2000, I spent a week travelling around the mountains with some of the CSGA guides, as part of their level 1 guides course. I listened and learned as much as possible. I wanted to sponge up as much knowledge from as many different guides as I could. I also discovered that personal mountain sense is developed over time, and it is best gained by gleaning snippets of wisdom from various knowledgeable sources — taking a bit here and there to add up to some sense of what to do or not do in the mountains.

On my final day out skiing with Shane, three days before he'd died, he had mentioned learning from Ruedi Beglinger, my original ski-touring instructor. It seemed right to search Ruedi out five years later and try to learn from him. If I wanted to be one of the best, it only made sense to seek out the best.

Chapter Nine

TWENTY THOUSAND FEET

"Don't let your phones distract you from the real purpose of life: figuring cut who the hell you are!!!"
— *Excerpt from letters to my family*

Through some twist of fate, I was re-acquainted with Paul Décarie, a family friend from Quebec. Paul oversaw carpentry for the guiding outfit Selkirk Mountain Experience and their various lodges, and he invited me to join him. In September 2000, I flew back into the Selkirk Mountains, landing at the same spot I had years ago. This was my chance to get to know Ruedi better, ideally impress him with my character and potential, and convince him to take me under his wing. However, he didn't remember me from those first days of ski touring back in my university days — though I never really expected him to remember a kid from five years earlier, I hoped he would.

Ruedi had an incredible legacy and was said to have skied more vertical than any other guide . . . anywhere. He was known to be stern and hard on his assistants, and yet he was the absolute best. If I could work up at his lodge and shadow him, I would learn so much. Of course, I'd have to develop a thick skin to withstand his rigorous and meticulous Swiss/German demeanor, but I'd gain so much if I could just keep calm.

Any chance I could, I picked RB's brain on what I should do to become a competent ski mountaineer and ski guide. When RB told me that he offered a one-week leadership course, I was ecstatic, writing in my journal: "A week with RB would be unreal. He knows mountains. I may be able to ski; I may be able to climb mountains with ease. [But] I don't know them as he does. He would be able to tell me where I stood. I am adept at learning; I firmly believe this man can show me the heart of the mountains." Five years earlier, I'd been blown away by his confidence and ease of traveling through the alpine, and I wanted as much of that for myself as I could soak up. By the end of the first week back, RB and I felt like friends, and I was working hard on getting into his leadership course. I knew how important it would be to my development — actually, to my *survival* as a skier.

The more I grasped about avalanche hazard, the more I understood that the Coastal Mountains were not the best place to learn — they were "too safe" because of the snow's warmth and weight, meaning the snowpack had fewer instabilities. It was great for skiing, but less risk meant less knowledge was needed to stay safe.

However, Revelstoke and the surrounding Columbia Mountains hosted some of the best snow in the world and had a tendency toward varying instabilities and persistent weak layers in the snowpack. With these increased hazards — these massive avalanche cycles — came the need to know more about mountain travel and how to make consistently excellent decisions. I decided to move to Revelstoke to imbue my mountain sense with the need to always be safe and make great decisions. These were not mountains to be complacent in, and I chose them to teach me.

In December 2000, I moved in with my cousin Magee and my buddy Myles in Revelstoke. Myles teamed up as my ski partner that season, but it was an atypically dry year, so the powder was less than epic. Instead, I put my time into learning how to move efficiently and how to set a nice skin track that is easier to follow and requires less power to use. The size of the step you take must change with the pitch of the skin track: faster, smaller steps when it's steep, and longer, stretched-out steps when the angle lessens. I focused on trying to glide and slide my way up the mountain, versus simply stomping. I also went on a few ski traverses, an incredibly arduous way to see the mountains. Ski traverses are essentially hiking trips through the winter-bound mountains, with the additional challenge of technical skiing and carrying the equipment you need to safely navigate the snowy slopes.

I loved the simplicity of these outings, how they stripped life down to its barest essence. Present-day society has pretty much removed the struggle to survive; if you want, you can cruise on unemployment and free handouts, and you'll have your basic needs met. However, on ski traverses, everything you encounter is set on killing you — well, not really, but almost! The cold is always waiting to zap your energy and freeze you to death; the threat of avalanches is omnipresent; and if you make mistakes, you are far from rescue — plus, we had fewer communication devices to help us get rescued in those days.

You must have everything dialed to ensure your success and must carry an enormous amount of gear. We had loads of clothing to keep warm, stoves to melt snow for water and for cooking, shovels, probes, and avalanche beacons, and burly four-season tents. With all this equipment, your backpack could easily weigh sixty pounds for a three-day trip. These trips were like small quests, and I always returned fulfilled. Awakening to freezing cold and getting up to make breakfast while staying warm and watching the sunrise — now this was living! The teams on these outings became tight, and we depended completely on each other, accepting each other's strength and weaknesses unconditionally. One of my longest and best partners, Aaron, was the perfect antidote to my enthusiasm; he always needed concrete reasoning behind our decisions, which made us a perfect pair.

The first winter, I completed three ski traverses. The first was the Spearhead Traverse in Whistler — Vancouver, BC's iconic ski traverse. It started at the Whistler Ski Resort boundary and followed a horseshoe of mountains around and back to Blackcomb Peak. I had spent much time on both ends of these mountains previously, but connecting them on a three-day trip was a whole new level, as the traverse links up twenty summits tied together by glaciers and ridges. It took all of our skills to climb safely through the tumbling glaciers, and to find safe camping spots away from avalanche slopes.

I also completed two more traverses, the Hurley Horseshoe

Traverse north of Pemberton and the Ashlu Traverse near Squamish. Mountains are constantly dangerous, and you must weigh the consequence of your actions at every point. Any error is compounded by your remoteness, so everything must be done correctly. As the saying goes, "Proper prior planning prevents piss poor performance." You have to think through the hazards and challenges you'll have to overcome, and then plan for all of these. If you do not, say, test your stove before you go and find yourself in the middle of a remote glacier with a stove that doesn't work, you'll find yourself in a world of hurt.

These trips were also part of the prerequisite to the Association of Canadian Mountain Guides' Assistant Ski Guide course, which I was hell-bent on taking to further my mountain skill set and safety margin, with the idea of maybe also becoming a guide. One thing that was becoming very clear was that I tended always to have more energy than everyone around me. I am not sure if it was my enthusiasm or the stamina I'd cultivated tree planting, but I could skin up mountains for hours and still have the drive to do more. When my crew was punched at the end of the day, I still had tons of desire left.

The most challenging job when you're skinning is that of the trail breaker, who has to push each ski down through the fresh snow, alternately, to create the track and who thus cannot glide or slide anywhere. Then the second person has a bit of effort, and for the third person, it's even easier, and by the fourth, there is a well-packed trench one in which you can glide and slide your way uphill with much less exertion.

I quickly realized that for our team to be the most successful, I should serve as trail breaker, putting my prodigious energy to good use. I was also hooked on the artistic skill it took to wind a safe, aesthetically pleasing skin track up a mountainside. The trail left behind is one that others will use, and the better built it was, the less difficult it would be for all.

The largest ski-touring day I had ever heard of around Revelstoke was 20,000 feet of vertical gain, which also meant 20K feet of downhill skiing. This was almost what heli-skiers, paying $1,000 per day, got on a regular day out — except this feat had been human-powered! I began to dream of hitting or even besting this number, trying to see what my daily limit was. My biggest day so far had been about 8,000 feet, but at the day's end I'd still had stamina in reserve and I'd still wanted more. Since my friends didn't have the depth of energy I seemed to have and they probably never would, I figured the 20,000 day was something I might someday try to pull off by myself.

In September 2001, I flew back into the Selkirk Mountains to join Ruedi at his main lodge, the Durrand Glacier Chalet, to help him build a sauna. The lodge sits atop a majestic ridge, with a view out over the steep, tumbling south face of Tumbledown Mountain. It was a pleasure to work there.

Up on the wall of Ruedi's room in the lodge, he'd hung photos of his first descents and first ascents in Europe, and he had photo books of the many traverses he'd completed — the room was an ode to his accomplishments. But what stuck with me the most was a poster in the outhouse. Originally an advertisement for this ski-touring-binding company Dynafit, the poster had been turned into a spoof ad for something called "Dynasausage."

Someone had cut out a photo of Ruedi holding a mottled meat sausage and glued it onto the ad, adding the quote: "I have ski toured nearly a million feet a season for the last 15 years," supposedly powered by the energy from the sausage. Ruedi — who was notorious for pushing people to do big days — confirmed these stats when I asked him. The ad was also a bit of a fuck you to the heli-skiing industry, as they had a special ski suit they gave their clients if they had skied a million feet — testimony, you might say, to spending more than $100,000 and having a lot of leisure time.

I returned later in December to take Ruedi's mountain-leadership course. Then I convinced him to bring me on as a helper for a few weeks to keep sponging up his knowledge.

The leadership course was an incredible experience. We spent all seven days on skis and skins, constantly feeling the snow and watching the hills change with the movement of wind and storms. RE had so much wisdom to share. He showed us how to create a toboggan to move an injured person down the slopes. He explained how to set a nice, mellow skin track that was effortless to follow yet efficiently gained the mountaintop. And he explained in detail how wind moved through the mountains, and how it changed the density of snow to predispose certain slopes to avalanches. Watching him weave his beautiful skin tracks around the mountains was so educational — how he would always stay in the safest zones, linking terrain to avoid any hazards. He almost painted his skin track, flowing his line effortlessly around the alpine features.

RB also passed along two huge takeaways that have kept me alive for years. The first was to "always ski from the top." This was not simply because mountaintops are the best, most logical places to begin your run, but because by starting up top you have literally zero threats hanging above you. Then, while you ski down, you stabilize the snow around you and leave fewer hazards in your wake.

RB's second piece of advice was, "The first three turns in a feature are where most avalanches will happen." This is because wind has its greatest effect on the upper reaches of all snow features, and where the convex roll has added the most tension in the snowpack. Imagine a waterfall, paused in motion; it's easy to imagine the potential energy in the falling water, but this water is also pulling on the water right above the falls. Convex rolls are like this — they aren't well supported by the snow below, and in many ways are being pulled by this snow. With this tension on top of the convex roll, if you cut this snow and there is an instability, it will likely react.

Taking the knowledge I'd accrued from RB's course, my avalanche course, and the CSGA course, I turned my sights back on the goal of a 20,000-plus-foot day. I really wanted to continue being mentored by Ruedi, and ideally this 20K would show him my potential.

On one particularly stable day in February 2002, it looked like I could head out and never have to break trail. The previous week I had watched skin tracks being set and had set my own tracks up the major high cols in Rogers Pass. To keep it interesting, I had a loop that initially went up Little Sifton, a 4,600-foot climb, then if I skied back down to the valley, I could go up to Bruins Pass, adding another approximately 4,000 feet, followed by a quick visit to Balu Pass and a ski out to the center, with around 10K done. Then I could drive down and start at the Illecillewaet parking lot and start again in a whole new zone.

It was time to test myself. I ventured out without partners, so I had zero safety net, but this meant I could also go at my own pace. I looked at it as a day of tree planting, and I worked the day exactly as I would have planting trees — tree by tree, step by step. I accepted the amount of challenge and hardship coming, and readied myself for it. Really embraced it. The wonder of what I was doing fueled me, hitting a flow state and just sliding up and down mountainsides. Everything so efficient that not a drop of energy is lost.

I breathed heavily, skinned continuously, and searched for my new maximum. All day I watched the little number on my Suunto altimeter increase as it calculated my uphill vertical. Quick snacks and efficient transitions had me shouting from the mountainsides. I often startled people as I caught up to them on the skin tracks, sweat dripping off my face, heart hammering, a maniacal smile beaming below my twinkling eyes. I was always ready with a positive comment to encourage others on their day out.

I wanted this. The more my legs tired, the more I started relying on taking rest steps, a technique high-altitude mountaineers use in which, essentially midway through your stride, you use your quad to power through from one leg to the next. The moment you can pass your weight over to the new leg, you straighten the bottom leg out and connect all the bones, creating a stable platform that requires no muscles to hold the body in place. In this position your muscles can relax briefly, recuperating power for the next step.

Past 8,000 feet, each effort added up to a new personal best. My inner coach was aggressive, yelling things like, "Do you want this, Greg? The only barrier is your desire . . . Do you really want this? If you do, let's go . . . breathe . . . breathe . . . breathe . . . Come on, keep gliding and sliding. Believe in yourself . . . you've worked hard and prepared for this."

On my second-to-last climb, I crested a col to find a group of backcountry skiers.

"Dude, you're moving! We watched you catch up to us from way down the valley — impressive," a tanned older man commented.

Getting my heartbeat back under control, I humble-bragged, "Yeah, it's just me, so I can move swiftly by myself. Man, it's been quite the day." And then, despite my better judgement, I added, "I've toured more today than I ever have — my watch just ticked over 18,000 feet up, and I'm getting close to my goal of 20K."

"Holy shit — that's insane," the man said. "We're crushed from our 4,000-foot day, and here you are, smiling away."

Almost blushing with pride, I detailed my day to them. Meanwhile, I was ripping my skins, switching my gear, and getting ready to go back down. Buoyed by their awe of my day, I wished them a great run and shredded off down the slope.

The rewards were waiting at the top of every ascent, where I could point my skis downhill and let gravity take over. I felt as giddy as a kid on a sled as I carved blissful, swift turns down the mountainsides. It was pure, uncut freedom, laughter recharging my tanks for the next big skin up. In just over ten hours, my watch ticked over 20,000 feet.

I'd done it. I'd proven to myself that I had insane stamina. And I'd proven that a positive attitude combined with desire would let me achieve my dreams and climb and ski more than I ever had in a day.

And yet, I still had to be careful, as my energies often blind me to risk. This manifested one day in March 2002, when I was ski touring in the backcountry. My day had been flowing smoothly, and my skin tracks were everywhere. Some 300 feet from a summit, I looked up and contemplated simply skiing from where I was, which would require me to cut out under the summit face, potentially undermining 300 feet of snow.

Ruedi's words echoed in my mind: "Always ski from the top — the first three turns are where most avalanches happen." And so, I opted to bootpack the rocky ridge all the way to the summit. From the top, my first turn was off the windswept peak, my second into slightly deeper wind-transported snow, and on my third the entire slope ripped out below my skis, 7 inches deep and 150 feet wide. In seconds, thousands of pounds of snow were careering down the avalanche path, gaining speed as the slide thundered into the trees, smashing some over, shaking others.

My little actions had created massive devastation, and huge snow clouds engulfed the forest below, all triggered by me. The energy I felt in that moment was body shaking, an elixir of fear combined with power. The feeling was so raw, so real . . . so intoxicating. The drug of adrenaline had me in its grip.

Chapter Ten

THIRTY THOUSAND FEET

"I take lots of risks and can easily be taken out at any point. One of my skills in life has been to mitigate these risks and accomplish wild, audacious acts."
— Excerpt from letters to my family

In tree planting, the days go long, sometimes twelve hours or, every once in a while, even longer, pushing you to your mental and physical limits — though the trancelike state induced by weed and its painkilling properties helped. I imagined skinning up and skiing 30,000 vertical feet would be a similar endeavor, requiring a zenlike, almost monastic mindset. There were rumors of someone in the States who had done a 30K day, so I knew it was possible but I also knew I'd need to train for it seriously if I wanted a decent shot. Fall of 2002, I increased the amount of trail running I was doing and added in more uphill running to strengthen my lungs and legs.

At home in Revelstoke, I also began thinking about logistics. I had all the maps of the surrounding mountains up on my wall and started to draw in the lines of where I had adventured. Each day that I returned from some new quest, I would pencil my little lines up and around the mountains, leaving behind a tangible trace of memory. Seeing where I had skied inspired me to seek places I had never been, and soon enough, I had lines drawn up and down many of the local mountains. It was these lines, in some certain order, that I'd need to connect to hit 30,000 feet.

At 3:30 a.m. on March 2, 2003, I drove up solo into the darkened mountains. This early, only their jagged ridgelines stood out, dark shadows silhouetted by the brightening morning sky. My plan was simple: I would follow the up-track that wound its way 2,900 feet up Grizzly Shoulder. From there, I could easily drop down for a quick second lap or go 1,700 feet higher to the summit of Little Sifton — thus each lap could add either 3,330 or 4,630 vertical feet, or something in between, depending on how high I climbed and how low I skied. I would leave my backpack at the bottom and hike with just a few snacks in my pocket, stopping at my pack after each run to get a drink, reapply sunblock, sort out my layering, and so on.

The skin track up Grizzly is perfect for vertical — it basically goes straight up, with no long, flat valley to deal with — and the ski down is the same. It was very efficient for gaining and losing vertical. Still, I knew that I needed everything to be smooth and function like clockwork. I was hiking up at 4:00 a.m., lit by a small headlight. I toured for around thirty minutes and set up my basecamp of food for the day. I quickly ate something, tightened my bag up, tucked it against a tree, and then headed up.

For the next 15 hours, I ran/skinned up and down this mountainside. I summited Little Sifton three times, once with some friends who had the same timing as me. Five of my laps were smaller, somewhere around 3,500 feet, measuring my stopping point against a small cliff band across from the slope. My goal was to hold a pace of around 40 feet of vertical per minute, or 2,400 feet an hour. All my training that summer was helping, and my quads didn't burn nearly as much as they had on my 20,000-foot day. All I needed to do, really, was stay in motion,

My skis were locked into the skin track. I breathed in deeply through my nose and then out through my mouth, expelling as I stepped up with my right leg, and then inhaling as I moved my weight onto my left leg. Tying my motions into my breathing has always put me into a meditative state. I think of my numbers and focus on moving, and soon enough my mind is off daydreaming, a million miles away, while my body does all the work.

My flow would end as I approached others on the skin track, bringing me back to Earth. Still, I enjoyed the human connection and the mutual support as I awkwardly passed them, encouraging them and then continuing upward with their "You've got this" echoing in my ears.

At one point, I noticed a large white mountain goat standing off to the side of the snow, munching calmly on alpine grasses. I looked up at him on his cliff as I whizzed by. He, in turn, watched me and then continued with his day. An hour and change later, I passed him again while climbing. I had to wonder what I looked like to him, a long-haired human with an ironic mullet I'd cut especially for a ski-mountaineering race a few months back — to showcase my redneck Canadian heritage — panting his way up the mountain, only to ski back down again, jumping off cliffs and shouting with enthusiasm. The goat probably didn't even give me a second thought! At one point, I skied right up to him and took a picture. He barely moved while I stood six feet away and snapped the photo. Then I skied off to set another new personal record.

The next day back at home, my quads sore and cramping from all that effort, I looked up the symbolism of mountain goats. Per one website, "The appearance of a goat spirit animal at a certain point is symbolic of new opportunities and greater heights you can reach in life." It seemed fitting given what I'd set out to do that day, and I was grateful to have had the majestic animal looking over me while I'd pushed myself to a new personal record: 30,000 vertical feet.

For me, it's easy to get caught up in my successes. With this new record, I had hit a point where I was feeling very fit and free; I'd developed a fitness that was exceptional and was doing things that were exceptional. The intoxication and power of it was like crisp, cold water from a creek. I drank it down and grew overconfident in my skills. And then my arrogance nearly killed me.

One day that winter, in late March, I was skiing on Mount Macpherson, a nearly 8,000-foot peak rising right above Revelstoke, feeling like a bird soaring above the mountains as I cut turns down the mountain. By noon, I was already 10,000 feet in, with plenty of time and energy left for more, gliding free through silky, untracked powder. Completely caught up in my energy, I failed to stop and re-check the snow stability as I changed aspects, going from a protected and supported basin to a hanging, wind-affected, unsupported face.

Three turns nto this new feature, I heard a large crack, and everything around me started collapsing and falling down the mountain. There was nowhere I could go — the snow was avalanching on both sides of me. Moreover, I was completely alone, and no one knew where I was. Sure, I was wearing an avalanche transceiver, but all it would do was help rescuers recover my body. Stupid enthusiasm.

"Goddamn it Hill, what have you done?!" I screamed at myself internally. I knew that there was no fighting this avalanche. I went with it and focused on staying calm and under control.

Caught in the sliding snow, I careered down the first 300 feet; I moved my arms in a swimming motion and kept my feet and skis below me, aiming downhill. Then the slope arced ninety degrees to the right, like a waterslide. I flew around the corner, caught in the flow, somehow staying upright and avoiding tumbling. Keeping my wits, I waited for an opportunity — patience at forty-plus mph while mired in a moving carpet of snow is tough to come by, but I controlled my fear and waited. Finally, I was able to ski right and escape the slide; peeling out, I was safe. I watched as the slide went another 1,000 feet, smashing into rocks and trees at the bottom of the slope. I'd escaped unscathed, but I'd certainly been warned: just because you're strong and you think you're safe — hell, you even tell friends to ski with you because you have a "safety circle" around you — doesn't mean that you always are.

Yet, I almost didn't care. It had been close, but in the end nothing had happened. I put my skins back on and climbed back up for another run. If I had died, it would have affected my friends and family, but I didn't yet have kids to raise or support, so I almost justified that it didn't really matter. I remember thinking: I am insignificant in the cosmos, so who cares? Just keep ripping and having fun, enjoying the drip of your favorite drug: risk.

PHOTO CREDIT: BRUNO LONG

Chapter Eleven

FORTY THOUSAND FEET

*"Gosh, some of this is so cheesy. I hope you remember that I
never took myself too seriously."*
— Excerpt from letters to my family

In August 2003, I decided to travel to Chile to ski its high-altitude volcanoes. I had worked hard all summer, planting trees as the lead highballer in the crew and saving mad cash, and I was excited about this trip. I would fly standby on one of my dad's Air Canada passes, with a stopover in Toronto and then Brazil. Since this was a spontaneous trip, I had not planned much My bags were checked and I was sitting in the boarding lounge when I heard over the intercom, "Could Greg Hill please come to the desk?" — where I was promptly informed that, since I didn't have a visa for Brazil, I couldn't board. There would be no Chile.

I called my stepbrother Adrian and told him I'd take the bus into town to meet him and hang out. When he picked me up, I saw two girls in the back of his car. One was blonde and one was brunette, and both were cute and bubbly. They were, it turned out, sisters. Kerry was lovely, but it was Tracey who caught my eye. Her straight brown hair framed her pretty face and highlighted her blazing-blue eyes; when she laughed, her shy smile sparked into a room-warming grin. Her eyes seemed to twinkle when she looked at me.

We went to Adrian's friend's house and walked around back into a secluded backyard to sit at a table. I sat directly across from Tracey, to gaze at her and engage her in conversation. Someone placed a case of beer between us, which I moved so I could see her. I liked what I saw. She was high-energy and emanated sheer happiness. More importantly, she was quick to laugh and found my corny jokes funny.

What made Tracey tick? How could I get her interested in me? I have heard you should always ask women questions. So when I finally had her attention, I asked her what she did for a living.

"I bartend," she said sheepishly, "but I'm educated as an elementary-school teacher. I just haven't had the opportunity yet. It's really hard to get a teaching job in Toronto. Especially since my education was in England."

She continued, "I've always known that teaching kids was my passion," her eyes brightening with emotion.

The night ended, and I went home to Adrian's place, where an old buddy, Yann, also lived. I asked them what they knew about Tracey, who at the time apparently had a boyfriend. Damnit! Still, the next day Yann and I went to the bar where Tracey was bartending, and I watched her at work. She had on a formfitting black dress that accentuated her silhouette and hinted at the thong underwear she was wearing — sexy, for sure! We got drunk, and I continued to flirt with her, convincing her to go to the zoo with me the next day.

That morning, before meeting Tracey, I showered and put on a special outfit: a pair of army-green shorts with a green safari shirt and a sun-blocking safari hat. Outfitted from head-to-toe like Steve Irwin, the 'Crocodile Hunter," I then skipped my way across the street to her. I am pretty sure this was the moment she fell for me, in all my resplendent goofiness. We drove to the zoo, our legs touching in the car, and then I spent all day trying to get her to laugh at more of my stupid pranks. Outside the orangutan pen, I jumped up and down on the benches screeching, pretending to be an ape. And I strutted around in my safari outfit, narrating in a faux British accent about the mating rituals of the animals: "Unbeknownst to his female counterparts, the male peacock will parade around, feathers fanned out, cawing loudly, desperately trying to get the females' attention" — just like I was doing with Tracey.

Unfortunately, my week in Toronto ended and I had to return to Revelstoke. I wondered how I could get back to Toronto and continue flirting with Tracey. Nothing had happened between us, but the tension was there, and I wanted to get to know her better. I thought that perhaps she was my damsel in distress. Maybe if I saved her and brought her to Revelstoke, she would flourish as a person and as a teacher

That September, of 2003, my cousin Benj was getting married near Montreal; it was easy enough to plan a stopover in Toronto afterward. Back in the city, I hung out with Yann, Alex, and Adrian — and got in some more Tracey time. It seemed like everyone in Toronto organized their lives around socializing, so it was only natural that Tracey hung out with us almost nightly.

I could see that we were building up to something. That week, I learned that she was newly single. Also, she was planning on moving out to Vancouver with Adrian, which made me pause and wonder whether there was potential for Tracey and me. One day, while we waited for the elevator in her apartment building, the tension reached its crescendo. We had played flirty eyes for so long and had so much body chemistry that I knew I needed to at least try. So I pushed her up against the wall and kissed her. As our lips locked, our passions unlocked. It was an incredible kiss; neither of us wanted it to stop, but then the elevator arrived. We broke apart, breathing hard as the doors opened; we got back in and pushed her floor number. The doors closed, and we flew into each other's arms again. The rest of the week was a blur of excitement and making out.

Meanwhile, Tracey knew nothing about the feats I was doing in the mountains and didn't seem too interested in that side of my life, which in a way came as a relief — I wasn't sure how I could explain my insatiable drive for skiing or constant risk-taking to her. I enjoyed that she knew nothing of the "Greg Hill" whom other people knew; instead, she was just getting to know me. We spent a great deal of time talking about our future aspirations. She yearned to start her teaching career and settle somewhere to start a family.

Our relationship continued by phone for the next month, and then I decided to fly to Toronto for Halloween. Adrian and Yann were throwing a party, and I figured, why not go?

Being young and fit, I chose a particularly revealing outfit. I was dressed as Tarzan — or, more accurately, barely dressed as Tarzan, donning only a loincloth and a furry vest I left unbuttoned. Walking into the party, I spotted Tracey, who'd dressed as a sexy policewoman!!! Immediately, I went to her, and when we locked eyes, I knew we were both in trouble. We partied late into the night and stumbled back to her place, intoxicated. Our defenses were down.

That night, we had incredible sex, and our relationship moved from casual to serious. All my life, I'd struggled with feelings of low self-worth and of not being loved — of being the ignored youngest child, of being the ski-bum fuck-up. But here, now, finally, in Tracey's arms, I felt nothing but pure acceptance.

In December of 2003, less than six months after meeting Tracey, I drove down to Vancouver to pick her up — after she'd relocated, as planned, to Vancouver with Adrian, and after some discussion between us, Tracey was moving into my house in Revelstoke. We loaded up my green Nissan Pathfinder with all her possessions, strapped her mattress to the roof, and drove into the mountains.

For Tracey, this drive was a great introduction to my wildman side. For the first sixty miles, we pushed through a crazy storm that had lain a sheet of ice over the landscape, with vehicles in the ditch everywhere and me hammering and driving as aggressively as I could to keep momentum through the mess. Higher, the ice storm turned into a blizzard, with sloughs coming off the cliffs over the Trans-Canada Highway, pounding the car. Unperturbed, I rallied on, learning later that the highway had been closed behind us and that there had been a fatality.

Tracey moved right into my house and my life. Like any new couple, we nervously figured out how our lives could work together while maintaining that I would continue to be me. I made it clear that I was going to be away a lot that winter, with my usual bouts of backcountry skiing, a trip to Europe to compete in the World Championships of Ski Mountaineering, and a mega, twenty-plus day ski traverse in the Monashee Mountains. No relationship was going to deter me from my path, I told Tracey it had to be this way, even as much as I loved her.

"Tracey, this may sound uncouth, but I need to be able to adventure," I said. "It's selfish, but this desire needs to be quenched or I would likely not be as optimistic as I need to be. I need to live unfettered."

Then I added, "You may not understand the hazards of the mountains, but just know that I'm doing everything I can to be safe. I've taken lots of courses, mentored with people, and at the end of each day I want to come home alive."

I didn't want to get too deeply into the complex pact I had made with risk — to the dark truth that I knew I could easily die yet would continue to push my limits nonetheless. It felt easier to keep her blind to these realities — to use her trust in me to push the idea that I was always safe out there on my skis. Adventure is defined by having some risk, but I wanted her to blindly believe that I could be 100 percent safe thanks to judgment and experience, even if the mountains could randomly dictate otherwise.

For the winter of 2004/2005, I had the goal of touring one million feet. I thought back to Ruedi's "Dynasausage" poster; if he'd been able to rack up that number while guiding and being slowed by clients, I was certain I could easily do it too, since I'd be moving at my own pace. This would, however, mean averaging 6,666 feet uphill for around 150 days, a number that on paper I found intimidating. Still, the snow was off to a good start, and with no job to slow me down — just my "Team Employment Insurance" membership paying the bills — I had ample time to ski. I had logged 50 days of skiing by the new year.

On January 15, 2005, my buddy Greg Todds, a phenomenal ex-pro snowboarder who'd appeared in many snowboard movies, was out in the backcountry near Trout Lake with other riders, all of them working to prep a jump for a photo shoot. He was riding these new boards he called "Noboards" — snowboards without bindings, like a surfboard. Greg loved their freedom and felt that it brought back the fun without the need for bigger and faster.

At some point, Greg wandered off, solo, to get in a run. But he misjudged the avalanche conditions and was swept off his feet and buried. The other riders witnessed the slide, but by the time they dug Greg out — he'd been buried for ten minutes — he was dead. This was a massive hit to all of us in Revelstoke, as Greg had been a larger-than-life person, one who'd pushed hard and huge in the mountains for years and had, in fact, recently been trying to pull away from the risk. He had two kids and didn't want to leave them. Going to his open-casket funeral and seeing the empty husk of body, without his energy and soul, was frightening. The depth of the loss but also the selfishness inherent to our mountain sports made me reflect on who would be most affected by my own death — would my family and friends be okay? And was all this risk worth it?

This was made patently obvious when I returned from skiing the day Greg died. Frank had already called to tell me the terrible news, which I was processing just as I drove up our driveway. Tracey came running out of the house and hugged me tightly, tears in her eyes.

"I thought you died today!" she sobbed. "When Taylor" — our friend — "phoned to tell me that Greg Todds had died, he said. 'Tracey, Greg is dead! Greg died in an avalanche!'" She was so shocked that she couldn't say anything, until Taylor corrected himself and said, "Greg Todds died while noboarding near Trout Lake."

"I felt so selfish because when I heard the name Todds, I felt relieved," Tracey continued. "Relieved that it wasn't you, Greg. Yet incredibly sad that it was GT . . . Don't you ever die out there!

I need you here."

Burdened with the loss of my friend, I continued to push big days and tried to keep my average up. I knew Greg would be proud of my continuing to strive for more. So I started aiming for 10,000-foot days; these typically took me around five to seven hours of constant effort, with only a few moments of inactivity. All actions were dedicated to moving upward — well, minus the times when I was skiing downward! If I was to hit my goal of one million feet for the season, I knew that I needed these more significant days to offset the smaller days out with friends.

If 30,000 feet in a day was possible, then maybe 40,000 feet was as well. I'd learned a lot on the 30,000-foot day, namely that I needed a climb of an appropriate length, so that I could recover between laps. Big, 5,000-foot climbs zapped my energy — too much up and then too much time skiing down in one push. My legs would tire out. Instead, I needed a 2,000-foot slope that I could lap.

So, I searched my maps and found a suitable arena in a heli-ski area called Choices in the Selkirk Range, a dish of terrain with four distinct 2,000-foot runs and a wide variety of terrain to keep things interesting. I'd mostly be skiing untracked snow; I knew that I could average 2,000 feet up and down an hour, so I was expecting somewhere around 20 hours of nonstop activity to get to 40,000 feet. For comparison, the Empire State Building is 1,454 feet from the ground to the tip of its antenna, so in attempting to climb and ski 40,000 feet, I would have to climb and descend 27.5 Empire State Buildings.

Myself, my stepbrother Ian, and a close friend of Ian's named Jesse toured in the day before and set up a basecamp at the bottom of the runs, where we bivied. Lying in my bivy bag, I fell asleep staring up at the stars, wondering what the next day would bring. I woke up at midnight to start my day. As my alarm went off, I lay in my sleeping bag, wondering why I needed to do this. I was snuggled deep into my bivy, with only my face peeking out. It was -15° F outside and I didn't want to get out, but I could see the moonlight illuminating the cirque around me and I knew I was set up for a wicked day of skiing — if I could just get out of bed.

The first climb, 2,200 feet up the arena, was the toughest, as I was laying down the skin track. I had, however, timed my outing with the full moon. Its pale white glow lit the terrain almost incandescently. Helping me discern features and keep myself safe while I set a decent track — one that was well angled, around 15 percent, so that I could glide upward all day on subsequent laps.

Once the track was in, I started lapping away. I'd chosen small, skinny skis instead of wider, more stable skis, namely because the smaller, lighter skis would make ascending easier. However, on the downhill, I was giving up control — you could probably best describe my lines as wilder, out-of-control skiing from the 1970s. But at the bottom, when I lifted my skis for the next lap, I knew that I had chosen well. With 90 percent of the effort on the ascent, I needed to save every drop of energy for climbing.

The day was perfect, with bright sun and light winds. I enjoyed four runs before Ian and Jesse joined me for one. Although I could not stay and hang, it was nice to have them as a safety net for my activities — Ian's simple presence in the mountains was calming, knowing he was there in case I misjudged or made an error in the delirium of my tiredness. Midway through the day, a heli-ski group joined us n the basin. They dropped in a few times and bore witness to my antics. When I heard the helicopter flying above me, I could only imagine how I looked to the people paying for this untracked-powder privilege: a little man running up and down, skiing the same runs over and over that they had paid thousands of dollars to access.

I was so proud — this was something that I'd wanted to prove to myself for years. That I could get in as much good skiing as someone who'd paid $1,000. I could equal the fruits of their self-indulgent fossil-fuel consumption with sheer leg power!

Have you ever looked out of an airplane window and been awed by the fact that you're hovering 30,000 feet above the surface of the planet? planned to climb up to this height and then go even higher and ski back down all of it, all under my own steam. It was a damned heavy goal. But by breaking it down into sizeable pieces, I could make it manageable. After each lap, I'd pause to have a quick b te, put some candies in my pocket, drink a quick pull of electrolyte mix and then get back to skinning. I also awarded myself a prize every 2.5 hours — or every three runs — stopping to eat a bigger snack, like a large Snickers bar or a "monkey wrap": peanut butter, banana, honey, and chocolate chips all rolled up in a tortilla.

Before this day, in all my years of adventure and tree planting, I had yet to go beyond fifteen hours of continuous activity. In many ways, such sustained effort was like peeling off the layers of an onion, stripping away more and more cares and concerns until there's nothing left but the core of your being. You start the day off as intact emotionally and physically as ever. At hour ten, you're tired and fewer things matter; by hour fifteen, you're almost a machine, just eating, drinking, and focusing on the goal; and by hour eighteen, nothing is left but you — who you really are — and the mountain. As the hours wore on, I wondered if I would find at my core a person happy and focused on personal progression or an insecure little boy angrily trying to prove himself to the world.

By the afternoon, I had 35,000 feet. If nothing drastic happened, I would meet my goal. A nunatak — rock spire — kept surprising me near the summit on my last few runs. Silhouetted by the fading light, it looked almost human, and I couldn't help but think that the spire somehow embodied Greg Todds and that Greg was watching over me, approving of what I was doing. Greg was someone who fully endorsed and had been excited about my energies and direction. With his support, I kept pushing hard.

By now I had peeled back all the layers of myself. Initially, I knew that I needed to prove to myself what I could do, but also prove to the world — to Dad, Graham, and everyone — that I was exceptional. That I was worth knowing. And to prove to Ruedi that I was worth mentoring and turning into his best assistant ever. By now all these reasons seemed valid, but what kept my legs moving in those final, exhausted hours? What kept my desire strong enough to keep wanting more?

Simply put, it was the knowledge that I could do what I was doing — that all my training and skill development had paid off, and that, really, this was pure and plain fun. I was smiling and moving upward. The wonder of the mountains, the wonder of what I could do — it was all so energizing. The person driving this wasn't an insecure person; he was someone who had found a passion that resonated deep in his core. Just past 8:00 p.m., my altimeter watched showed that I'd climbed 40,000 feet. I took a final run down by the rising moon, my headlamp off, making turns on pure instinct, my quadriceps burning.

Throughout that season, I kept grinding toward my goal of 1,000,000 feet; ticking it would quantify how much my time and energies were worth, and would show the world (and my family — in particular, my high-achieving father and brother) that I was more than just a ski bum. I skied off 40 different mountaintops, completing 37 10,000-plus-foot days. Yet at the end of April, when I typically gave up skiing and went tree planting, I was still not done. Fortunately, I was tree planting outside Revelstoke, which let me keep ski touring on my days off. On May 19, 2005, on my 145th day of ski touring that season, I squeaked past the million-foot mark. I was out on a solo mission on the north-facing Sapphire Glacier, where my four runs put me over the "finish line." I whooped with happiness and satisfaction on my final run down. When the snow shrunk to nothing and I was walking down through a green forest, I savored what had been one of the best experiences of my life.

Chapter Twelve
FIFTY THOUSAND FEET

"Sometimes you just have to go to know ... The key is knowing when."
— Excerpt from letters to my family

In late fall 2004, Tracey became pregnant. We weren't planning on it, but when a condom breaks and the morning-after pill doesn't work, it feels like fate. We had only been together for fourteen months, and I was unsure about committing to Tracey for life, but our relationship seemed to work. She let me be the madman I needed to be, which was, I'm sure, something few women would have been willing to do. The fact that this baby didn't care about birth control and insisted on coming into this world made us both say, "Why not? Let's give it a go!"

On August 25, 2005, our daughter, Charley Amelia Hill, was born in Revelstoke, and our lives were changed. I had no idea how profound an experience having a kid would be; I was madly in love with our newborn, as was Tracey, who had always wanted to be a mom.

Life was working out for me: my ski career was blossoming, I had a great partner and now a daughter, and I was becoming famous, soon to be profiled in National Geographic Adventure magazine as one of their 2005 "Adventurers of the Year" for my one-million-foot season. In the meantime, an article in the magazine Ski Canada came out in which the author called me "King of the Hill," with five pages devoted to me and my pursuits. Men's Fitness ranked me as "one of the top fittest guys in the world." Finally, perhaps for the first time in my life, I felt validated. Validation is simply another form of acceptance, and therefore it felt amazing.

There was, however, a dark side to all this attention. Over the years, I'd heard secondhand stories that Ruedi doubted my accomplishments — that he felt I was lying about climbing and skiing 30,000 feet or 40,000 feet in a day. Ruedi allegedly claimed that I was calculating the up and adding the down to make these days — essentially doubling my footage, so that, say, on the 40,000-foot day I'd only climbed 20,000 feet. I was a little unnerved about this, as much of the reason I'd gone after these audacious goals was as an homage to Ruedi. I'd been more than willing to accept his militant leadership style, as I knew I could learn much from him and hone my guiding and mountain skills, but it saddened me to hear of these whisperings. Where was Ruedi coming from?

This all came to a head one day in January 2006 courtesy of a mutual sponsor that Ruedi and I shared, Genuine Guide Gear (G3), who provided me with free skis and gear in exchange for exposure and testing feedback. The company's head of sports marketing forwarded me an email from Ruedi in which he'd stated his claims, asserting that I'd been doubling my numbers, calling my honesty and professional integrity into question, demanding I issue a written retraction and apology, and adding barbs like "Further chasing vertical with a sick and competitive attitude will lead to a very sad ending" and "I do not respect Greg Hill in any ways [sic]."

It was horrible to be called out so seriously and to have my honesty questioned. What had I done to Ruedi to deserve this? I was beyond hurt; I didn't know why he thought I was counting the up and the down and adding those numbers together. Ruedi had been on one of my mentors, and I'd learned from him how to count my vertical — just the up, not the up plus the down. All I could surmise was that Ruedi found it hard to believe that I had climbed 40K feet in a day, and so he'd projected his disbelief onto all my achievements. For him to say that I was a liar cut me to the core. Perhaps he was angry that I'd mentioned him as an inspiration in the National Geographic Adventure article without asking his permission first, but this seemed like a trifle. For him to reach out to my sponsor and ask them to drop me felt way out of proportion. The vertical gain had been recorded on watches and was backed with maps, so there was plenty of proof there — if Ruedi needed it and asked for it, instead of going behind my back with all of this.

On January 5, 2006, Ruedi sent me a letter directly, restating his same assertions. I was pleased he had written me instead of emailing others behind my back, but I had trouble with some of his rationale. His assumptions were unfounded and disrespectful. The notion that my math must be flawed because I could only do half of what I said c aimed — while he was able to do twice that and more — left me flabbergasted! Without ever asking me, he'd decided that I'd lied about everything. Still, at least the lines of communication had been opened, and Ruedi and I continued the discussion on email, hammering out a few minor details that had been misreported in the National Geographic Adventure article — namely that I was a full ski guide and not an assistant guide, and that I was a forester instead of a tree planter, facts I agreed to correct in a letter to the magazine.

Still, I remained upset over this issue, and it had all made me stop to consider why I do these things. Was it solely for the glory? Was I really a self-aggrandizing person, like Ruedi had said?

When I first did 20,000 feet, the goal had been to see if I could do as much as I had ever heard of anyone climbing in a day. While I pushed to accomplish it, I was buoyed by the feeling of doing more than I had ever done — the awe at being able to do this was what kept my energies high. The 30,000-foot day was the same — I was trying to find the limits of my potential, plus it was incredible to be so fit and able to ski so much. The excited inertia I got from the descent would power me back up on the ascent. I happened to get some press from this, but I didn't look for it — the 30K day was simply a fascinating feat to others.

As I peeled back the layers during my 40,000-foot day, I realized that I do these things for one simple reason: I believe I can! I enjoy training with a goal in mind, and then attempting that goal. Sure, the magazine articles and attention were nice — most of us appreciate being recognized for our accomplishments. But when I peeled back the onion skin, that was not the person driving this machine, the person who kept my legs moving and lungs heaving, who kept me pushing. That person was a guy who loves digging deep, finding his limits, and then pushing past them. He was a person inspired by the magic of life and the world we live in. That million-foot season, I hadn't spent 145 days imagining beating Ruedi; I had spent 145 days inspired and excited to be in the mountains, and to be alive. To me, mountain-scapes perfectly capture the wonder of life at its most beautiful, dangerous, and awe-inspiring.

In June 2005, two famous high-altitude skiers, the Marolt Brothers, invited me to come to Colorado the following March to try for a record for vertical feet climbed in a twenty-four-hour period. They were putting on a race at a small ski resort — Sunlight Mountain near Glenwood Springs, on the Western Slope of Colorado — where I could make the attempt.

In the lead-up, I worked hard on my vertical speed. That fall, I searched out our steeper trails and worked running uphill for 3,000 feet nonstop, calculating what my maximum uphill output might be. I knew these speeds weren't sustainable, but continually pushing into my hardest efforts would make the longer, easier efforts, well, easier. This was going to be the biggest and longest push I'd ever tried, and I needed to put in the training. As I ran uphill, I'd scream out loud, pushing deeper than ever before.

I also worked extra hard all summer while planting, visualizing the 50,000-foot goal and imagining the effort needed. The next step, 40K, was amazing, but this would be next level — another 25 percent. I would need to work my butt off. I even started going to the gym and working on my leg strength, powering them up.

Once I had snow to tour on, I was hammering out 10,000-foot days as quickly as possible. I finally cracked the four-hour mark and was pumped — I was getting faster and faster. With skins on, I worked on finding the perfect balance between effort and exhaustion, homing in on a speed at which I could inhale deeply as my legs relaxed, and exhale as I powered them back up, timing my breath precisely with my steps. In while powering up, out while pivoting my hips and sliding my thigh forward; in while pushing up on that thigh, and out with the pivot and shift. Finally, this would be my chance to put the naysayers to bed. If I could do at least 40,000 feet in front of bystanders, it would prove that all my other vertical claims had been true.

Upon first inspection, the racecourse didn't seem ideal. First off, it lay between 8,200 and 9,800 feet, a much higher elevation than I was used to, which presented an added challenge. Also, the course started off too flat for the first half mile, then was too steep for the next half mile, then was too mellow again for the final half mile, instead of being one continuous pitch that gained the 1,640 feet along its length. Oh, well — it was what it was, and I could not change it. I needed to fully accept this so there would be no resistance during the challenge.

If I wanted to set a new personal record — climbing 50,000 feet up in 24 hours — I would need to average 2,083 feet an hour, or 35 feet up per minute, all day. Yet this didn't account for time spent descending, which I estimated would be about 4 minutes per run. So, realistically, I needed to climb 2,400 feet an hour while ascending to make up for time lost to transitions, descending, and stopping for snacks. This was an uphill speed that I had kept for my previous big days, so it should have been feasible . . . if nothing went wrong. The elevation was the biggest unknown, and it filled me with questions.

There were around 100 people total racing, many as teams, alternating laps, and then the soloists. The starting line was a mishmash of people: snowshoers with their snowboards on their backs, teams dressed up with wild colors and hairdos, and then the serious ones, on small skis, with tight, aerodynamic bodysuits and devilish grins. On race day, the second the starting gun went off at 10:00 a.m., I was in the lead group and moving steadily upward. The cold Colorado snow was frozen under our skins and glided really well, but you had to pay attention, or you could easily slip backward or sideways, especially up the steeper section. Although I had put months of training into this day, it was now all about this moment.

"Find your pace and settle into it," I thought between gasps. "Breathe in deeply through your nose — quick, deep, powerful breaths, and time them with your stride . . ." I jockeyed for position right off the bat. This was my race, and I wanted to lead it the whole way.

I cheered myself on some more, internally: "Push with your arms, focus on using those triceps for extra push . . . come on . . . !"

I picked up my cadence to quickly get ahead of Steve Romeo, another racer who might be a challenge. Steve and I had been buddies for years, and he had the potential to go big this day.

The sharp sound of my skins was loud on the cold snow, as they slid and glided upward: *tstsht . . . tstsht . . . tstsht . . . tstsht . . .* I charged up the steeps, hamstrings strung tightly as they powered me forward. "Man, do I want this! I have trained and am so fucking ready to push as hard as possible today!" I coached myself. I hit the upper flats and stretched out my stride, mimicking Nordic skiers. The views were insane, a straight shot up the Roaring Fork Valley to the twin summits of Mount Sopris, which reaches nearly 13,000 feet, towering above the grasslands and piñon-studded foothills below.

"Breathe and believe in yourself, Greg," my inner coach again encouraged me. "Breathe deeply and relax — let the oxygen flow through your body and don't get caught up in the stress of the situation or the desire to go faster. Just relax and make it happen."

I reached the top and ripped my skins, roughly stuffing them inside my zippered jacket. I clicked my heels in, remembering that the right heel was poorly mounted and that I could not get a perfect lock. And then I was off, sliding downhill all while zippering up my top, poles squeezed between my knees before I transferred them to my hands. I carved fast and furious turns down the slope — I love skiing fast on groomers, and this was it. Jacket flapping in the wind, my energies elevated by the competition, I yipped and hollered my way down, careering through the corral, making sure my number got registered. A quick glance at the clock showed a lap time of 31:05, much quicker than my average needed to be across the duration of the event. Wowsers.

Down at the base, Tracey helped me with my snacks and passed me another set of skis so that I wouldn't have to do anything but eat, drink, clip into new skis, and move again. This was a new idea, using two sets of skis, getting Tracey to prepare a set so that the skins were warmed up and the glue would be guaranteed to stick while I was hiking up. Not that transitions take long, but saving a minute on every lap could easily add up to an extra lap over the twenty-four hours.

Tracey was as stoic as ever. Maneuvering around with our daughter, Charley, in her arms, she worked some serious mom magic to help me at each pit stop, and was so essential to my efforts that day. It was the first time she'd seen me in "business mode," so I imagine it might have been somewhat shocking. I was not warm — I was short and to the point, saving my breath only to convey what I needed. There was no time to be chatty or considerate.

Every few minutes and after each lap, I would re-analyze my pace and ensure that it was on point for 50K feet. Keeping my optimism high as each lap blended into the next, I would chat with and encourage everyone I passed on the way up. I kept looking at my watch to ensure that my vertical speed was somewhere around 40 feet up per minute, feeling my confidence swell with each passing hour that I maintained above this pace. This day,

I could do 50K. Everything was set up for it: I'd embraced the sheer, grueling punishment of the endeavor, I had done all the work, and I could believe in myself and just let my body do what I'd trained it to do instinctually.

The laps melded into each other as the hours wore on. I checked my watch regularly and skinned as quickly as possible, trying not to go so hard that I lost the ability to speak, due to rapid breathing, on the uphill climbs. If I went too fast and couldn't talk to my fellow racers as I passed them, I would burn myself out all too soon.

"This is possible — you've got this," I kept thinking, looking at the numbers on my watch and knowing I was ahead of par for 50K. My legs still felt light, and my boots and skis were the lightest possible. Step after step, I maintained my core so that my skins stuck to the icy snow. Glide and slide; slide and glide.

Slowly the day turned to night, and the temperatures plummeted — I am talking -15° F in the depths of night! Working within the small pool of light cast by my headlamp, with only the tiny beam casting on my ski tips and a small snowy area visible around me, I entered a trancelike state. My mind was stuck in a loop of breathing, checking my watch, doing the calculations, relaxing, and staying focused. My body just kept moving, never questioning its prime directives.

I also had to work hard at staying warm, a key part of which was the Arc'teryx clothing options I'd brought — breathable and warm layers that allowed me to maintain a bubble of warmth yet not get sweaty. (Sweating at these temperatures is a quick route to hypothermia.) Tracey was always there, too, ready to accommodate anything I needed. At twelve hours in, I'd logged more than 25K up and down; 50K was looking more and more like a possibility.

At seventeen and a half hours in, someone caught up to me! So far, no one had passed me; it had been me doing all the passing. Confused and concerned, I asked, "Dude, did you lap me?"

"No, I've been chasing your silhouette for hours now and I've finally caught up," the skier said. "My name's Jimmy, by the way."

"Nice to meet you. Holy moly, has this been an intense time," I said, then added, "Jimmy, we're at 36,000 feet toured, and we're on track for 50,000 feet if we keep this pace up. Want to do a few laps together?"

"Sure, let's do this," Jimmy said.

As I learned while we skied through the night, Jimmy was ten years older than me and lived in Colorado. His biggest day up to this point had been 20K, so he was deeply into a new personal record. I cannot remember much else of what we said, other than that we connected wonderfully and used each other to keep moving, distracting ourselves with conversation while we pushed our bodies to the limit. It was a "six-hour date," during which we lapped the mountain, in roughly forty-minute intervals, pushing each other to keep moving, keeping that conversational pace, and then finally watching the sunrise together as we hit 40K and then entered new territory for both of us.

At 9:30 a.m., 23.5 hours after starting, Jimmy and I skied through the finish line, side by side, having each climbed up and skied down 50,000 vertical feet of terrain. *Fuck yeah!!!* was all I could think, my brain fried and body totally exhausted, my quads so locked up with fatigue I could barely stand.

Jimmy and I promptly retired to our rooms, where we recouped before the ceremonies. After hours of exertion in the cold air at elevation, I started to cough, hacking up a black tar–like phlegm. Barely able to stand in the shower, I coughed and coughed this junk up. At the same time, Jimmy was taken to the hospital for his own respiratory issues.

A few hours later, we had the ceremony, and the Marolt Brothers wanted to give me the record, which made absolutely no sense. Jimmy and I had worked for it together, and that's how it would go. We split the record and the winnings, which were not much — $1,000 each — but what we won was a new personal record, and likely a world record for vertical climbed and skied in a twenty-four-hour period. Booyah!

And to all the naysayers — including Ruedi, who'd doubted my big days — I believe there was finally enough evidence to allay their doubts. Jimmy and I had climbed 50,000 feet up and skied 50,000 feet down, and it had all been documented publicly, at a race. To put that into context, the next time you're in an airplane, look down and imagine hiking up to your current height, skiing back down, then climbing half that distance again and skiing back down again.

Scan the QR code to see a video of Greg in action!

Or imagine climbing up and down the Empire State Building thirty-four times.

PHOTO CREDIT: BRUNO LONG

Chapter Thirteen

?90,000 FEET

"My goal in the mountains and in life is to face my fears — to overcome them and see what comes of it."
— Excerpt from letters to my family

Having completed my million feet in a season, I decided on a different style challenge for the 2006/2007 season. My million-foot season had been 7.5 months long, so nowhere near fast enough to attempt two million in twelve months. If I were to do this, I seriously needed to hone my efficiencies. I kept the idea close to my chest, telling no one; I've never been one to talk up my accomplishments before they happen anyway.

Instead, a more approachable goal — and one that could perhaps be part of clocking two million feet in a year — would be to again go for a million feet in one season, but do it across a hundred 10,000-foot days. This would break down to five to ten hours of heart-slamming activity with each outing — a strenuous day at work, one demanding singular focus and akin to climbing up and down the Empire State Building six-plus times in a row.

I documented much of my efforts with blog posts (I'd built a website for my skiing, greghill.ca) in case anyone wanted to follow along, and as a sort of record for myself. You can see the evolution and learning and a life in motion as the season went along, like the time in deep snow on the Macpherson Fingers when I figured out that smaller steps and quicker breaths were more efficient for skinning up than my preferred big, lunging steps and deeper breaths. Or documenting skiing with my parents, and the birth of our son, Aiden, who came into the world weighing a massive ten pounds. Or how I kept motivation high by slaking my thirst for deep, untracked powder. (" . . . [The] feeling of skiing through powder is what keeps me going. It's the closest I can come to flying, and I love it. Swooping down a mountain like a bird would fly — fast, fluid, and non-stop," I wrote.) Or trying to balance the reality of needing to make a living ski guiding — and not lose too much energy or motivation to my day job — with the need to also get out and push these big days. As I neared the end of my goal, I "stalled out" at 990,000 feet, and the following blog post of the same name encapsulates much of those events.

> I had plans to finish my millionth foot before I flew to England for a wedding, but I stalled and did not finish it. The day after the Spearhead Traverse (during which I toured from Whistler Village up Blackcomb and summitted Spearhead Peak, Blackcomb Peak, then Decker, Trorey, Pattison Tremor, Ripsaw, Mount Macbeth, Whirlwind, Fissile, and Flute — 11 summits and 20,600 feet of skiing, across roughly 30 miles of travel — all in 13 hours, 32 minutes), I drove up to Cypress with thoughts of touring 10,000 feet on the hill, but the pouring rain washed away my drive. I sat in the car and realized that I would prefer to finish my million feet on a lovely, sunny

day. Not a rainy day. I sat and pondered for a while before I drove away.

I won't have time to do a hundred 10,000-footers, but as in high school, I am happy with an 80 percent. The season was exceptional, and I will never complain about not achieving my 100 days. It gives me another year to attempt it. I learned more and realized what is needed to achieve this lofty goal and may try again. As for this year, I explored a lot and skied more new lines, and I am psyched that more discovery is left out there.

That previous season, during which I'd skied 990,000 feet in around six months, showed me that my dream of two million feet was firmly in the realm of possibility. As the 2008/2009 season drew near, I became more serious about my goal, until I realized that the sheer cost, time commitment, and logistics were at the time probably too much, with two young children at home. I put the dream on the back burner.

Instead, I focused on becoming an adventure filmmaker, starting a series called "Skin Flicks." Your typical ski movies, with colossal cliff drops and crazy, wild lines, were referred to as "ski porn," whereas my films would instead focus mostly on skiing accessed by skinning up. This project was a great way to use my extra energy in the mountains, and I began to film many of our adventures in our backyard.

The thrill of exploration was so strong that I bought eight topographic maps and carefully lined up all the lines and taped the maps together. One night, I was stretching on the red shag carpet at home and looking up at all the lines I had diligently drawn in over the years. I could see a void: just north of Revelstoke lies a 400-foot hydroelectric dam, which creates a 75-mile-long lake. Here, the mighty Columbia River becomes Lake Revelstoke, which blocks easy access to a lot of the Monashee Range. During the summer months of tree planting around here, I'd gazed up at these peaks and wondered about canoe access. One mountain in particular, Hat Peak, always caught my eye, and I began to imagine a way up it. Hat Peak boasted one of the longest descents I could find around Revelstoke — at 7,500 feet, it was massive, plus it was hard to access across Lake Revelstoke. That night, I got up from my stretches and peered closely at the map. I could see the moraine lines bisecting the valley; it all looked like fairly simple terrain, with some serious glacial rolls. Perhaps I'd found a way to its summit.

Ian and Aaron were as excited as me when, in January 2008, we loaded the canoe onto my Pathfinder.

Highway 23 travels north of Revelstoke, paralleling the Columbia River where it's been dammed into Lake Revelstoke. The highway had a hard snow base, driven over by endless logging trucks. I drove slowly to make sure we were not sliding off the road. The snowbanks dwarfed the car.

"Something new — this is exciting!" Aaron quipped.

Ian, in his quiet, stalwart way, said little, but his energy was palpable.

Forty miles later I pulled onto the side, plunging the truck as deeply as into the six-foot-tall snowbank as possible to get it off the highway. Ian threw our bags up onto the snow, while Aaron and I unloaded the canoe.

"Yeeee-heeeeeeeeeeewwww!" I hollered, my energy exploding out of me

I pulled out my paper map, trying to connect what I saw of the mountain to what was on the map. My studies the night before had shown me a small creek we could paddle to. From there I followed the terrain up, matching my interpretation of potential ways up Hat Peak.

I located the moraines and studied the terrain above, wondering about what this choice exposed us to. It all looked manageable — there were no endless, massive slopes, but more like more smaller ones connected with benches. The glacial rolls looked real, but we could avoid any open crevasses by going around on the many snow slopes.

Familiarity breeds confidence, and I was feeling strong.

After the 1.2-mile crossing of the lake, we hopped out of the canoe and started skinning up. The electric hum — the titillating thrill of not knowing what was ahead — increased as we wandered past massive twin cedars, split with a V. Their ancestral beauty drew me in for a hug — yes, I am literally a tree hugger. A few minutes later, we came upon a wolf kill, the gray fur of a moose strewn across the snow amongst bones, blood, and many wolf prints. We were truly "out there."

A steep and challenging section in the trees had us cutting a skin track up a steep boulder field, and then boot-packing up a small, tree-lined couloir to access the moraine. So far, our pencil line up was working out.

The snow was as settled as we'd hoped — cold and seven days old, just calmly stuck on, giving us the confidence to skin up the short pitches and onto the glacier. Nervously, I tied into the head of the rope, then thirty feet later Ian, and thirty feet later Aaron, the rope linking us in case we erred and skinned over a deep crevasse.

I glanced at my map, identified the slopes, calculated the exposure from the mountain above, then balanced it out with the stabilized, old snow. All seemed great, so I skinned off with the boys in tow, the crevasses easy to see in the bright light coming out of the blue sky above us.

Looking up at the summit, I followed the crenellated ridge to the south where I hoped to access it. The small cliffs we were going to have to climb were minor, but the exposure looked huge. The glacial bench I was standing on, munching my PB&J, was mellow, with a 300-foot bootpack to the ridge. It looked perfect. But the more I chewed on my sandwich and mulled over the idea of climbing that ridge, the more I knew we were unlikely getting to the summit. Those little cliffs on the ridge were beyond my alpine-climbing risk tolerance.

Meanwhile, whenever I could, I was filming these moments for the Skin Flicks. I wanted the footage to capture our passion, the hum of excitement, the thrill of self-discovery and exploration we were feeling up there. When we finally booted up to the ridge, we stood there and high-fived, thrilled to be living it. There were no guidebooks for these adventures, no GPS, no 3D navigation apps, no tracks to follow — except occasionally those of the mighty wolverine, whose tracks I have followed to many high cols.

A second big adventure that season became another one of my better-received Skin Flicks. At the time, Golden and Revelstoke had each developed a hardcore crew of shredders. There wasn't real competition, but we liked to egg each other on. The Golden crew called themselves the Dogtooth Rangers, and these skiers and snowboarders were known for their daring descents, coupled with airy ascents. We had all shared skin tracks and powder-filled moments. When we heard that they were questing for the Comstock Couloir on Mount Dawson (11,079 feet), the second highest peak in the Selkirk Range, I knew we needed to join them.

The Comstock perches on the side of this highest mountain in Rogers Pass. This couloir is mythical, haunting all views, hanging ethereally in the background. The couloir starts just below the summit and thunders straight down through lots of rock bands, with a large cliff at the bottom that always looks "just" filled in. It had to be the biggest unskied line around.

The Dogtooth Rangers Isaak Kamink, Mark Hartley, and Ty Mills were rallying to ski the line in the high pressure that was sitting over the Selkirk Mountains, during a run of bluebird days with no precipitation and a stable layer of snow blanketing the range.

My friends Conor Hurley, Aaron Chance, and I couldn't go the same day as the Golden crew, so we ended up in the parking lot at 4:00 a.m. that next morning, skinning up by headlamp, cold morning breath puffing like smoke. We labored up to Asulkan Pass, a three-hour grind. By 7:30 a.m. we were looking across at the Comstock. I squinted at the cliff band at the bottom, just making out a continuous line of snow that wound through the cliffs. I could see that it looked skiable. Yet the cornice at the top was hidden in a layer of cloud, almost visible but not as clearly as I wanted. We skied off the pass into the valley; about midway down, I was able to make out the Golden boys' skin track, winding up to end in a few yellow tents perched at the treeline. We met them here after skinning back up, hoots and hollers of welcome uniting us as one team.

"What do we think about this cloud layer? Are we still going to give it a try?" Aaron asked the group.

With this group, it would have been easy to get caught up in our manic energy and maybe not discuss things enough, so I welcomed Aaron's more conservative antidote to my exuberance.

"They look like wispy lenticulars — maybe they'll blow through," I said.

"Let's go take a look," said Isaak. "There's still lots of time to make those decisions and lots of information we could gather between now and then."

"Maybe with weather like this it might stay cool enough for us to bootpack straight up the couloir? Maybe the cornice isn't getting warmed, and we can risk the exposure?"

Different options and ideas buzzed around like flies, our final decision indeterminate.

Mark set off, spilt boards on his feet. We couldn't see the line, but we could feel its presence as we toured up the moraine. It was calm and cold, the cloud layer still locked in above us. Two years before, we had toured up this way toward Mount Selwyn, so our familiarity with the terrain made our decisions easy, but the fear of the unknown ahead had me vibrating.

Would it go? What would it feel like to look down below my skis, at 2,500 feet of steep line tumbling away? Would a ski cut suffice? Or was it such a huge panel of snow that there would be no controlling it from above? An endless loop of questions swirled through my brain, like the clouds around the summits above.

"Without seeing the cornice, I'm skeptical about bootpacking straight up it," I said to the group. I always want the least hazardous way to the top, and hiking directly underneath a cornice for three hours in a chute seemed very sketchy. Aaron saved the day by suggesting we take a line off to the side, up the Selwyn Glacier, that might give us a better vantage on the couloir and the cornice, as well as lead to the summit.

The boys agreed and we skied off the col, sticking a couple of steep turns in light snow on a short, steep pitch. A few more arced turns and we were on the glacier putting on the rope and our skins. I tied in and went first, my skis putting in a fifteen-centimeter-deep skin track. The cold snow on this north-facing aspect was light and consistent. I looked at my paper map, matching up the elevations with my Suunto altimeter watch as we ascended into the clouds, my rope team partner just visible thirty feet below me. My skin track into oblivion continued for a while, and then light started piercing through the clouds in small windows. Maybe, just maybe, we'd break through the cloud layer and could ski this thing.

Finally, I spotted the small cornice hanging off the col, and aimed our skin track there. The light was getting better, and I pulled out my camera and filmed the gentlemen walking the skin track under the cornice, capturing an iconic moment for Skin Flicks. Later, I would capture more indelible footage, shooting back across the summit ridge as the boys crawled "au cheval" — straddling the arête, like a man on a horse — across a hyper-exposed, rocky, and snowy section with a mind-numbing drop to either side into the cloudy void. It is still one of the wildest places I've been in the mountains, a spot of class-four technical terrain that was made even gnarlier by the full-on winter conditions.

From the summit, we slip-slid down a ridge, Mark peering over cliff bands to find the best way to the col above the couloir. Eventually, the clouds parted enough that we could finally see the cornice. Up close, it was far smaller and more manageable than the monster we had perceived from thousands of feet below. Isaac pulled out his cordelette — a small length of Perlon rope used as a belay anchor — and we swung the loop over the massive teardrop of snow, sawing back and forth to cut through this Styrofoam-like chunk of ice.

"Here she goes!!! Yeehaw — let's see what happens!" someone hollered.

We peered in, watching the 400-pound cornice smash into the slope below with an audible *Ummmfff* before it started tumbling. Entraining the snow around it, the cornice slid into the clouds, vanishing down the chute. The snow was simply sloughing, and there didn't appear to be any avalanche hazard in the loose snow — save the slope's avalanche-friendly 50-degree pitch.

Wanting to film looking back up as the boys skied in, I quipped that I should go first, and snuck in seven deep and steep turns, each controlled and almost coming to a stop as the snow flowed like water and poured over my skis. I then hid beneath a dark-gray cliff band and filmed Mark shredding his turns into this line.

Once we were all in, it was a series of leap frogging, pulling-in, controlled turns, making sure our sloughs didn't hit any of our team. Basically, the leader would move a bunch of snow with his turns and then find a spot away from the fall line, ideally under a small cliff or something protected. Then we would follow one at a time, never exposing each other to our turns. All was going well and the snow was soft and stable, perfect for steep turns. But the choke was yet to come, and we all wondered if it was just a cliff band covered with a skiff of snow or an actual snow slope. We could manage the cliff band with some rappelling, but hoped we wouldn't need to. Mark again took the lead as we approached the choke. He slashed a few tight and quick turns across the fall line, searching for a way through the bottom cliffs.

The drip of adrenaline had been trickling all day, and now it was a constant shot.

"I'll holler once I'm through," Mark yelled up to us.

Scan the QR code to see a video of Greg in action!

Mark pulled through the choke, looked back, and started shredding the steep fan. He'd made it. The tension we'd been feeling all day released — all the unknowns and endless questions had now been resolved, and relief poured through me. We'd made the first descent of the Comstock Couloir, completing the biggest unskied line in Rogers Pass. The combined skills of our team, a bonding between the two towns, had made this possible. I was beyond excited to get home and edit this footage into a Skin Flick. It was going to be by far the most exciting one I'd created, since this was by far the most exciting adventure I'd been on.

I thoroughly enjoyed filming our adventures, and tried my best to be creative and give a window into our world. There were some serious new descents, and at the end of the year 2009, I compiled our excursions into a movie, *The Unbearable Lightness of Skiing*, a playoff Milan Kundera's meditative book *The Unbearable Lightness of Being*. At the time, not many people understood what backcountry skiing was all about, so I tried to explain and demonstrate what it was in this compilation of those two adventures — Hat Peak and the Comstock Couloir — and other highlights from this season. My film, much to my pleasure, was accepted to the Banff Mountain Film Festival, and ended up on a world tour. It was among my finest accomplishments.

My professional ski career was also growing — I was actually getting paid to be a skier! The "sponsors were happy." I have never been good at asking for money or knowing my value, but I was accidentally sent another athlete's contract that year instead of my own and saw how well paid an athlete could be. This empowered me to ask one of my main sponsors, the high-end mountain-apparel company Arc'teryx, for a modest salary.

Things were finally happening, and I was blown away by it. Around that time, Tracey and I got married (with our little children slaying our assembled friends and family with their overwhelming cuteness as flower-bearers), I started presenting at film festivals, and I was invited to give a slideshow at the Vancouver International Film Festival in Kelowna. I presented to a crowd of 700 people and had a blast recounting my adventures.

My previous stage experience — as an actor in high school and at university — helped, and I was comfortable and entertaining, or so I hoped.

My movies put me ahead of the curve of self-produced pieces and brought about one sponsorship change. In 2009, the German ski company Dynafit signed me as an athlete. At the time, they produced the best backcountry equipment and had created the revolutionary pin binding, a game-changer in the backcountry. This binding was very light compared to all the previous backcountry bindings — there is an old saying, "A pound on your foot is worth five on your back," so any weight saved on your feet is huge, and these bindings were one-third the weight of previous generations. But what truly set the pin binding apart was the way it worked. Bindings up to this time had had a frame attached to your foot that you lifted with every step, but pin bindings got rid of that. The pin style had a small, indented pocket on either side of the toe of the boot that got pinched by the binding. This pinch was very strong and became a fairly effortless pivot point, which allowed backcountry skiers to glide and slide much more like cross-country skiers, paving the way for most of the incredible adventures happening in the mountains at this time.

What was insane was that Dynafit got in touch with me because they wanted to make the perfect backcountry ski for the North American market. And they figured I was the man to develop it with. Me — little nine-fingered Greg Hill from Sutton, Quebec. I'd never been so excited. We were going to call it the Stoke, after Revelstoke and the stoke that I brought to the backcountry.

In May 2009, I flew to Chamonix, France, to test out the prototype. This ski was the first wider yet lighter ski made for the backcountry. I met up with Bene Bohm, the CEO of Dynafit, and a few of us climbed and skied Mont Blanc in an eleven-hour push from the valley back to the valley. I filmed this adventure, and couldn't contain my excitement to be on the Stoke ski on its maiden voyage up Europe's highest mountain: a stratospheric 15,777 feet. My companions were all on the skinniest ski mountaineering skis, while I was on a wide backcountry ski. Yet it was light enough to keep up with the Euros on the way up. Standing on top of Mont Blanc, I clicked into my signature ski — mine! — a ski that we'd built to specifications that I thought would be perfect for ski mountaineering. How were they going to perform? I took a couple of tentative turns off the icy summit. The ski was wide at 106mm but felt sturdy enough to handle shitty conditions, which is very important, because the next 1,000 feet were these crazy waves of frozen snow known as sastrugi. The waves were as awkward as they come, but my skis slipped and slid through them with ease.

I had to think hard about the descent. I had only seen the face briefly on the way up, and I knew that the line wended through the towering ice walls, but I was on edge. It's a complex process, memorizing a slope from one view and then flip that view as you ski back down. You look for specific, landmark features to guide you down the run, but one, small miscalculation can quickly land you in the wrong spot.

Scan the QR code to see a video of Greg in action!

On Mont Blanc, once we'd passed the sastrugi, the skis were in their element in untracked, north-facing snow. We arced turns down the hanging face, pulling left on the correct glacial bench powder sliding smoothly beneath my skis' bases. We skied quickly under lots of overhanging ice walls, slipped lightly across small crevasses, and then skipped our way down the dirt trail to the car. It was an auspicious start for this new ski.

With 2010 on the horizon, my dream of challenging myself to climb and ski two million feet in a calendar year had reached a fevered pitch. I could no longer keep putting it off. The desire had grown for years; my experience and mountain sense were elevated, and my fitness was honed. I would never be more ready — well, except for the financial reality of taking a year off from tree planting, our main source of income, and somehow paying for my family to live, including spending four months in South America during their winter. I probably needesd $80,000 to pull it off.

Tracey and I had decided to keep her home with the kids until they went to elementary school. Though Tracey worked a few nights a week as a waitress, I was still the primary breadwinner. My sponsors gave me around $30,000 a year, but this was not enough money to both support a family and realize my goal. I would make some money ski guiding, but I also needed lots of free time to accrue vertical. I had zero ideas about making it work, but I knew I had to give it a go. Otherwise, I would never have been satisfied.

The first step was going to be asking/telling Tracey. One night in early December 2009, we were drinking a nice bottle of red wine on the couch. I waited till I knew she had consumed more than half the bott e and would be loosened up, and then I started painting a pictu e of the year ahead and explaining how it was a life goal — and how we could travel to South America as a family and live in Chile and Argentina. I made it all sound very adventurous and romantic. I am not sure if it was the wine or the colorful idea, but Tracey agreed, and just like that the two-million-foot year was or.

Chapter Fourteen

TWO MILLION FEET: PART ONE

*"As your father, I want you to be the person you dream of being.
Become that person, and dream as big as possible."*
— *Excerpt from letters to my family*

On January 1, 2010, I drove up to the Macpherson Trailhead, a local backcountry skiing spot. The mountain looks like a ski resort, but in reality it's these perfect avalanche slopes that roar down between old-growth cedars. Sitting in the dark alone in my truck, I breathed deeply, relaxed, and started my Suunto altimeter watch. I left my truck at 6:00 a.m. and worked on getting in my daily 5,500 feet quickly. The challenge had begun.

It was a dark and crisp morning — the access starts through our Nordic trails, so my first feet were on a groomer, which felt fast and smooth. I was jittery with excitement. Today was the start of the biggest challenge of my life, with so many hours of dreaming to reach this point. This was my journey to Mordor, my ultimate personal challenge. I slowed my cadence, letting my signature Stoke skis glide and slide their way uphill. Breathing deeply, I embraced what lay ahead — in, out, in, out — timing my breathing to match my stride. On top of my first run, I kicked my tails into the deep powder snow, looked down the fall line, and let out a huge holler. Then I was off, flowing down the hillside like a kayaker in the rapids, the snow billowing over my knees. I didn't have to get ahead at this point — just hit par and not tire myself out too early, relying on my mantra of "Breathe and believe" to get me through this and the many other long days ahead.

"Breathe and believe" is all about relaxing and not stressing — a relaxed state will ensure success. You breathe deeply and slowly so that the oxygen can flood your muscles as well as your brain. The believe part is a little more complex: it requires years of training and hard work to develop a skill set you can believe in; it's something you build brick by brick through training, practicing, and dreaming. You cannot honestly believe in something unless there is a deep understanding of it, which comes from sustained dedication — as with Malcolm Gladwell's notion of the 10,000 hours you need to put in to gain expertise at a given skill.

The first month started at a mellow pace, one I knew I could pick up as needed. Most days, I was able to get out and ski tour for at least five or six hours, fueling my psyche by reaching amazing summits with friends. Summits are the absolute best — they provide the most reward out of all the aspects of ski touring, A peak is a defined finish, one that provides a concrete and tangible goal. Often, I'd be so elated up top that I'd let out a scream, my voice echoing off the silent mountainsides clad in snow spread in every direction.

Settling into my challenge, I understood that to maintain harmony at home, I needed to balance family life with my objectives. There are many hours in the day that don't get used, like those between 8:00 p.m. and 8:00 a.m. I when everyone is usually in front of the TV or going to bed. Instead, I used this time to get in my vertical, heading to the local ski hill, Revelstoke Mountain Resort. It was an ideal venue — there were no avalanche hazard, the trails were groomed, and I could quickly skin 5,500 feet up on a very direct path. I didn't exactly have permission, but there were no rules against it either — and besides, late at night, there was hardly anyone around.

One night around 8:00 p.m., I set out via headlamp, skinning up the ski hill. Wearing my lighter and smaller skis, I could get a quick cadence going, as I did now on the freshly groomed run called Snow Rodeo. It was glorious movement — no deep snow, just gliding and sliding my way uphill, breathing hard and setting a pace of 2,400 vertical feet an hour. Up top, I let out a quick holler at the moon and stars, ripped the skins, and headed down, carving turns on perfect corduroy. (When a ski hill is properly groomed, the snow is a consistent flat corduroy of half-inch ribs of snow.) Corduroy is incredibly pleasant to ski — it's so soft and consistent that it holds the edge of your ski almost without fail. That night, I knew there was no one around, and the snowcats would have lights going. If I saw them, I could slow down and go around. Often, to groom steeper slopes, snowcats attach cables to anchors, using these to pull themselves upward easily.

The steep pitch on Snow Rodeo, about a third of the way down the run, is the best pitch on the hill, as it steepens perfectly and holds a consistent angle for a solid 500 feet. Skiing powerfully and carving my way down the pitch, I was going around 40 mph when I got here. I ripped a left turn at high speed, curving underneath some trees to reach the top of the next pitch. Then, suddenly, a thin horizontal shadow cut across my limited light, probably four feet off the ground, and didn't disappear as I shone my light directly on it.

Holy fuck — duck! At the last moment, I leaned back and limboed my way underneath a steel snow-cat cable! The cable felt more like a metal rod as my ribs smashed against it. There was no give as it pushed me over and grazed my body, pulling my hat and headlamp off. I skidded to a halt, feeling an immediate flood of guilt and anger.

You idiot! You almost ruined this entire challenge when you had barely begun, I chastised myself.

Assessing my injuries, I determined that nothing was terribly hurt, other than possibly some broken ribs. I'd been very lucky — at that speed, the cable could have killed me. I stood up, picked up my gear, put my shitty headlamp on, and then sheepishly found a mellow snow road to slide the rest of the way down. I was so ashamed of the incident that I didn't write anything on my blog or really tell anyone. I want people to think I am competent, and this near miss had reeked of total incompetence.

By February 4, 2010, I'd logged 175,300 feet climbed. My ribs still hurt when I bent down to put my boots on, but I'd otherwise healed from getting flossed by the cable.

Most ski towns have their trademark mountains — ours is Mount Begbie (8,967 feet), which you can find on our newspaper's header and in the logos of many other local businesses. It has three steep, rocky peaks, like a podium, with the middle one being the highest. With its unique profile and hanging glaciers, Begbie catches the morning sun and the evening light, seeming to float above town. On February 23, I set out to climb and ski off Mount Begbie. Since the skin track was in, I decided to see how fast I could climb and ski the peak, round-trip. That day, I put on my skinniest skis and skinned as quickly as I could up to the summit. The 7,100-foot climb took 2 hours and 25 minutes, and then I skied down in 25 minutes, setting a personal best (PB) of 2:55. I'd left the house while the family was asleep, worked my butt off for almost three hours, and then I was home by 9:00 a.m., when the day had barely begun for everyone else — a mountain climbed before breakfast!

I have never been good at asking for money, probably due to the insecure side of my character, and never really knowing my value made it hard to quantify what I was worth to my sponsors. Yet I knew that this year I was doing something no one else had done before, and that I had the skills to document and share it. On a whim, I reached out to an online store called Backcountry.com and connected with their sports-marketing boss. I figured, since this was going to be the biggest backcountry year ever, that perhaps they wanted to help me out. Every last bit of money would help.

One day in later February, my friend Aaron and I were working our way up to a new summit when I got a call from Backcountry.com. They said that they were in for $20,000 US and would also support me with media help. It was just the call I'd needed, and I dove back into my goal with a financial weight lifted off my shoulders.

My shiny, titanium Suunto altimeter watch had a cumulative number on it that would add each successive day, so I had a running total. Every night when I set my alarm, I would look at this number. When I awoke in the morning, I would strap the watch on my wrist and think about what par was for that day. Day 80 times 5,500 feet = 440,000 feet. I would then compare this ideal number to my actual tally, to figure out whether I needed to push that day or could just keep steady. It was a constant loop in my head, and I invariably thought about my goal a lot.

On March 24, I was guiding up at the Whitecap Alpine backcountry lodge when I hit 495,000 feet; just another 5,000 feet would get me a quarter of the way to my ultimate goal, which I ticked later that day with a solo lap up Mount McGillivray. Up top, I filmed myself, saying into the camera: "Just ticked over 500,000 feet on March 24. I am about a week ahead, and what's the first thing I think? Awesome! Time to focus on a million. It's been amazing; it's been excruciating; it's been challenging. It's been exactly what I am looking for. Something to really focus on, something to commit to, and wow, I have to do that three more times . . ." You can hear the doubt in my voice, the emotional drain of realizing I was only one-quarter of the way there, with tons of hard work still ahead.

That May, I realized there was something important I needed

to do. By this point, I had triggered many small sloughs, walked narrow ridges, and looked thousands of feet down vertiginous mountainsides where a fall or avalanche meant certain death. But I'd always been lucky; so far I'd survived. However, what would happen when my luck ran out? One night, after Tracey and the kids went to bed, I wrote her a letter on the computer, for her to find if I died. I'd also compiled some film clips of me up in the hills, solo, so that my family could see the beauty that drew me to these dangerous places.

> Dear Tracey,
>
> I am crying while I write this. Crying because I have dreaded this outcome forever. Always hoping that I was just being paranoid and I would live out my life with you. But I guess not . . . My life is so great, my wife so beautiful, children so fantastic. For years, I have stood on summits and thought of you, shouted your name to the mountain gods, and expressed my happiness over and over. As I write this, I am filled with one huge regret — not being able to live out our lives together.
>
> I AM SO SORRY. I had an inkling that my good luck would run out one day. Initially, you will be very mad at me and upset, but hopefully, at some point, you may understand. I write this to help you understand.

The mountains have always made me feel more alive and lucky to be who and where I am. Sunrises, pristine powder slopes, snowstorms, sunsets — I have spent many hours wondering if it is all worth it if it kills you in the end. And it is. I could not have spent days in an office or years wandering the city. My soul is bound to these mountains, and will remain here forever. Look to the mountains and smile, knowing my energy is still vibrating among them.

All that I am hoping with this letter is to help you overcome the anger and resentment you will feel. We all die — some early, some late. I have died having lived a life worth remembering. Just remember me, and let my happiness and desires fuel you.

Love,

Greg

For the month of May, when the snow around Revelstoke is usually disappearing, I needed to figure out some other way to get my skiing feet in. I concocted an adventure to Canada's highest mountains — the Saint Elias Mountains in the Yukon, a thirty-three-hour drive from Revelstoke — with four friends.

Looking at maps, I believed that we could go toward Canada's fifth highest mountain, Mount Steele (16,470 feet), and possibly even summit Mount Lucania (17,192 feet), the second highest. We'd take an air taxi from Silver City on the rocky shores of Kluane Lake to a basecamp just south of Mount Steele in the heart of the range. Judging by the maps, it looked like there were 2,000-foot climbs all around our campsite, and with endless late-spring daylight, I would be able to crush loads of vertical during our three-week stay.

After a three-day drive and three days of waiting to fly into basecamp, we were finally on the plane, which was just big enough for the pilot plus two of us and our gear. The plane flew through a massive range of wild, steep, and rugged mountains, stretching, clad in ice and glaciers, to the farthest horizons. I mind-skied hundreds of lines as we flew deep into the range.

Face glued to the windows, I spied endless adventures — steep, wild couloirs, glacier-capped mountains, and peak after enticing peak. At basecamp, watching the plane fly away, I started to look around; the 2,000-foot slopes I had hoped to ski were riddled with crevasses. Then, probing in the snow around camp, we realized that little snow covered the glacier, and our thoughts turned to the grim possibility of falling into a crevasse. There were deep, dark holes everywhere, hinting of endless falls into the frozen abyss. I could feel my dream of spending days lapping and crushing vertical slipping away. To protect against crevasse falls, we'd need to stay roped together at, which made for slow going. Still, I couldn't argue with safety, as I certainly wouldn't reach two mill on feet if I was dead in a crevasse. In the end, during our trip, all we did was summit Mount Steele — we downclimbed and rappelled the icy crust, and then when we finally put our skis on, the skiing turned out to be subpar, on hardpacked snow and glacial ice that made for terrible turns. After the climb, we were tent-bound for three days, and I could almost feel my numbers slipping away — on my altimeter watch, I could literally see them going nowhere. I fell behind par and started to worry. When a weather window came, we radioed the air taxi to pick us up, heading home early.

Driving home, I was grumpy and annoyed by my friends. We stopped at the most amazing place, Liard River Hot Springs, where a crystal-clear river winds through the woods, with geothermal heat emanating from it. We ate magic mushrooms and relaxed in its waters. More accurately, the team relaxed. But I was pent up with anxiety — specifically over the fact that I was now roughly 40,000 feet behind — a worry the 'shrooms only exacerbated. I had maintained close to par since the beginning of this goal, and I didn't know how easy it would be to get vertical in Chile. One day missed was a vertical mile added onto a future day. These successive bad days were adding up to thousands of feet I'd need to recoup somehow.

Back home, with ten days in Revelstoke before we flew as a family down to Chile, I got creative in my search for June snow, finding a handful of shady slopes where I could lap it up, grinding off huge, 12,000-to-14,000-foot days. Still, even as hard as I tried to get back to par, I was still coming up short.

In Chile, Tracey, the kids, and I first based out of the small town of Termas de Chilan in the Las Trancas Valley, where we arrived at the end of June. An acquaintance and world-famous snowboarder, Craig Kelly had skied here a few times and recommended it. There were four summits accessible from the same trailhead, all volcanoes higher than 10,000 feet that offered up skiing on all their aspects. Moreover, the area was known for its geothermal activity — hot springs you can ski-tour to. It seemed like a skier's paradise.

Using Google Earth to plan my days, I was antsy to get back on my skis, and it wasn't long before I was out touring. I began to explore the Nevados de Chillán ski resort as a way to access the volcanoes above. It was so burly down there, with nearly constant winds — and gusts up to 60 mph — blasting across the mountain. I kept my Gore-Tex jacket cinched tightly around my face and used goggles to protect my eyes from the stinging snow/ice crystals pelting me. But still, I was getting nuked. It had to have been almost perpetually windy here, because the ridges were all exposed, black volcanic rock while the snow stuck to the gullies and protected areas.

I pulled out my camera and filmed these first impressions: "First day of ski touring in Chile, and it's definitely really windy. I can't quite decide how long I am going to stay out here. Definitely [fifty mph] — I don't know what to say. I have to figure it out. I keep worrying about my goal and losing days, and [the] days are hard to get back."

In my first week, I had experienced nearly nonstop winds. Doubt pervaded me once again. I was not having the heroic moments I'd been wishing for. Yet the days were simple; the resort was only a 10-minute drive from our cabin, and I was spending the hours away from my family almost exclusively hiking and skiing, racking up vertical feet.

One day, at around 8,000 feet of vertical already climbed, I skied into a valley and found a natural hot spring, where I undressed and had a long, relaxing soak. As I decompressed, I started to realize that my energies were building again and that I had the drive to make this happen. I was finally coming back from the low point I'd hit in the Saint Elias Mountains.

I realized that skiing here was all about the activity and the incredible places I could go versus the snow quality. Being a spoiled powder hound from Revelstoke, I'd assumed I would find great powder skiing, but I'd found wind-blasted, mostly awkward turns with occasional soft snow. No, what was best here was the setting; I'd uncovered the ambiance unique to living and breathing mountains, with fissures that steamed constantly, like sleeping dragons breathing smoke. Or that had metal summit so blasted by the wind that the snow had been carved like a horse's mane at full gallop on their windward side. Everything was different, and interesting. It was an entirely new landscape that I had to approach with a different mindset.

On July 2, the halfway mark for the year, I was only 50,000 feet behind — a number I'd proven I could tick in a 24-hour period at the event in Sunlight in Colorado. It was seeming more and more like 2,000,000 feet just might happen.

I started to develop a two-pronged attack, going out skiing early before the family woke up, spending the day doing family things with them — visiting hot springs, taking small hikes, checking out markets in the city of Chillán. Then I'd go back out at night to ski via head amp. The mountains are different here, and I had to flip my way of thinking. The south faces get less sun and better snow, versus the north faces at home in the Northern Hemisphere. It snowed a lot in the Andes, but then the wind would steal the powder, blowing it away to vanish into thin air. It was hard to understand how it could snow for days, but then I'd go into the mountains only to find zero powder. Still, with diligence and serious focus, I kept putting in large days — 8,000 feet or more, sometimes ten days in a row — to chip away at my deficit.

On July 13, I hit one million feet climbed. But truth be told, I wasn't that elated with this benchmark, realizing that I was a full 11 days behind, with a huge amount of vertical still to go. My stats at this point were: 141 days on snow; smallest day: 130 feet; largest day: 23,070 feet; most runs: 13; unique summits climbed: 44; total runs: 526. These numbers were testimony to an incredible amount of dedication and adventure.

I also mentally reviewed the close calls, of which there had been many. Since I had to be out so often, I was always pushing conditions. I recalled the time when an ice chunk bounced down a gully and glanced off my face, leaving a fat lip. Or the time I managed to ski-cut a large avalanche and was luckily in the right spot — above it. There were also, I'm sure, many unknown close calls, times when I hadn't realized I was standing on a fragile cornice that could have collapsed and sent me plummeting to my death.

The weight of the consequences was heavy, although I kept those fears from Tracey. Still, I had to unburden myself of them somehow, and making a short film seemed like the best way. I didn't feel like the letter I had written was enough, so maybe I could convey my feelings better on video.

One calm sunny day, I set the camera up facing a narrow ridge, with a large mountainside in the background. Then I climbed and scrambled out onto a snowy perch. Sitting there, I pondered what to say. After a long pause, I kicked my heels together, took some deep breaths, sighed, then started in.

"My heart is in my throat—" A deep exhale, then, "How do you start this?"

I paused and breathed again, a few more quiet moments, and then stared straight into the camera.

"Hi, Charley, Aiden, Tracey," I said. Another deep sigh, then: "I mean, I know that this seems like a crazy thing to do, but I think I would be crazier to think I couldn't die out here. I understand that there are so many hazards out here, and no matter how smart I am, how wary I am, there is a chance I could die.

"Aiden and Charley, you are both so young — three and four — and I want to make sure I can give you something, leave you something to show you who I was in case I do pass away.

Ha . . . and I don't want to. I love life far too much to do that. I mean, I love it. I live a life that is unparalleled, it's amazing. But because I run out into the mountains and do everything I do, I run a chance of dying. And I want something for you guys . . . I have lost four friends in the mountains, and I would be super-naïve to think, 'Oh, it won't happen to me!'"

I talked into the camera for seven minutes total, attempting to explain the wonder and but also the great responsibility that came with adventure.

Chapter Fifteen

TWO MILLION FEET: PART TWO

"We dreamed them up and became our dreams because we believed in ourselves. Believe in yourself."
— Excerpt from letters to my family

Every moment of every day, since the start of the year, I'd been preoccupied with a tiny number on my watch. I'd look at it in the evening before I went to bed, the little black digits on the gray screen taunting me with how far I was behind. I'd wake up at night for a pee and couldn't help but glance at my watch and think about the day ahead. And I'd look at it first thing in the morning, feeling a hollow pit of anxiety form in my stomach seconds after waking. And, of course, it was there every moment of every day while skinning up, a constant reminder to pick up the pace. Even during my downtime, trying to relax while floating in the local natural hot springs with the kids, I'd look at my watch and will the number to magically grow.

(Actually, while sitting in one of these tubs one day, I brainstormed a super-easy way to cheat on my goal. The density of water is such that if you turned an altimeter on and pushed it under the water, you could do thousands of feet in seconds of simply moving your watch up and down — three feet down in water is a change of approximately 3,000 feet in the air. So bringing the watch to the bottom of the hot springs and back up twice would have been a 6,000-foot day. Ha, it would have been that easy . . .)

The only consolation for all this admittedly self-imposed pressure was the sheer beauty of these mountains, especially the volcanoes, some of which were still active, like Villarica, which tops out at 9,383 feet above the town of Pucón and is one of Chile's most active volcanoes. The red glow from the summit is visible at night, with the mountain's insides roiling and boiling, and occasionally spitting magma high into the sky. At the base, like all the volcanoes down there, Villarica had incredibly strange and unique trees — the araucaria or monkey puzzle trees, which are like the truffula trees from The Lorax fused with some kind of prehistoric reptile. They have large, scaly trunks that lead to spiked branches crowning the top of the tree, 100 feet up, and I took my time wandering through them on my way up Villarica. The day I topped out — climbing my first living volcano — a solitary plume of smoke whirled off the summit into the pale-blue winter sky.

For as many magical days as there were like the one on Villarica, I also had plenty of days where my ambitions were thwarted. Back then, I was working off trip reports and Google Earth, and nothing ever seemed as easy as on my home turf around Revelstoke. Things that appeared close, like the Volcán Llaima, about forty miles as the crow flies, tended to not be as simple to access as they would have been in Canada. They sometimes took hours of car travel to reach, with false starts, dead ends, and constant re-routing to get around snowed-in roads and blizzard-bound mountain passes.

A journal entry from that trip shows my frustrations with the ever-oscillating emotional ups and downs of my quest:

> Today I went up and down nine times, for 9,360 feet. My motivation [also] went up and down a few times. I awoke, and watched the rain hitting our windows and felt down. Then when I drove out of the parking lot I felt up, and then once I was hiking, I was down again, wondering if I would be able to tour enough to hit 1.27 million feet this day. For the first 3,000 feet I was down, and then I suddenly realized I would be able to tour the requisite vertical and I felt up again. And I rode that feeling right till the end . . .
>
> In the overall course of this goal, the 1.2–1.5 million [section] should be the hardest; once I have hit 1.5 and have less than 500,000 feet to go, it will be exciting. For now, I am trying to focus on how good that's going to feel and push through to that point. My sister Christy once said that while running up a hill one should focus on the feeling you'll get when you crest the hill — and use that feeling a little early to get you up the hill [just like I am now while trying to get to 1.5 million feet].

I also noted in my journal that all this exertion was making me skinny. In fact, my ring finger shrank as I shed pounds, and my wedding ring fell off — taking me hours of searching to relocate, after I realized it was gone — while the family and I walked along a pebble beach, one of the daily excursions I took with Tracey and the kids to vary their routine of play time, short walks, and just hanging around while I was out skiing.

One of our stops in South America was Las Leñas, one of the continent's best-known ski resorts, high in the Argentinean Andes. Sadly, our rental cabin was filthy, with cigarettes left in ashtrays and just plain old dirty all around, and there was no town to speak of for Tracey and the kids to visit, so they felt isolated. The dry, desolate desert wasteland surrounding the cabin was a weird place to walk. We often stumbled upon horse carcasses and those of other animals. Apparently, a recent and large volcanic event had brought smoke and ash into the valley, killing most of the wildlife, which by now were mostly bones with shreds of skin and hair still attached. The harshness of life was apparent everywhere.

The Andes here were high and wild, with steep couloirs, jagged ridgelines, and rocky spires. The combination of these features created ribbons of snow that arced beautifully down the mountainsides, while carving around these spires all looked very playful. The most interesting thing for me was finding a fossil while up at 12,000 feet. It was a concentrically curled ammonite, about two inches square. Imagining that these high mountains had at one time been the floor of the ocean put everything into perspective. When my race to two million feet began to feel all-important, I would stop to acknowledge that the mountain I was obsessing about had once been under the bellies of giant underwater creatures. More surrealism came in the form of the condors, whose nine-to-ten-foot wingspans had them casting giant shadows over my skin tracks, startling me.

Two and a half months in, my little sister, Jesse, met up with us in Argentina to hang out with the family and do some ski-touring, being the most outdoorsy of all my siblings. Then it came time for the family to fly home to Canada so Charley could start kindergarten. When I asked Aiden if he understood what was happening, he said, "You are going to stay here for a month, and then you are going to die, Daddy."

Woah — what?! Those words, from a four-year-old, struck deep in my soul.

"No, Aiden. I'm going to be here for another six weeks, and then come home to you guys in Revelstoke," I told him. With tears in my eyes and fear in my heart, I hugged them all goodbye at the airport in Santiago.

With my family gone, Jesse and I were alone, and I could focus strictly on getting vertical, without feeling guilty about doing extra runs or hiking up another thousand feet to increase my daily total. The best thing I could do now for my family was to climb and ski as much as possible, so that I met my goal — the one we'd all sacrificed so much for.

About three weeks after the family had left, I set my sights on Sierra Velluda, an 11,762-foot stratovolcano in Chile, a fearsome peak that floated high over the landscape, its buttresses, ridges, and cliffs looking almost impassable from the valleys below. Joining me on the climb was a keener named Donny Roth, who'd contacted me through my blog. I'd spent two days exploring around and used Google Earth to figure out the best way to the summit — a north-facing couloir — up which we bootpacked to the top of the peak. From there, we looked down the south face, at the upper 1,500-foot headwall that hung above some big cliffs. It looked impassable. Fortunately, I knew there was a small couloir that linked this hanging face to the remaining 6,000 feet of the descent.

"Hey, Greg, are you sure this goes?" Donny asked.

"I know it looks like we're about to ski off the edge of the world, but there is a small couloir we can sneak through," I told him. I showed him the picture I'd taken of the face again, to placate his fears.

I pointed to my previous high point, and added, "From down there, I could look up and analyze the snow — and I didn't see any wind affect, or slab properties, just small sloughs." However, as I peered down, all I could hear was Aiden's words echoing in my head: ". . . then you're going to die, Daddy."

Were we making the right decision to ski this wild line, or was my ego blinding me because I wanted this first descent? There had been no avalanche hazards for a few days and no new winds, and temperatures were constant. It felt like everything was stable, but still, I couldn't forget Aiden's prophetic words. Paranoid thoughts dashed through my mind, making me question all the rationalizations that had brought me to this point. Was I pushing the limits to fuel my addiction? Did I need to feel like death was a real possibility? Were things different now that I had kids?

At the same time, I also couldn't forget the excitement and emotional return that came from stepping out and risking everything on lines like these. The IV of adrenaline had been pumping lightly all day. With these competing thoughts ricocheting around my head, Donny and I skied down the face, arcing deep powder turns where the snow tumbled off those certain-death cliffs. Nothing bad happened, and we hooted and hollered down the mountainside.

Phew, today hadn't been the day.

I used my final three weeks in South America to push my total up past 1.6 mill on vertical feet (the 80 percent mark), putting in huge days — logging 1C-plus-K days on sixteen of the eighteen days I skied. In retrospect, I should have stayed down there longer, enjoying the abundant snow, but I had to make it home to my family.

When I walked out of the terminal and into the arms of my family, it felt so good. The fear that had lingered since Aiden had uttered those ominous words was finally gone as I hugged his little body. He didn't remember what he'd said, but perhaps he had kept me alive while I was out adventuring — the extra fear and reality of his words.

By the time I made it back to Revelstoke, in October, winter had yet to arrive, even as my cup was refilled with the love of my family and friends. I headed out nonetheless, struggling through the forests and mountains around Revelstoke. There was not enough snow to really ski, especially because I did not want to hurt myself. Typical early-season snow has not settled, and your skis often plunge through, hitting rocks or trees underneath. This makes it easy to twist a knee or even break a leg. I persisted, but all the gains I'd made in the Andes were gone quickly and I fell back behind par.

Fortunately, December brought in a proper volley of storms, and conditions improved dramatically, with loads of epic powder that made every extra run well worth it. My partners were all super strong, but this goal was not their goal, so often they wouldn't want to do that extra lap in the dark. I carried a bag, which we dubbed the "Bag of Commitment," filled with Clif energy products. Clif Shots were 100-calorie gels, while Clif Bloks were tasty, candy-type energy chews laced with caffeine. If anyone went into this bag, they were committing to more runs. It was a great way to re-inspire my friends and get them to keep pace with me. At one point, I did the math for the year to date — in 261 days of skiing, I'd averaged 7,520 feet a day and taken 1,019 runs. However, I was also noticing that I was slowing down and was just generally exhausted, with not a lot of ummmfff left in my steps and with lots of cursing going on during the climbs. With two weeks left in December, I still had 99,500 feet left to go, which I was pretty sure I could make happen as long as conditions stayed good and

I didn't get injured. Still, t was going to be down to the wire.

When someone dies being adventurous, people usually say something like, "At least they died doing what they love." And yes, while I agree, I think a more accurate way to phrase it would be, "At least they lived doir g what they loved." Because a life lived with passion has increcible value to the individual, bringing them more in those moments than a long and empty life. I thought about this a lot in 2010 a year that, for me, truly exemplified this idea. Of course I didn't want to die, but I was willing to live a year — and a life — full of risk to feel like I'd truly lived. I was willing to wear that mantle with each and every step I took toward two million feet in the wild, untamable mountains.

All the doubts, all the worries, all the questions were finally put to rest on December 30, 2010, at Rogers Pass. Here is an excerpt from my journal that day:

> It started off as it should: I got to the parking lot first, dilly-dallied around till a few girls got ahead. Passed them and then I broke trail for two thousand feet up onto the Bonney moraines, [making] sure the skin track was since I knew friends and family would be following my track today. At the top of the moraines, I looked down and I could see lots of people heading up. So I skied down a quick lap and saw quite a few friends. We toured back up to the top.
>
> I chose the Bonney area because I knew that lots of people could hike the 3,500 feet in and we could all enjoy untracked powder all day.

I pulled in a couple of great laps, [and then] did some simple math at the top: 2,000,000 - 1,998,500 = 1,500 feet. So I skied down 1,500 feet and then hiked back up and met Tracey, my mom, Don, and some great friends on the top just as my watch was ticking over.

"So, are you there?" my buddy Frank asked.

Pulling up my watch, I showed them all the number: 2,000,000 feet.

"Yeah, there she is . . . Woah . . ." Lots of whooping from the twenty or so people standing on the small peak.

"Woah, I guess I am going to get emotional . . . Holy shit . . ."

"You're a nut bag — you're, you're crazy," Frank joked.

We all bantered some more, and then — despite thinking this moment wouldn't be such a big deal emotionally — I started crying, the tears freezing on my cheeks in the zero-degree air. All the tension of never knowing, a year of questioning and always doubting. Finally, it was over. The release coursed down my face as I cried and smiled through my tears at my friends and family.

So much had been invested in this silly goal that finally achieving it was overpowering, while having Tracey there to witness the final moment, with friends and champagne, made it all the more incredible.

It was such a cold day that we didn't linger up top, but instead started skiing down. Was my two-millionth-foot turn any better because of all the effort? Perhaps. But what felt even better was getting to the bottom of the run and putting my skins back on for another lap — a carefree lap that was simply extra.

Since my dad, stepmother, Betsy, and many other important people in my life didn't have the skills or ability to get into Rogers Pass, I chose to finish off the year at the Revelstoke Mountain Resort on December 31. This way, everyone could take the chair lift to the top while I hiked up, and they could all witness my last upward steps of 2010.

It was an epic finish. The burden was off my shoulders as I toured up the ski hill, the air feeling rich, my legs light and springy. The weight of my worries was gone. I had lived my dream, overcome endless obstacles, summited seventy-seven different mountains on two continents, and lived a year unlike any I will live again. Now I was finishing it off with what felt like all of Revelstoke cheering me on.

When I reached the top of the chairlift, there was a huge banner that read "2 Mill Hill" and a gathered crowd of about 100 people cheering. The tears didn't come that day, but the elation continued. I shared my yearlong adventure n a slideshow at the ski lodge, relaxed at home, and then we had a celebratory party at the local strip club — well, sans the strippers. That night, my friends and family gifted me a framed photo of myself in silhouette standing on a small, rocky peak near Mount Avalanche, and all my friends had signed along the border. I took the picture home and hung it by the stairs in the basement, where it remains to this day. On January 1, 2011, my family and I went back to the hot springs. As I lay there soaking away the worries of my year, I knew that my cup was truly full. I was following Shane's advice and "living a life worth remembering."

PHOTO CREDIT: TOMMY CHANDLER

Chapter Sixteen

MANASLU

"Since mountain travel is so amazing, so incredible, there has to be the darker side."
— Excerpt from letters to my family

Backcountry.com was amazing at promoting my story, and I ended up with hundreds of pages of articles, in multiple languages, in various magazines and websites. The world celebrated my year. Men's Fitness claimed I was "one of the top 25 fittest guys in the world," an accolade I will never forget. I'd finally achieved something truly unique: I was "2 Mill Hill."

However, my lack of business acumen meant I still didn't make much money, so started to ask for more. And sponsors started calling. Salomon, the French ski company, was wondering if I would join them — they wanted to create a backcountry side to their brand. I jumped at the opportunity and left Dynafit. During my final meetings with Dynafit, the CEO, Beni Bohm, had suggested that I participate in and help film a speed-record attempt on the 8,000-meter peak Cho Oyu, as part of a small group of elite ski-mountaineers who'd skin/climb up and then ski down. At 26,684 feet, Cho Oyu is the sixth highest mountain in the world, and straddles the border between Nepal and Tibet, its slopes relatively broad and gentle for a Himalayan giant — it's the easiest to climb of the fourteen 8,000-meter peaks. Even though I was no longer a sponsored athlete with Dynafit, I was still invited on this trip, which was slated for 2012. Since I had climbed and skied Mont Blanc with the crew in a day and had filmed the entire eleven-hour excursion, they knew I was strong enough to help them document this feat. This was an excellent opportunity, even though I wouldn't be paid for my efforts. But I didn't care at all — in my mind, life experiences trump financial gain.

As the date grew closer, there were some issues getting into Tibet, the side of the mountain we'd hoped to be climbing. China had closed its borders to foreigners because there was unrest amongst the Tibetans. Two Tibetan monks had set themselves on fire to protest the oppressive Chinese rule a few weeks earlier. Given this state of affairs, it was tough to say if Tibet would open in time. We continued forward all the same.

The plan was to land in Kathmandu, Nepal, with a much larger group of seventeen people and climb Mera Peak, a 21,247-foot mountain in that country, using the 20-mile trek into and up the peak to slowly acclimatize us to the higher elevations. Then, most of the group would go home, except six of us who would stay to attempt Cho Oyu, if possible. If not, we would attempt Manaslu, another of the Himalayan giants, standing 26,781 feet high — an option I was less eager about, as Manaslu was considered one of the most dangerous of the 8,000ers. Judging from the map I'd bought and the route we would take on Manaslu, I could see no hiding spots. The route, up the mountain's northeast face, wove through crazy-steep ice walls fractured into seracs, and we'd have to spend a lot of time exposed to a massive slope below these features while moving between Camp II and III. There were no ridges to hike on or terrain features to hide behind — it would be all or nothing. This worried me greatly.

On August 21, 2012, I landed in Kathmandu after sixteen hours of flying from Vancouver. I was so pumped; exploration and adventure in a new country awaited, not to mention the possibility of climbing an 8,000-meter peak! I was also fired up to hang out with Eric Hjorleifson, or Hoji, an incredible Canadian freeskier. The rest of the gang was mostly European, with a few Americans sprinkled in.

I was not prepared for the craziness of Kathmandu — it was totally unlike any place I'd been. There appeared to be no rhyme or reason for how the traffic — or anything — worked. Everything was dirty; they burned trash in the street or left it in huge, rotting piles for the dogs to eat.

I glanced up at the electrical poles and couldn't imagine how anyone knew where any of it was going! There were hundreds of cables running every which way — total insanity. Electricity would go on and off at random times, and all the modern conveniences we take for granted were non-existent. Honking horns blared as we drove to our hotel. Traffic stopped as a large cow wandered listlessly across the road.

We roamed the streets after settling in at the hotel, our minds thrust open with wonder. There was much to process.

The main road through the city was being expanded by six feet on either side, so workers were dismantling the fronts of buildings to accommodate the development — with no safety protocols whatsoever. A worker stood on the concrete, sledgehammering, hammer blow after hammer blow reverberating off the steelhead as he swung at the concrete, wearing nothing but open-toed Crocs.

Everywhere I looked, people were living in ways so foreign to my Western sensibilities. A dejected group of young boys sat along the curb, sharing a gasoline-filled plastic bag they'd wrap around their faces and inhale from. The high was a brief reprieve from their lives on the streets. One boy had no use of his legs, and after his turn at the bag, one of his friends hoisted him onto his back, and they disappeared into the chaos. There was incense burning, street vendors haggling, streets packed with people, and rickshaws weaving between it all. What looked like havoc to me somehow worked fluidly for the locals.

The first real challenge was staying healthy, which involved stringent rules: don't eat uncooked vegetables, drink only bottled water, and engage in frequent, almost obsessive hand washing. I had to think and act like a germophobe.

The next bit of excitement was our flight into Lukla, rated the most dangerous airport in the world, on a plateau at 9,337 feet deep in the Himalayas. The runway was short (1,729 feet), the approach was wild, and the landing was a notoriously dangerous feat, even for experienced pilots, with factors like wind shear, fog, snow, and all manner of mountain weather to contend with. From the air, as we came for landing, I looked down on tiered gardens that levelled off the sides of the lush green mountains, where the locals grew their crops.

Most Everest attempts start in Lukla, so it's become a bustling little town used as an entry port to Everest Basecamp, which lies 38 miles away. From here, travel into the range is primarily on foot, so climbers will hire local porters to carry their loads. I was awestruck as I saw my first porter walk toward me. He probably only weighed 110 pounds but was carrying a load that was twice that, multiple boxes adding up to the size of a fridge attached to his back. The man carried a small, single-legged seat on which to perch and lean up against walls to brace himself, while his load was anchored across his forehead with a strap. It blew my mind; part of me wanted to ask him if I could try, and the other part knew that I couldn't match him.

Midway through our hike to Mera Peak, it became apparent that Tibet was not going to open, so we'd be trying Manaslu instead. We'd suddenly gone from the "easiest of the 8,000-meter peaks" to "the fourth most dangerous of the 8,000-meter peaks." I was apprehensive but hoped that if I followed the mountain rules and tricks that had kept me safe for years, I could mitigate the hazards. As much as I like risk and want to walk the edge, I also like to hedge my bets and keep risks manageable.

To reset and prepare for the next leg of the trip, we flew back to Kathmandu to relax and reorganize for a couple of days, though we didn't want to stay too long here, only a mile above sea level, and lose our acclimatization. When you acclimatize, the pressure in your arteries increases, which forces blood into areas of the lungs that are not typically used. You learn to breathe deeper, and the body produces more red-blood cells to carry oxygen. Our bodies adapt, but it takes time. Acclimatization, however, regresses much more quickly, so we didn't want to linger at lower elevations.

With the group size now down to six, we boarded a helicopter and flew up to a village called Samaguan, in the Gorkha District directly under the imposing Mount Manaslu. The team were all Germans or Austrians: Sebastian "Basti" Haag, Beni, Constantine Pade, plus Reiner and Robert (whose last names I cannot remember!), and then me, the oddball Canadian. I was nervous, but I was awed when Manaslu peaked out of the clouds — like a jagged tooth, it floated above every mountain around it. Everything about the peak looked beyond my skill set, with steep, ice-covered rocks and snow faces that looked so steep that they shouldn't have been there.

This team was stacked with crazy ski-mountaineering athleticism. Basti and Beni had been relentless in their attempts at speed records up and down mountains. In the Himalayas, they had already set two different round-trip records. In 2006, they'd set a speed record climbing and skiing off Gasherbrum II (26,362 feet, the thirteenth highest mountain in the world). And Beni and Basti also held a similar record in speed ski-mountaineering on

Muztagata (24,757 feet) in China. These guys ate big mountains for breakfast.

Constantine was a young recruit of theirs, much less experienced but very fit. His good results in ski-mountaineering races placed him as someone who could keep up with Basti and Beni. Meanwhile, Reiner and Robert were friends of Beni's and very strong in their own right — they were not here to set any records, but instead to strengthen the team and encourage the record-setters.

I had some serious boots to fill if I planned on documenting this feat properly. I knew there were few, if any, videographers who could climb and ski mountains like I could. However, I was worried about the altitude and my ability to capture the story behind their challenge. was up for it, but I knew I'd have to tap deep into my core to find the endurance.

After the trek up from the slate-roofed village of Samaguan, we settled into the very busy Manaslu Basecamp (elevation: 15,748 feet) for a few days of acclimatization, setting up our tents higher on the moraine, away from the larger, guided groups that had taken over the prime real estate below. To pass the time, we had a few fun wanders up onto the Manaslu Glacier. One day, while watching people walk by, I noticed Glen Plake. Glen is a legend amongst skiers; he has years of pro skiing under his belt, and he's best known for his giant, flashy mohawk. I had met Glen a few times in the past, so I went over to chat with him. It turned out that he and his friends Greg and Remy were there to ski off the summit. They were looking to be the first to skin/climb up and ski down Manaslu without oxygen — which happened to be our goal as well, except we had the added component of the speed record added on. There could have been some competition, but I didn't feel any. As the only skiers on the mountain, we immediately bonded over the possibilities, and had Glen and his crew over for tea.

Our team was finally acclimatized and feeling strong, so we headed up to Camp I at 19,000 feet. It was a long and excruciating ski tour, gaining around 3,000 feet of elevation along its 3 miles. The first bit was super wild, with these deep, open crevasses that we skinned right across, their dark maws piercing 150 feet into the ice, disappearing into blackness. We followed thin walkways of snow weaving around the crevasses.

The team had no speed goals for the day, so we did not set a super-fast pace. But regardless, the elevation was taking its toll on me, and I found myself digging deep to get up to Camp I. We were carrying huge bags to set up camp, plus I had all my filming gear to capture the action. I brought along my trusty Sony camera, knowing that it would get the shots. Similar in size to a loaf of bread, it was always awkward to fit it into any bag. Along with that, I had my carbon-fiber tripod, which I'd strap on the outside of my bag. Since Beni and Basti were to be the heroes of this trip, I needed radical footage of them climbing. I would ask them to wait and quickly get ahead so I could film them in action, skinning across narrow crevasse bridges. Or I'd let them get ahead of me and film them against the Himalayan backdrop.

As I looked up at the fixed ropes above Camp I, the climb's technical crux leading up to Camp II, I began to have serious concerns. I could see a lineup of people working their way slowly up the 45-degree slope, which was exposed to immense blue ice blocks teetering above them. I did not want to get into a queue of climbers and remain exposed for the hours it would take to move through here at a snail's pace. Our team was lucky in that we were all very fit, which meant we could cruise through these seracs, spending only brief moments directly below the towering chunks of lethal ice. I worried that something tragic would happen with all the people clustered in this area, and we vowed as a team to time climbing these fixed ropes for when traffic was nonexistent, which was typically either before 6:00 a.m. or after 9:00 a.m.

I also had to wonder about the many guided clients' abilities to recognize alpine hazards. There is a tendency for clients to turn off their brains while they're with their guide, assuming that, because the guide is so experienced, there's no way they'll get into any trouble. But, of course, it's still the mountains and shit still happens. I wondered how many of these clients had wanted to climb their first 8,000-meter peak and had signed up for Cho Oyu, only to end up here like the rest of us when Tibet's border closed — maybe not even knowing how much more hazardous Manaslu was. Had they made peace with the possibility of death — had they made the Adventurer's Pact, in which you accept death as part of the equation?

That afternoon, we skied back to basecamp, which was super fun, nothing wild, just sliding on snow and weaving around all the crevasses we had crossed. What was interesting to me was how quickly I felt better — for every 100 meters I descended, I could feel myself getting stronger.

The following morning, we journeyed back up to Camp I to spend the night at altitude and get better acclimatized, with the goal of pushing on to set up our tents at Camp II (~21,000 feet) the following day. I spent a fitful night at Camp I — fitful because of the decreased amount of oxygen, a hypoxic state in which your body is a little worried and doesn't let you fully commit to sleeping, causing you to awaken every hour or so, almost struggling for air. That next morning, we headed up to the fixed ropes, letting the crowds go first. I was excited to finally cross my first ladder bridge. I'd spent years walking on glaciers but had yet to scratch my way across an aluminum ladder in crampons, with hundreds of feet of darkness lurking below.

On Manaslu, as with all the 8,000-meter peaks, the climbing Sherpas had done so much work to make the route as easy as possible for guided clients. The Sherpas do all the grueling, risky labor of bringing the ropes up, crossing the crevasses, stabilizing the ladders, and anchoring the lines. We, the tourists, just hike up, clip into the ropes with jumars (mechanical ascenders), and work our way up in relat ve safety. About 400 feet above Camp I, I stopped to film our group crossing a ladder, and then I crossed myself. My crampons made the going awkward, and I paused midway across the 18-foot-wide crevasse to peer into the abyss and ponder what would happen to me if I were I to somehow fall in.

As we climbed toward Camp II, the pitches of snow were getting steeper, the e evation was making breathing more difficult, and all I wanted to do was slow down. I couldn't, however — I needed to push hard to get video of the team climbing the fixed ropes. Step, breathe; step, breathe; push, push, breathe. I would look around for a good angle for filming, rush over to get into position, ask the boys to give me thirty seconds to set up the camera, then stand there, breathless, filming them as they came up the ropes. The whole day went like this, with me getting more and more exhausted the higher we climbed.

As we climbed, I also evaluated the hazards involved with these slopes. Fortunate y, the fixed ropes passed mostly above the overhanging seracs. But the pitches of snow, running from 150 to 300-plus feet long, were canted at 45 degrees, which is a steep, avalanche-prone angle. Partway up, I started thinking about the warming daytime temperatures and how these would affect the safety of these slopes; all my years in the backcountry had trained me to consider every last hazard, as well as how quickly conditions coulc change on a big mountain.

"Hey, guys, it's starting to get warm, and I'm worried about these slopes," I told the team. "I think we should either go down now before they get too hot . . . or wait until they have cooled back down this afternoon." But nobody seemed that concerned, perhaps lulled into complacency by the presence of the fixed ropes. So maybe I was just being overly paranoid. Everything had been set up in advance for us — where to camp, walk, clip in, and climb the ropes. Everything had been decided by someone else — and, oddly enough, by people we didn't even know! We didn't need to make any decisions and didn't have to think for ourselves. It's scary how the internal alarms are quieted and how we rely less on our inner wisdom in these situations, but it happens.

After 3.5 hours of slogging, we arrived at the traditional Camp II, a large, flat glacial bench at 21,300 feet. All around us, giant avalanche slopes fed into this singular spot. While looking at the map earlier in our trip, Hoji and I had noted there was no escape. There was something ominous about the spot — in 1972, a group of fifteen climbers on a Korean expedition camped here and had been swept to their deaths by a massive slide.

From our position, I assessed the slopes for their inherent risk factors and determined that there were fewer hazards to our right. We skinned up a hundred meters, then over to the right, finding a small ice pedestal, surrounded by a deep moat, off to the side of where a major avalanche would flow. There were some slopes above, but they were so steep it didn't look like they would collect snow, plus they ran out into a bench that trended toward us and that had a convex ridge that would redirect the snow; in a slide, if snow got moving, the wind and powder could reach us, but the slide's mass would fall into the moat. The site looked nearly perfect, an oasis of safety in an ocean of uncertainty. We set up our three tents here, stomping out a platform in the snow.

On September 12, we awoke early. I lay there cocooned in my down sleeping bag, just my mouth and nose poking out. I took a few deep breaths and accepted the uncomfortable moments that were about to come, and then got dressed. Even the most minor tasks — putting on my clothes, eating breakfast, donning ski boots — were challenging at these heights.

Since everyone else on the mountain was boot-packing, we had the pleasure of putting in a new skin track up the massive mountainside. We left camp by the light of our headlamps, a small circle of light illuminating our frosty exhalations as we slowly skinned upward. Within 300 feet, we were skinning through old avalanche debris, buried under 7 inches of light powder. I worked on staying relaxed and breathing deeply, and not moving too quickly. The higher we climbed, the thinner the air became. Settling into a slow rest-step-skin pattern, we worked our way up the slope. Conditions were great, and we skinned up to about 23,000 feet before stopping for the day.

While we were working our way up, I'd spotted the tents of Camp III. Some 1,600 feet above Camp II, this camp sat almost dead center in the slope, under a headwall, with seracs and steep snowfields looming overhead. It was not a place I could have slept comfortably — not because of the elevation but because of the persistent exposure. Previously, there had been a different Camp III, higher and much farther right; it was possibly a less perilous spot, though a more grueling climb from Camp II, one that perhaps most clients weren't prepared to make — akin to completing a marathon only to jump right in to a second marathon.

A few tents had been pitched slightly higher, hidden underneath a larger, 15-foot ice wall, which could feasibly act as a shield and redirect an avalanche should one occur. This looked like a much better site to me, albeit still concerning.

We continued skinning, and I eventually had to lean over and throw up. Sitting there crumpled, exhausted, and having just lost my breakfast, I still managed to enjoy the sunrise at the highest elevation I had ever been to. I watched as the sun crested the Himalayan peaks to the east, its peach-colored rays spreading out as it rose. Meanwhile, fresh sunlight descended the face above us, everything getting lighter till all the snow around me had turned a rosy color. I was filled with wonder. What a spot! Rousing my energies, I stood back up and continued skinning after the boys.

Not much later, and with no reason to go any higher that acclimatization day, we stopped at 23,300 feet and pulled off our skins, in preparation for skiing down. The soft Himalayan snow skied as well as we had hoped, making for perfect, easy turns until we hit a patch of avalanche debris under the powder that made for bumpy going.

The old debris was evidence of an avalanche cycle that had gone through a few weeks earlier. I guessed that these slopes often slid, which only made me further question the placement of Camp III. But much as I wish for myself, I don't like telling others how to live — we each make our own decisions and must live with the consequences. However, these clients had let the decisions be made for them and might not have fully understood the risks. Still, what was I going to do — march into Camp III and demand that everyone relocate?

Back at our Camp II, I took the time to again evaluate our little haven, analyzing it again from a new angle to ensure it was the best spot. The slopes immediately to the left were not as steep, with very little potential energy. Meanwhile, the fluted slopes directly above were, as I'd noted earlier, so steep that most of the snow would continually shed in small sloughs, rarely building up enough to become a giant avalanche that could release without warning.

After another pause, we kept skiing down from Camp II. The powder was super fun, yielding bouncy, spring-skiing-like turns. Skiing down to the fixed ropes, I dreamed I was going to rail slide across the ladder! As if! I have never been a rail slider in the terrain park, much less above a huge, dark chasm, but it was a fun notion to entertain for, like, half a second.

Below the ladder — which we walked across — I watched Constantine ski a little more left than we had. The slopes became a little steeper and more unsupported, and he triggered a small avalanche.

Constantine kept skiing without realizing what was happening behind him — he had no idea that a small slide had almost caught him, threatening to drag him into the crevasses below. Scarier than the slide itself was what it hinted at: a weak bottom layer of rotten, un-bonded snow. Like anything without a good foundation, a collapse would be the most natural result, which meant that any snow that had fallen this season would be sitting atop this weakness. It could crush it down, bridge over it, or sit precariously on top. Everything depended on how the subsequent layers had formed.

Back at basecamp, it started to snow and snow and snow. We sat out the storm for a week, occupying ourselves with card games, while I read *Game of Thrones* books three and four. Worrying about their acclimatization, Beni and Basti ventured out on a couple of days. The terrain up to Camp 1 was not really avalanche terrain, so I joined them for one of these crazy, wet adventures. We left wearing our Gore-Tex jackets, huddled in their protective comfort, heavy, wet snowflakes sliding off our shoulders. I buried my head in my hood and followed the boys. We were quickly on the glacier and roped up together, following wands placed earlier by the Sherpas. The boys put the skin track in for us, and I was content to simply follow. It felt great to be active again, and, in time, we made it up to Camp I. This kept my acclimatization level up, or at least it didn't set me back.

Glen, Greg, and Remy dropped by a few times during this

waiting period, and I brought up my thoughts about the Camp III placement.

"Wasn't the typical Camp III farther right, closer to the ridge? Where it is now seems pretty exposed," I said.

"Well, it's not perfect, that's for sure. Our tents are the highest on the right, hidden below the serac," said Glen, referring to the higher camp I'd spotted. "It's possible that the ice feature would push the flow away from us. Regardless, I'll wear my beacon while I sleep."

I said my bit and decided not to belabor the point. However, it was clear that Glen knew the location was less than ideal, but was still willing to take the risk, while Remy was a fully certified mountain guide who likely knew exactly what the issue was.

Basti, not being good at relaxing and also worrying about his acclimatization, wanted to go ski the pitches by the fixed ropes between Camps I and II mid-storm. Wind and new snow typically equal avalanches, I told him — conditions up there were likely very dangerous. Basti, however, didn't want to wait until the sun came out, as he knew that would for sure start an avalanche cycle. He tried to get others to join him, while I kept pointing out the storm cycle of avalanches that was probably occurring up higher. But Basti wouldn't listen and headed off solo despite my concerns.

Basti stayed in radio contact with us at basecamp as he made the climb. After a nervous few hours — at least on our end — he'd reached the steeper fixed-rope pitches, where I knew the risk of a slide was greatest. Basti skinned up higher, and then something spooked him. He got on the radio and asked for us to make sure he checked in every five minutes. Otherwise, we should come looking for him.

Sitting drinking tea, we waited anxiously through the tense minutes between calls, knowing that Basti was so far from our help that if something went wrong, he'd likely die. Eventually, after 1.5 interminable hours, he made it back to basecamp.

During one of our many card games during the storm, we'd talked of many things, but one conversation sticks out for me, in which Basti adamantly put forth his idea that the mountains are there to be conquered.

"It is me versus the mountains," he'd said. "The challenge is to conquer them and then feel better because you have won."

"Are we not trying to work with them to summit? The main challenge being within oneself and overcoming personal limitations?" I countered.

Basti mulled this over and then countered with, "The mountain puts challenges in your way — elevation, snow, cliffs — and it is up to you to be better and stronger than these obstacles. And then you get to the top and you have won."

I didn't necessarily agree, and said, "I personally feel that I'm working with the mountain, understanding it, and then working through these challenges. I chose to challenge myself in the mountains, and the limitations are mine and mine alone — the challenge is me. How far can I hike? How hard can I push myself? Do I know enough to overcome these hazards safely and summit this mountain?"

When the storm cleared, all we wanted to do was get back up on Manaslu. We didn't know what had happened to our tents, the snowpack, and all the other people and equipment on the mountainside. We waited out the first three days of sun, watched the winds whip across the summit ridge casting huge tails of spindrift, and looked for natural avalanche cycles or any indication of what was happening on the slopes. The guided parties started back up toward Camps II and III. Remy, Greg, and Glen walked by to head up the mountain as well. They were not planning on going to the summit yet — just getting back to their high point. We needed to get back up high as well, to sleep at 21,000 feet so we wouldn't lose our acclimatization.

On September 22, we arrived at Camp II, from where I could see the Camp III tents still pitched directly in the center of the slope.

This seemed ludicrous. To my mind, sleeping with your beacon on was far from a solution — it means that you're still in avalanche terrain. One of the biggest rules of the mountain is to limit exposure time. It makes a lot of sense: the less time you're there, the less time you have to get caught. You are not limiting your exposure time if you're sleeping on the avalanche slope — in fact, you're maximizing it! Not to mention the fact that everyone in your camp could be buried, with no one left to dig survivors out, rendering the beacon useless.

Our tiny island of safety had changed with all the new snow, and our tents were just tiny tips of color poking out of the snow. I took off my heavy camera bag and pulled out my shovel to dig out our tent, cutting through the new snow, slowly and gently exposing the yellow fabric. The tent had been bent and warped by the mass of snow. I continued to dig, getting the door out, and I was glad that none of the poles had broken. The tent slowly popped back into its dome shape; somehow, it had survived!

"Hey, Greg?" Beni asked. "Can I borrow your shovel?"

I was dumbfounded. Where was his? Then I looked around and realized no one had a shovel but me — what the fuck?! A shovel is as synonymous with alpine travel as skis are with skiing. So many situations in the mountains require a shovel, from digging your tent out to excavating a simple toilet to, more dramatically, digging your friends out of an avalanche. The avalanche beacon I'd been carrying around was useless if my partners couldn't dig me out after finding me. Why hadn't I noticed this earlier?

This total lack of preparation had me gravely worried. Typically, partnerships in the mountains develop slowly over the years. They form when you're comfortable with your risk tolerance and satisfied with your partners. Ideally, your partners' strengths complement your own, making up for any weaknesses either party has. There develops an unwritten code that your partners will be prepared to save you, or you'll be ready to save them. Having a situation like this, in which there was zero room for error, was foreign to me, and I became increasingly unsettled. Our first-aid kit was the size of a bible, essentially a prayer that nothing would go wrong. Gulping back my apprehension, I lent Beni my shovel, and we reclaimed our campsite from the snow.

Before going to bed, we discussed our plans for the next

day; perhaps we'd go for the 26,247-foot (8,000-meter) mark, climbing onto the peak's upper plateau. So much depended on how the snow had stabilized, information we could glean only while ascending the slope. The stability could go either way: the new snow could have compressed the weak layer and bridged any weakness, allowing for safe travel; or the fresh snow, combined with the wind, could have created a slab of snow sitting precariously atop this weak basal layer.

Wrapped up in my sleeping bag, I breathed deeply, acclimatizing, wondering what the next day would bring.

Our alarms woke us up at 4:00 a.m. on September 23. The -22° F temperature made us question the wisdom of this early start. I lay there in my cocoon, with just my mouth exposed, breath crystallizing on every surface it touched. "Do we need to go higher today?" I asked myself. At these elevations and temperatures, the thought of getting dressed, putting on my ski boots, and laying down a skin track was daunting.

Next to me in the tent, Robert likewise stayed huddled in his sleeping bag. Calling out to the boys in the other tents, we all agreed to postpone our ascent, deciding instead to stay put and sleep some more, and then ski back down to rest at basecamp for another attempt later.

It's rare to sleep well at high altitude, so I lay there, rolling in and out of a light sleep. After about a half hour of this, the tent walls suddenly started flapping. A crazy wind battered the nylon, picking up intensity until the whole tent was getting blasted. How was this even possible — could the winds go from zero to 50 mph in just three seconds? The tent shook even more, struggling to hold its shape, then the wind died as quickly as it had arrived.

An eerie calm followed. I couldn't quite grasp what had happened.

"Why did the wind instantly pick up, blast us for fifteen seconds, and then stop so suddenly?" I asked.

"Avalanche . . ." Robert whispered, his German accent thick with fear.

Of course! Shit! How big was it? Were people involved? My mind was racing.

Then, from out of the darkness came shouting, too far away to discern what was being said, though you could hear the voices pitched with concern. It sounded like people were out looking for lost friends, probably shouting out names. It was evident that many people had been caught in the slide. Our little team hollered back and forth between our tents — we were all accounted for — then sprang into action.

Pulling my ski boots on, I stood outside the tent and peered into the darkness. Tiny headlamps bobbed around on the slope beyond our camp, the worried voices still screaming for their lost compatriots. This was big. Looking below, we could see that people in Camp II were awake, but we were a hundred of feet higher and closer to the site of the avalanche.

We grabbed what little we had to help — my one shovel, a small first-aid kit, extra warm layers, and water. But then we decided to wait until we could see with the coming dawn, to make sure there were no more hazards hanging overhead — what good was a rescue effort if we were killed too? Fifteen minutes later, once it was light enough, we set out, skinning furiously up the slope and trying to understand the extent of the disaster.

We encountered the first bit of avalanche debris within 150 feet of our tent. The avalanche flow had followed the curvature of the terrain and flowed past our camp, right down into Camp II. By the pale morning light, it looked like it had just grazed the first tents below us. We could see headlamps moving down there as the climbers emerged from their tents to survey the damage.

We skinned higher, and our headlamps lit up a down boot. Soon enough, there was manmade debris everywhere — tents, clothes, sleeping bags, lone boots, everything strewn about and partially buried. The lighter stuff had been carried the farthest down the slope, riding atop the snow. Now that I could see the slopes above in the morning light, I was stunned by the size of the avalanche. A crown ran line the whole way across the main slope, at least three feet deep and hundreds of feet across.

Some 100 feet above our camp, we met up with the first group of survivors. A group of Frenchmen sat atop the snow, cold, in shock, and barely able to grasp what had just happened. My French, which I'd learned in my French elementary school, came in handy now. They had, they told me, all been sleeping in their tents when a wall of snow thundered down out of nowhere, picked them up like flotsam, and carried them down a thousand feet. Curled up in their sleeping bags, there had been nothing they could do. I handed them some water. They pointed to bits of material buried thirty feet away. "There, that is a tent; there must be people in it," one man said.

Struggling with what to do, we decided to triage and help those who were obviously alive and above the snow, even if just parts of them were exposed. We knew deep down that those who were buried had very little chance of surviving — at this point, they would have already been buried for around thirty minutes.

It was gut-wrenchingly difficult to decide where to go and what to do amidst the eerily quiet chaos. The tent that the French guy had pointed to was completely buried, with just a tip showing; it would take a while to dig out

Immediately, our group started helping dig out those whom we could. We provided water, warm clothing, and any care we could. Soon enough, rescuers from Camp II came up and started helping. They were far more prepared with oxygen tanks and radio communication to Manaslu Basecamp, which helped them initiate a helicopter rescue. There were people partially buried with broken ribs and dislocated arms whom we dug out; it was essential that we get and keep everyone warm in the bitingly cold morning air at 20,000 feet. Others had been so injured that, despite our best efforts, they still faded away. Through some miracle, many only needed sleeping bags and warmth to stabilize.

I started to help a woman named Catherine who was barely conscious, though her tent mate beside her on a sleeping mat was slightly better off. He was conscious and complaining about his sore back, so we focused on her. We pulled an oxygen mask down over Catherine's face, hoping that the extra oxygen would help keep her alive. I talked to her, asking her to stay with us. She did not respond to verbal stimuli and did not seem to notice us touching her. Her partner began to tell us their story: while sliding down the mountainside, he had felt his body bouncing off Catherine's and had ended up on top. Through whatever random twist of fate, he was relatively unscathed, while Catherine had borne the brunt of the impacts.

We kept checking Catherine's weak pulse until, eventually, her heart stopped. We needed to move on; it was four degrees below zero, and other climbers needed our help. Before then, I'd never seen anyone die, and the moment was profound both in its finality and its brevity. We hoped that Catherine at least felt no pain in her last moments. We discussed starting CPR, but we had no real way to keep her alive at this altitude, in the freezing cold. We had to move on and help those who had a better chance of survival.

A volley of bellowing from farther down the slope brought me to where Robert was digging out a man. The man was alive and yelling — his shoulder had been dislocated, but he was more concerned with the green sleeping bag wrapped around his legs and that was lodged in the avalanche debris. His partner was in that sleeping bag, and we worked hard to dig him out, hoping he was still alive. We each took working furiously with the shovel until we were exhausted, handing off the tool to the next guy. I don't know how much time passed, but eventually we realized we were unearthing a dead person. His partner could not comprehend that his friend was gone, and that there was nothing we could do. Once we had dug the man out and placed his inert body on the snow, I moved on, searching for other places to be of assistance.

The variety of injuries was astounding; some people were "okay" after their 1,000-foot tumble, while others were so riddled with internal injuries that their life escaped them quickly. Some had arrived floating on top of the debris, while the tent beside them was buried in the suffocating snow. There were injured people stuck in their tents with their tent mate's dead body wrapped around them. There was barely a hairline of difference between life and death. Some people had been talking to their tent mates as it happened, getting ready for the climb that day, and when the avalanche stopped, their partners were nowhere to be found. Given how much time had elapsed, I knew that anyone who had not been found by this point was most likely not going to survive. Those who were lucky were alive, and the unlucky were dead. Overtaken by grief, I sat down in the hardening snow and filmed myself.

Choking through sobs, I narrated: "Oh, man, I didn't know any of them, but it is so fucking sad. They all come out here trusting their Sherpas and everything, and they camp in this huge avalanche path. And how many died today . . . I don't know . . . ten? . . . Oh, God . . . we are so lucky because we decided to sleep in, hang out, and wait. One hour difference and this would have been us . . ."

We spent hours helping, mourning with people as they watched their friends pass away mere inches from them. We dug a landing platform and moved the injured people close enough for them to be plucked off once the helicopters arrived. We also dug out the deceased and tried to locate any other missing people.

Periodically, I wondered about Glen, Remy, and Greg — what had happened to them? I was pretty sure they had been up at their own Camp III. Tucked up under that fifteen-foot-tall serac, they had been as protected as they could be. In an avalanche, their placement might have left them untouched. It was too far away to tell what remained of their tents. Where were they now?

Up to this point, I had recognized no one — they were all the nameless people I had seen on the fixed ropes or wandering around basecamp. Three hours into the rescue, I saw someone resembling Glen, looking lost, dazed, and completely unnerved, making his way haltingly down the steep pitch above where everything had collected. I ran up and gave him a huge hug.

"Glen, thank goodness you're alive! What happened? Where are Remy and Greg?" Questions tumbled out of my mouth faster than he could answer. His body language communicated what he was reluctant to say. He had not found either Remy or Greg, and with several hours having passed since the avalanche, they were surely dead — their bodies probably never to be found.

The rescue operation was well underway; the helipad was built, the guides had contact with basecamp, and helicopters were on route. Those who were able to be helped were helped;

those who were beyond help sadly were precisely that.

I realized I was just dead weight now, but one thing I could do was to get Glen down to my tent and offer him some coffee and something to eat, and be an ear for his sorrows.

I began to boil some water, waiting for Glen's survival story. I made coffee and just waited, knowing it would come soon. Then, he began:

"When we went to bed last night, we were saying, 'This is the worst friggin mountain you could ever climb. Because there is nothing ever safe on it. Every camp is a mess.' But we were committed, so we stayed put. We were in our tents having trouble sleeping. Strong gusts kept smashing the tent and shaking it. I was reading my bible and breathing deeply when a loud gust rocked our tent. 'That's more than wind,' Greg said. 'It's an avalanche.' A second later, we were hit, and we began to get smashed around and tumbled downhill. I figured that was it, and I was immediately mad at myself for having died in an avalanche. I struggled against the pressure and chaos around me. There was little I could do, caught in my sleeping bag; at least my arms were out so I could protect my head and try and orient myself.

"Eventually, it stopped, and somehow I was still alive. The first thing I saw was a picture of my wife. I started pushing against the tent walls, freaking out, punching the sides of the tent, moving the snow. Then I found the tent door and unzipped it. Cold air flooded in, and I started yelling, 'Greg . . . Greg?! Remy? Remy?!'

"There was nothing — just silence. I turned my beacon on, waited for a signal, and kept waiting. But it wasn't picking up anything. There should have been two beeps — Remy's and Greg's — but there was nothing.

"I freaked out and started pulling on any piece of fabric I could, hoping to see Greg's sleeping bag, but it never was. There was no sign of Remy or his tent. He'd just disappeared.

"I contacted basecamp and let them know I was okay, and then decided to get out of the crevasse I was stuck in before I fell even farther in. I walked my way out and got my first view of the devastation. All of Camp III was gone, and the debris had swept into Camp II.

"I spent the next hour searching all around, assuming the forces had swept Remy's tent the same way and that Greg had to be nearby. He'd been in the same tent as me. I thought hard, back to last night when we'd talked about the beacons. Remy had said that his was in his tent, and Greg also needed to turn his on. But somehow, neither of them did!

"After an hour or so, I gave up hope that I'd find them and began hiking down to meet up with you guys. All I could think was, 'Oh, not Remy . . . . Man, he has kids and a wife back home. What a disaster!' I've lost friends before, but none who were so close."

For an hour or so, Glen and I discussed the risks and realities, and how we hoped Remy's wife understood those realities. All I wanted to do was help Glen process. In my mind, there was no way his friends had survived.

To deal with this bittersweet twist of fate, Glen wanted to walk off the mountain, taking his grief and hiking back down to basecamp under his own power. I helped him ready himself, and then I watched as he started making his way down the glacier, heartbroken.

Looking back up to a buzz of activity on the slope, I could see that I was no longer needed at the avalanche site, so I took stock of my thoughts. We had gotten lucky — not just with our tent placement, but with our timing. We had narrowly escaped through fate or laziness, whichever had made us decide to stay in our bags that morning. When the avalanche roared down the mountainside, we could have been mid-slope, skinning up in the dark.

Thinking about my safety net — my teammates — I realized that I didn't want to be part of the expedition anymore. I have never ditched a team before, but I'd always felt weird with this group. Maybe it was the nonstop German being spoken, which I could only grasp little bits of, or the way they approached mountains. I firmly believe in working with the mountain, being challenged by it to overcome your own limitations but not fighting against it. But Basti highlighted that it was an ego game — him against the mountain. This "I am better than the mountain" approach was so counterintuitive to what I felt, and it seemed dangerous, especially considering what had just happened.

I knew that we had been lucky, and if you want to learn from mistakes, you need to own them. This was not a case of continuing as if nothing had happened. If I stayed to climb Manaslu, I would be ignoring the truth of this tragedy. If I walked away, I could own the mistakes and think deeply about them, and hopefully never make them again.

To my mind, the mistakes had been plentiful: Due to the pressures of the expedition, we'd ignored all the wind we'd watched blowing across the ridge that set up the wind slab which avalanched. We were also not really prepared for any sort of self-rescue or any issues, with only one beacon, one shovel, and a tiny first-aid kit. We had nothing to truly help with in the aftermath of the avalanche, though fortunately the other teams had had oxygen and such. We had a small time window and needed to push the conditions to try to be successful. I almost felt as if the objective was more important than anything else, which is not my typical way of thinking.

I also recognized that the partners with whom I've adventured have always had the same risk tolerance as me. Whereas, with these men, I felt like success was everything and we were not prepared to settle for anything less.

Knowing this felt right, I packed up everything I needed from Camp II. My backpack was massive, but I skied off with it, slowly and carefully, down to Camp I, where I grabbed even more stuff. I must have looked like a wild bag lady, with gear clipped onto the sides of my pack, hanging off helter-skelter; with almost too much to carry, I began to ski down to basecamp. My emotional burden was heavy, heavier than the bag on my back. I had just witnessed people dying and seen dead bodies pulled out of the snow, and been stunned by the reality of risk.

If we hadn't huddled deep in our down bags, we would have added to the body count. I was so focused on filming and being as strong as possible that I'd overlooked that wind slab developing. Basically, I'd crossed my fingers and hoped things would be okay, which is not a viable long-term strategy in the mountains.

Tracey, Aiden, and Charley, plus the rest of my family and friends, expected more out of me, and I expected more as well. Never again, I vowed, would I let luck determine the outcome. We had made a good decision about our camp spot, but I had still been considering going up toward Camp III that very morning. I'd been one random decision away from dying.

The guilt ate at me, bouncing around my head as I jump-turned my way down the fixed-rope pitches. My ego likes to protect itself and can convince itself that it makes no mistakes, but I knew we'd made some mistakes and then gotten lucky. How good would my one beacon have been had I worn it, with no other beacons and only the one shovel in our group? Very pointless, I figured.

The despair of the rarified air lifted a bit as I skied lower; the increased oxygen made me feel better, even as my survivor's guilt increased.

The first thing I did was call home and let them know that I was okay. Disastrous news travels fast, and I wanted to put the flames out before they grew into a brushfire. It was super early in

British Columbia, but my stepfather, Don, would be up and most likely checking the news.

"Hey, Don, sorry to wake you, but I knew you'd be up," I told him over the satellite phone at basecamp. "There's been a major avalanche here and many people lost their lives. Can you reach out to everyone and let them know I'm okay? Before the news gets them worried. Thanks. Love you all. I have to go."

A few hours later, I tried to phone Tracey and connect directly with her. She had just returned from camping, and her phone was buzzing with messages. As she struggled to process why there would be so many messages, I reached her on the phone.

"Hey, honey, its me," I said. "I'm fine, but there's been an avalanche. Lots of people were caught in the slide, but I wasn't. I was one of the first responders." I tried to keep my tone nonchalant, so that she wouldn't worry, and then continued, "Sorry I can't talk for long, but just know that I love you and the kids. I'm flying back to Kathmandu and I'll call you then, and we can chat more."

"Okay, I love you. Talk soon," Tracey said.

Afterward, as Tracey listened to her messages — from friends, coworkers, and various news agencies — she realized the size and severity of it all and broke down crying. The harsh reality of all the risks I take had been splashed across media outlets worldwide, awakening a deeper fear in her.

I cannot remember exactly what happened when the rest of the team came down — that whole day was one, big terrible blur. I just know that when I told them I needed to leave, they understood completely, although they did try to get me to stay because I was the filmmaker for the trip.

I hate letting people down, so I was open to discussing more. Beni figured the avalanche hazard was gone, and with the good weather in the forecast, he would have a good shot at summiting and setting his record. I agreed with him that the main hazard was gone, but the weakness in the slope was still there and could certainly build back up with wind-loading on top of the shitty basal layer, especially if more snow came in.

Part of me wanted to honor the dead by not traipsing over their graves in the days immediately following the disaster. I know that following a deadly car crash in a city, everyone drives through that same intersection without a second thought. This felt different, though — I had grown to like Remy and Greg, who'd been so unlucky while we were so fortunate. It's not that it felt dishonorable to climb over their graves; it was more that it felt dishonorable not to give ourselves time to grieve them.

We discussed it back and forth, but my feet were planted, and I wanted to get home. Beni understood that we'd exceeded my risk tolerance, and that I would not be able to continue with them. For him, nothing had changed, and he wanted to attempt his world record. I fully respected his single-minded focus on his goal, but I would not stay to witness it. In his stern and stoic way, Beni protected his ego by separating himself from the event. Something huge and cataclysmic had happened — but to them, not us. They'd been unlucky, while we were not.

"We were so very lucky that we chose to stay in our sleeping bags and not venture up for another ski from 23,000 feet," I argued, as we gathered in our tent. "We were so close to making a mistake that could have cost us our lives! I feel like we need to take this warning and learn from it. We'll learn way more by walking away and analyzing our actions."

"Greg, I will agree that we did get a little lucky, but we were not in the wrong," said Beni in his blunt, Teutonic way. "Mountains are dangerous, and that is the truth."

"I guess I feel like we were unprepared and almost got caught. I've spent my life taking courses and trying to be prepared, and we just weren't. I feel like the record you're searching for is more important than making good, safe decisions."

With a heavy heart, I packed up my belongings and organized my escape plan. Many people were heading back to Kathmandu from Manaslu Basecamp in the wake of the disaster, so it was easy for me to catch a helicopter ride.

As I hugged everyone goodbye, a part of me understood that I had not forged a strong connection with these people. That through language barriers and differing opinions on risk, we were not meant to be partners in the mountains.

Immediately upon opening my email in Kathmandu, I was bombarded with messages from media outlets. How had they known I was involved in the avalanche? How did they get my email address? Regardless, I wanted to placate people and share my thoughts. I have always wondered why the media gravitates so strongly to these mountaineering tragedies. If fifty people die in an earthquake in a village, it gets a brief mention. But if a handful of people die in an avalanche while climbing, it gets big-time international attention.

My theory on this is pretty simple: These mountaineering stories are so fascinating because we chose to be there. We invited risk into our lives, and it bit us hard. This was not about villagers living their regular lives, and then — *bam* — the earth shook and their houses collapsed on them. It is as if the media gloms onto these tales to prove that we fragile humans should not take risks, that people should not step out of their comfort zones: "Oh, look at these idiots — they risked it all and suffered the consequences!" seems to be the almost-gleeful attitude.

The world wanted to know everything, and I emailed and talked with several people on the phone. After I flew back to Canada, I was interviewed by CBC National at the airport and answered phone calls from all the Canadian media outlets. In my humble Canadian way, I did my best to clarify why we do what we do, and that it was important not to judge others for what had happened or for their decisions. I knew that this event would echo in my consciousness for years, perhaps permanently changing my relationship with the mountains. Eleven people died that day, with dozens more injured. A serac had cut loose in the dark, dislodging the six feet of fresh snow sitting atop that slope, and lives had been ended or changed forever.

PHOTO CREDIT: BRUNO LONG

Chapter Seventeen
PAKISTAN 2014

"But don't fear failure, as it can help you. Uncertainty is great — it creates challenges and promotes evolution of yourself."
— Excerpt from letters to my family

In 2014, a fellow Salomon athlete, Ptor Spricenieks, invited me to participate in an expedition to Pakistan, with all the expenses to be paid for by Salomon. Ptor and I had loosely known each other for years, but had never really adventured together.

The objective was to climb a 6,200-meter peak, Gashot, with a fabulous virgin ski descent off it — a stunning snow shield on its northeast aspect. It was a steep and continuous snow field pitched at a consistent 45-plus degrees for 3,000 feet. If you could ski it under good conditions, you would be set up for perfect turns that would go on forever.

Taking to heart Kurt Vonnegut Jr.'s saying that "peculiar travel suggestions are dancing lessons from God," I decided to join Ptor.

Yet for some unknown reason, I had a deep-seated fear in my gut prior to the trip. Because of this ominous sense, I began to draft a letter for my kids, who were nine and eight at the time. I had a healthy connection with them, and I couldn't imagine what it might be like for them if something were to happen to me and they had to grow up without a father. In the letter, I tried to explain why I was willing to take such big risks.

Dear Aiden and Charley,

My two most amazing kids, you have brought so much to my life. Thank you.

I have started this letter numerous times and always faltered. Faltered because part of me is worried that by writing this I will manifest my future, or lack thereof. I write this so that you'll know who I am, so that you'll understand that I have lived a life unlike many before me. That I have experienced so very much, and that if I pass away early, it's because I have lived too much already.

When I was working on my latest record [my "March Madness" challenge—see below], in March, I was pushing my physical limits so hard that I overlooked certain dangers. It was a very eerie avalanche hazard, one that was hard to predict. At 5:00 p.m. I was up on Cheops's West Shoulder (in Rogers Pass), all alone, enjoying the mountains. I had already skied this slope earlier in the day, and then skied several other runs. Enjoying the last rays of light, I slid down the mountainside. Going a little farther left than in the morning, I pushed into steeper and rockier terrain. Since I always ski everything with the thought that it could slide after me, I looked back uphill for a moment. Something was weird — I could see small cracks forming in the snow. Shadows lengthened as the slab pulled away from the mountain. It took only milliseconds to figure out what was happening; I had to ski to the right and away from the three-foot-deep slab avalanche I'd triggered, and I had to do it now!

The slab of snow was gliding down the mountainside while I was skiing on top of it! The fractures grew, and smaller pieces began to break off as they gained speed. Arcing a turn on what was left of my slab, I skied farther right, jumping onto another chunk of slab, balancing there. Then I eyed the bed surface and jumped off onto the hard snow underneath, edging my skis hard. I skidded to a stop as the rest of the snow surged past me.

What began as a pleasant solo ski under alpenglow had precipitated into one of the largest avalanches I have ever skied, escaped, and survived. I stood there, watching as a massive cloud of snow erupted off the first bench 1,000 feet beneath me and then continued to crash 3 000 more feet to the valley below. Something I'd triggered had had enough destructive potential to bury a train.

It's partially because of that close call that I wanted to write this. Who cares if I curse myself by writing it? At least I will have given you two a way to figure out who I am. During your life, you will hear many differing opinions about your wild father. So, I thought I should at least give you mine . . .

Prior to the trip to Pakistan, I had spent the month of March 2014 climbing and skiing more vertical than I ever had before — some 330,000 feet up around Revelstoke, my "March Madness" challenge. Then, in April, I took the full ski guide exam and got certified by the Association of Canadian Mountain guides. After nine years in the industry, I was now no longer an assistant guide. Swelling with confidence — which is never a good sign — I said goodbye to Tracey and the kids and headed to Pakistan. Ptor was a character who saw the world differently than most people, and I knew the trip would not be boring. I was delighted to hear more about the "happiness box" he was creating — his invention, he said, would somehow only capture happy thoughts and then spread happiness energy to the world.

Also on the team were the skiing filmmakers Daniel Ronnback and Bjarne Salen. I knew little of Daniel, but Bjarne was a legend, having filmed on the craziest lines in Chamonix and all around the world.

This was shaping to be a trip of a lifetime, but I still had constant premonitions of something going wrong. I couldn't discern if it was just a generalized and understandable fear about heading into the world's highest mountains, or if this was something more. Whenever I inhaled, I felt congested and a little scared.

Almost one year earlier, on June 22, 2013, an expedition

to Nanga Parbat, at 26.660 feet the ninth highest mountain in the world, had been attacked by Islamic militants, with eleven people (ten climbers and one guide) killed high in the mountains of Pakistan. The original motives of the militants had been to kidnap members of the expedition party, who were from China and various countries in Europe, and hold them for ransom. Instead, sixteen militants stormed the Nanga Parbat Basecamp, robbed the climbers, tied them up, and then executed them.

Our team would be following the same valley — the Dimroi Valley — before branching off to our destination. So, it made sense that my foreboding thoughts were more centered on being kidnapped or killed by extremists than on making a mistake in the mountains. Culturally, Pakistan made me feel uneasy; as a Westerner, I would stand out and be an easier target for kidnapping — or worse. To add to my anxiety, we would be the first expedition to this valley since the murders. How could I assess this type of hazard? This was a huge unknown, with far more factors beyond my control than I was accustomed to. Staying vigilant was the best I could do.

In Islamabad, we were picked up by our tour organizer, Liver, and his employees. They treated us like friends, and I felt immediately secure with them, even amidst the chaos of this massive metropolis. Immediately, we went shopping for some shalwar kameez outfits, which are traditional for Pakistani men, since we wanted to blend, although our height — being taller than most of the locals — and awkwardness in the garb surely made us stand out. The next day, we rode in a van stuffed full of skiers and our equipment along the infamous Karakoram Highway, a

500-mile road into the rugged heart of the range. Each district would provide a guard to accompany us through their protected zone, as the road ran through Taliban-controlled territory.

Gazing out the window, I witnessed a world unlike any I'd seen. Each village we drove through was crammed with very vocal, active men who were all dressed like the images of terrorists I'd had drilled into my head by Western media, and there were no women in sight. I would scout the crowds, wondering how I could pick out anyone who had ill intentions toward our group. It was impossible — everyone had long beards, wore the shalwar kameez, and possibly hated our Western guts.

One of my life's maxims has always been to look past stereotypes and connect with the person, versus making general assumptions about them. However, in Pakistan, because of my ingrained fear of terrorist acts, coupled with the recent murders, it was difficult. Even as every male I'd connected with in the country so far had been nothing but gracious and friendly, I still found myself plagued with misgivings, my thoughts surely colored by the biased post-9/11 coverage of the Islamic world by Western media. When an image is flashed at you for years, showing long-bearded men with guns, these men labelled as the enemy, it's hard not to be brainwashed.

What a shitty way this was to experience a new country, and yet I felt powerless against it.

In the meantime, ours was as much a journey of sight as of smell. At times, I would be swept up in the flavors of mouth-watering spices, tantalizing tastes conjuring up images of fantastic meals. Then, seconds later, the aroma would turn foul and the stench of rotting organic material in the gutters or the odor of burning meta or melting rubber from some burning trash pile would permeate the van.

Most of the buildings in these villages were concrete boxes, 12 feet wide by 30 feet deep, with an assortment of everything and anything for sale. It seemed like each concrete box had a specialty that t delivered to the town — one could be a bicycle-repair place, while in the building next door a man could be seen pounding and bending metal, then there might be a small restaurant with people all siting on their haunches enjoying roti with curry. The locals wore mainly drab colors — everything was just grays and browns, with some off-whites.

The brightest things were the cargo trucks, which had been exquisitely painted, with bright-red religious quotes in calligraphy — ntricate, beautiful art. I couldn't help but stare as they rolled by. The road streamed north, curving in and out of valleys; the farther we went from the capital, the rougher and more dilapidated everything looked.

The terrain up high was barren, devoid of life, with rocky slopes tumbling down mountainsides. Everywhere I looked, I could see the industriousness of man. Every house or village had diverted water from miles away, building paths and aqueducts to bring the precious liquid to their area, creating forests, gardens, and greenery in otherwise lunar terrain. Everything looked harsh and inhospitable, yet the people here had eked out an existence against all odds.

I spotted the proud owner of a few buildings along the steep roadside, standing tall and watching us drive by. I'm sure that he was just as curious about our reality as we were about his.

We rounded a corner, and up ahead came upon a small, colorful pickup truck with seats in the back filled with young, smiling boys. About twenty of them had crammed into the truck bed and were on route to school. Their childish energy was palpable. They waved excitedly as we drove past, and we waved back. After two days of travel, we arrived at the head of our valley, from where we would drive a four-wheel-drive vehicle to the end of the road and then begin our hike in, with porters helping carry our loads.

Honestly, I was uncomfortable with this whole idea of hiring porters to carry my gear so that I could climb some obscure peak. How odd we must have seemed to them. They must have questioned why we would travel halfway across the globe to climb up and ski down some mountain in their backyard that they'd never even considered climbing; it probably seemed pointless. Yet the money we brought in was a big deal, and what we paid for ten days of carrying was substantial. For this trip, we had hundreds of men and boys crowding around, trying to get hired as porters. These men's day-to-day lives were so difficult that they had no need to invent struggle, while we Westerners had such soft lives that we needed to create struggle — such as climbing mountains. The contrast between our lives and theirs was even more pronounced as I looked at a young boy wearing a battered, old World Wrestling Federation backpack he'd gotten somewhere. What was his image of our world?

After another day's drive — across sketchy bridges and above white-knuckle drop-offs — our hired Jeeps piled high with our bags, basecamp equipment, food for three weeks, and then finally the porters and us, we reached a village at the end of the road, deep in the Karakoram.

I appreciated watching the porters' daily devotions to Allah, saying their Salah prayers five times a day, stopping our convoy for lunch but more importantly to face Mecca and pray to their god. Though I have only a tentative, incipient relationship with religion and spirituality, watching the porters pray as well as their dedication never failed to impress me or get me thinking.

Here in Manukush, it was as if we had time-warped to another era, leaving electricity and technology behind. I couldn't resist a stroll through the village, watching, observing, and attempting to decipher the ways of these mountain people. Ahead of me on the trail, a woman walked toward me — the first female I'd seen in five days. I kept my eyes down and tried to remain unintimidating. Seventy feet later, I peeked up, looking left and right. Where did she go? The woman had literally disappeared.

The trail I followed was a dirt path, winding around fruit and nut trees. At their bases, I could see the tiny rivulets that had been diverted from the stream to water them continuously. Given the robust size and apparent ages of the trees, I could tell that they — and hence the village — had been here a long time. Soon I — as a tall, long-haired white guy walking casually around their village — attracted curious children. I usually connect quickly with children, and these laughing little ones were no different.

Using a variety of hand gestures, they showed me around and brought me to a cemetery to show me a human skull!

One of the older boys whipped out a cell phone, flipping it open to show me a picture of Gashot, the mountain we were vying for. Pointing at it and me, he gestured that this was where I was going — how he knew this, or why he had that photo, I will never know. He impressed all the younger kids and me with his technology. It was such a wild contrast, this village full of spartan, windowless huts and with limited electricity, yet then this child with a modern flip phone. We communicated through grunts, hand gestures, and whatever full-body actions I could think of, finding common ground.

Our expedition stayed the night in a school that had been built by the Tyrolean mountaineer Reinhold Messner, to give back to the mountain communities that had helped him in his quest to summit the highest mountains. (Messner was the first person on Earth to summit all fourteen 8,000-meter peaks, a feat he accomplished without relying on bottled oxygen.) The children I played with all knew how to spell their names in English as well as how to say a few basic phrases. A part of me wondered about the implications of teaching these children English and about the world outside. It would inevitably mean the end of their culture, as the youngsters learned of this other, "better,"

more fascinating world beyond the stone walls of their village. I pondered who was better off: these people, with their harsh, yet simple existence; or us, with all the stress and trappings of the modern world? Happiness seemed to come naturally to these children, and it would be a terrible thing to compromise that.

Past the village, we followed a beautifully built trail higher into the mountains. Its stacked rocks looked like they had been placed centuries ago; everything felt timeless, and the amount of effort that had gone into creating this trail was impressive. If a cliff blocked the trail, they had either built up a rock pathway sometimes twenty feet tall or stuck trees into the cliff face and balanced rocks between them to craft a walkway above the river. The porters carried most of the heavy gear, freeing us up to enjoy the hike. I thought about how these people would not be affected in a nuclear holocaust. Their existence likely wouldn't change at all, other than there would be no more foreign hikers coming through.

Every action up here had a direct survival function. The dung from all the goats, donkeys, and maybe even humans was collected and piled into the gardens as fertilizer. Each plot of land grew early wheat or perhaps potatoes, followed by corn. The fields where the animals grazed in the spring were planted once they moved to higher pastures. Higher, we came to another village, one that — even with its 1,000 residents — almost seemed like part of the hillside, so well did the houses blend in.

Rounding the corner, I saw our destination, Gashot mountain. It floated above the meadows, steep and imposing, its upper reaches clad in hanging glaciers, the bottom still out of view behind the terrain before us. The ski line was visible too, and it looked bigger and more intimidating than I'd imagined, a planar stretch of snow canted at fifty degrees that ran for thousands of feet.

My heart was in my throat, and my legs wobbled with fear. A few steps later, I could see the bottom of the line, where the snow ran out. It brought an end to the feature, which no longer disappeared into the unknown, taking away some of the intimidation. My excitement began to build.

"Holy shit!!! The line looks insane! It looks doable, but, damn, that is a serious piece of mountain! How do you think we can get up there?" I anxiously asked the group.

I gulped. In my mind, I always like to find the ascent that has the fewest hazards, the easiest way up. But here, everything looked difficult and scary. On either side of the face, the terrain was steeper and more convoluted, with hazards like canted mini-faces, crevasses everywhere, and unsupported serac and ice features.

"Everything around the shield looks precarious — the most supported and best way up is the ski line. We also need to know exactly what the snow feels like on the shield," Ptor mused.

"I agree it looks like the easiest way . . . but, damn, it looks nerve-wrackingly steep."

Every snow slope above the shield was mellower and not exposed.

"It looks like above the shield, we can maneuver back and forth between all those crevasses, and the slopes do mellow out," said Ptor. This would be a godsend, since by then we'd have climbed into the 18,000-to-20,000-foot range.

Up at basecamp, I decided to show the porters what they'd been carrying. I pulled my skis and boots out of a bag, pulled out the skins, and did a live demonstration for them. Twenty of them surrounded me and laughed when I pretended to skin up the mountain and then ski back down. I could only imagine how silly our reckless (and ultimately pointless) pursuit looked to them. Our logistics man, Mirghani, dealt with the porters for us. For some reason, they got quite upset when it was payment time, but we didn't know why. After lots of yelling and pointing, we eventually found enough different bills that every porter could see that he had the same amount as his fellows. With a disgruntled *hmmmppff,* they walked off down the valley, leaving us to our adventure.

Basecamp was sandwiched between two rock ridges, nestled amongst little trees and rocks around 12,000 feet. We could look west down-valley and watch the sun set behind endless Himalayan ridges, as well as see the greens of the valley we had just left behind. The other direction was directly up toward our goal. The snow didn't look too far from basecamp, maybe a half mile, where it deepened as it worked its way up the ridge of the moraine. We spent our four days acclimatizing, moving camping gear and equipment up the moraine and onto the glacier. We situated our advanced basecamp in an area that could not be affected by any slopes around it. This was not going to be

Manaslu all over again. We climbed up to 15,000 feet, but with no immediate need to sleep high since we were still adjusting to the lack of oxygen. On the surface, everything was going great, but I still woke each morning to the same sense of foreboding I'd had since signing up for the trip. Since this was Ptor's trip and he was more experienced in the big ranges, I wrote in my journal that I would simply support him and defer major decisions to him. For now, this seemed like the best way to keep my worries at bay.

On May 14, 2014, we toured back up to our advanced basecamp, enjoyed a rehydrated meal of pasta and sauce, and sat in the setting sun. It was sublime! We decided that we would try to summit one of the 18,000-foot peaks to the north of Gashot the next day, which would not only be an excellent acclimatization exercise but also a chance to ski.

Ptor woke me up the next morning May 15, around 5:30 a.m. Huddled deep in our down sleeping bags at 15,000 feet, we were all a bit slow to get moving, but soon Bjarne, Daniel, myself, and Ptor were all fueled up and ready. By 9:00 a.m. we were skiing down around the glacial seracs to reach the toe of Gashot.

A tremendous two-hour ski tour led us to a plateau at around 16,500 feet, encircled by a ridge of 18,000-foot summits. We searched for the line with the least amount of commitment to it. We headed toward one that was built of smaller slopes that were not convex, in which each slope supported the one above it. The snow did not look wind affected and was possibly powder. From here, we could see the line off Gashot, our primary target, directly opposite us and less than a mile away. It really was a perfect ski line; I can see why Ptor had wanted to cross the world to ski it. Once you were on the shield, the pitch never changed — it looked like a perfectly planar ski line, just a very steep one, at altitude. But we couldn't focus on it yet since the acclimatization had to be perfect — rushing anything in these mountains inevitably leads to disaster.

Bjarne pointed the camera at me and asked, "Greg, what do you think about this place so far?"

"Today, I'm psyched that we're going out skiing and there's a little bit of fluffy powder. Here, look at this!" I picked up a handful of airy snow and blew it off my hand; it exploded like a dandelion, snow crystals lazily fluttering through the air.

I continued, "Himalayan powder waiting for us — I'm psyched. And that thing is wicked looking!" The echoes of my shouting bounced off the surrounding mountainsides, my childish excitement impossible to miss.

On the way up, I hadn't noticed any recent avalanches off anything, but there was some wind at the higher elevations. Aside from that, the mountains were dormant. In the last ten days, it had snowed around eight inches in the alpine, and most of the steep lines had sloughed off, while the others looked settled. Our skin track easily climbed up through the glacial roll, and then we boot-packed up a steeper section near the top of the acclimatization peak. Here, I noticed a widespread crust about eight inches under the new snow. I guessed it was from the high pressure in late April, but it seemed like the snow above had not formed into a slab — just light, dreamy, unsettled powder.

A rocky scramble brought us to the summit, likely a virgin peak we'd just made the first ascent of.

We were making a movie on Ptor and his life, which meant he was the star of the show. He skied off first with a quick hop off the summit and over a few rocks, and then gracefully carved nice powder turns in the upper face, cutting loose a few slow-moving sloughs that went nowhere. Next it was my turn, and soon enough I was enjoying my first turns in Pakistan — they were great, flowy, cold-powder turns.

We had left Daniel lower on the slopes to film one of us skiing down the ridgelines — a position that offered great footage with the Gashot line in the background. I was surprised when Ptor chose a more direct line down the cirque, which did away with the incredible backdrop. Since he had skied down already, I decided to ski the ridgeline to make sure we got our scenic footage.

I worked my way over to the line — the light was flat, and I couldn't really define the convex roll at the top. I stuck to the ridge and slid over to the top of my line without any ski cuts. Still, I wasn't overly concerned. Ptor had said that he felt that the Karakoram snowpack stabilized quickly and that there were few slab avalanches, and I'd accepted his assessment without question. That day, my internal alarm should have been going off, but it wasn't. The line I was thinking about skiing, a planar face beside the ridge, looked tantalizing in what little light we had, but it wouldn't offer many escape options once I committed. Skiing left might work, and would hopefully bring me to the edge of the line where I could stop myself. Or I could go hard right and to the other side of the gully, away from any overhead hazards. Neither was ideal.

"Here I am in Pakistan, awaiting my first run. It looks amazing. I can't wait to rip it up!!! Yeeee-hawwwww!" I said, filming myself with my GoPro camera while we waited for the sun to come back out, so we could get better footage.

I put my helmet back on and waited for the next sunny patch. It soon arrived, and Bjarne told me to drop in.

My first left-hand turn was simply to gain speed and approach the ridge. Then I slashed an elegant right-hand turn, spraying up snow for the photographer. The light was right, and the snow felt fast and fun. I quickly carved into a nice left-hander, working my way out onto the face. Another right-hand turn and I was flying down the ramp. Then looking to the right, I noticed that the snow was breaking up into large, rapidly accelerating slabs. Meanwhile, below me, the snow was also moving and breaking away in slabs!

Holy shit! An avalanche was following me right down the middle of the face. Not just following me but all around me, everywhere, the placid white panel of snow breaking apart into larger planes. It was too late to go left and regain the ridge — there was too much snow above me and following me. With no time for long, involved decisions, I chose right, aiming for where the snow was not yet in motion, straight-lining ahead of the avalanche. Then the avalanche caught up to me and I immediately struggled to stay balanced, skiing on top of a massive, mobile slab. Lower down, I jumped onto another slab then skied as quickly as possible, trying to cross the gully to safer terrain beyond. If I could get there, the snow, I hoped, would continue downhill without me. I needed to stay calm and make the right decisions.

Then, suddenly, I knew I wasn't going to make it — the cascading snow had closed off my escape. I tried to jump the waterfall of snow, but I didn't make it. Like dipping your paddle in a very fast river current, I was instantly grabbed and thrown down-river, my skis like anchors dragging me into the snow. I felt my left leg twisting and then a hot, stabbing pain shooting down my ankle as a sharp flash of light popped before my eyes. I tumbled, trying to protect myself as I bounced off the gully walls.

Caught in a whitewash of snow, I continued to tumble, never really knowing which way was up. At some point, both my skis came off, which let me roll into a ball to protect myself. My head banged hard off a few things — rocks probably — my helmet bearing the brunt of the blows. Caught in the whitewash, I caromed off the gully walls; my back smashed against something, and then my head. I tumbled over and over, always trying to remember which way was up and to be ready to head toward the surface. I was going so fast that I wasn't sure I'd succeed.

I was blasted upward, my head out of the snow. Fortunately, through all my guiding, I have taught my clients what to do in case of an avalanche and imprinted those skills myself. The central concept is to get your hands around your face to create airspace around your mouth. This can be a lifesaving air pocket while your friends search for you. I was able to get my right hand up and near my shoulders, but at this point, I was primarily trying to stay balanced. I managed a backstroke arm movement that allowed me to keep my head near the surface. It felt like I was succeeding.

Treading snow furiously, I kept my head up near the top of the flow; it was gradually slowing, but also going from a fluid state to something more like concrete. The snow got heavier by the second, and I was no longer able to stay vertical; I felt myself tipping over. "No — please!" I fought hard to stay upright and keep my head clear, just managing to do so as the avalanche slid to a stop.

I cleared my face with a few desperate hand swipes. I was going to be okay! However, I couldn't breathe properly; there was an obstruction in my throat. I inhaled and exhaled slowly and calmly around the ice chunk lodged there. Finally, the heat of my body melted the obstruction enough that I could cough it out — it was roughly the size of a large strawberry. Those first few, full breaths of clean, cold mountain air had never felt so delicious.

Now I did a full-body scan. My head felt like I had hit it pretty hard, but fortunately my helmet had taken most of the brunt. My left arm, pinned in the snow, felt strange, but I couldn't determine if anything was wrong, while my right arm was totally fine. Meanwhile, my right leg felt okay, but I could feel increased heat around my left calf.

Because I am reasonably calm in stressful situations, I sat there and awaited my rescue. I probably could have continued to dig with my right hand, but it seemed pointless now that my head was out of the snow and I was breathing. So instead, I sat and got mad at myself. I'd been ski-mountaineering for sixteen years, and in all that time had never really been caught in an avalanche, though I'd skied away from quite a few. This, I reasoned, was all because I'd followed a handful of hard-and-fast rules to minimize my exposure.

But on this day, I'd broken some of my cardinal rules. First, I'd succumbed to "Kodak courage," throwing caution to the wind to make sure we got good footage for Ptor's movie. Second, instead of ski-cutting the slope and managing it properly, I'd skied right into the slope for a better photo. Goddamn it, Hill — you know better! I hollered at myself in my head.

I always tell myself that I will make the right decisions, but there is so much behind every action — my need to be a hero, my addiction to adrenaline, and just plain, old foolhardiness. I had said I wouldn't step out and that I would lead Ptor. But then, at the first opportunity, I'd gone and almost died!

I screamed a few times, but I wasn't sure the others heard me. I was facing a steep wall of snow, so I had no view or idea of what was going on. I assumed they were all safe because I had been the only one exposed to the slope, but really, where were they?

Time ticked by slowly — enough time to feel, and then quickly discard, self-recriminations and guilt — and then, about five minutes later, Ptor came rushing over. "I found him. He is okay!" he screamed up the hill. Then he pulled out his shovel and began to dig me out. He was way more frantic than I was, so I tried to slow him down a little. A few minutes later, and everyone was there. I'd been the only one caught in the slide.

As I watched them all dig, I thought about the GoPro on my helmet and the fact that it had likely recorded the entire event — the skiing, the slabs breaking away, all the tumbling, and, finally, the rescue. How awesome was that going to be — how often do things like this get recorded, and the adventurer survives?

They dug more. I warned them about my left leg and helped them to dig out my arms. My left arm had been held in place by the ski pole; it hurt, but overall seemed okay. My right leg, newly excavated, was also fine.

We all worked on my left leg. It felt relatively normal, but as it emerged from the snow, I could see that my toe was pointing up toward my face at an odd angle. My friends dug slowly, supporting my left leg with their hands. Then it flopped over like a dead fish, simply sagging in place. It looked like my lower leg had been disconnected from the upper part.

"Okay, Greg, we need to straighten out your leg," Ptor said. "This is going to hurt like a bitch."

I gritted my teeth and breathed deeply as he pulled my leg slowly and extended it. I almost fainted from the pain, but held on.

He held my foot away with traction as we maneuvered my leg into a better position. There was no blood flowing out of the boot or anything to suggest external bleeding, but clearly my leg was broken, and I wouldn't be able to get out of there under my own power.

Ptor rummaged around his bag and pulled out a small, ripped pair of Levi's 501s that had been sliced along the sides. I immediately understood that you could thread ski poles through these holes to create a splint.

"Ptor, we can splint my leg if you want to go call in the rescue," I said. "I think that is the most important thing we can do." I was definitely not walking out of there.

Ptor pulled out the satellite phone and punched in the code. But there were no satellites in range, so he needed to ski lower to find service. Ptor skied off in search of a rescue while Daniel, Bjarne, and I were left to rig bandages for my leg, using Ptor's first-aid kit.

Since it appeared to be a fracture of the tibia and fibula, we needed to figure out how to apply traction, to pull the bones away from each other and perhaps prevent any further damage. With injuries, you usually try to support the joints above and below the damaged area, which would mean bracing my ankle and knee. We ran two ski poles through the jeans and then along the back of my leg up to my knee, plus two longer poles on top that went past my knee. Using webbing, we then wrapped the upper part of my leg tightly to the ski poles, tying some cord around the foot and pulling the ankle away from the knee. Bracing myself for the pain, I encouraged Daniel and Bjarne to pull harder. When they got good traction with the rope, they tied the ends to the pole baskets. It felt decent; the bones were well tractioned, and the splint seemed stable overall.

Now that the injury was dealt with, we started to manage my discomfort. They placed skins under my legs for warmth and down jackets under my bum, and then moved me forward so that we could re-arrange my backpack. As we sat and waited, I reached up to turn my GoPro off, only to realize it had been lost in the slide. Damn, that would have been some great footage!

While we waited, I got the guys to pull out my camera so I could film myself.

"Yeah, here are the consequences: a really sore shoulder and a broken leg, and you know, almost death, really. But to live a life . . . life is so fleeting . . . it could come and go, and nothing can happen in your entire life, or you can live one to the limit and have shit like this happen. But this, compared to all the great things that have happened, is minuscule . . . so minuscule. It's been so many, many moments."

"Hey, Bjarne, when do you think the helicopters will rescue me?" I asked. It was only 1:45 p.m., with seven hours of daylight left. "Probably a little too early, but I am hoping 4:30," I continued. I had zero idea how the rescue would work or how long it would take. I guessed the helicopter would have to come from the closest city, Gilgit, but I really didn't know. We had never really discussed the process of a rescue!

"I guess 6:30."

"6:30 — seriously? Come on, that's way too long from now."

"Well, it is longer than we hope. At least that way it will be a relief when they come earlier." Good point.

I wondered what Daniel's guess would be. He had hiked across our small bowl and up to a high point to see if he could spot Ptor and/or anyone coming up to help. Daniel waved back at us, but he didn't seem to have any new information.

It was hard for me to see the size of the avalanche, but I knew I'd been fortunate to end up on the side of the flow. This allowed me to keep my head out of the snow, with some breathing room. Just 50 feet below was a terrain trap, a pit where the debris looked to have piled up 20 to 25 feet deep — what would have been my grave. Overall, I'd been extremely lucky. I hadn't been killed, and I hadn't sustained a compound fracture, which would have meant shock and dangerous blood loss, especially with a rescue unknown hours away. Had I gone into shock, I most likely would have died.

Over the next few hours, I kept imagining the sounds of helicopters. I would perk up and feel like I'd heard them, only to be let down when I realized it was nothing. The sun was out, and we were all relatively comfortable; I was wrapped in Bjarne's and Daniel's warm clothes, while they stayed dry in their windproof layers. To warm up, they would take turns walking five minutes uphill to the viewpoint.

When 4:30 p.m. came and went with no helicopters in sight, we started to realize that perhaps we needed to plan for an overnighter. Around 5:00 p.m., we sent Daniel down to advanced basecamp to grab what bivy gear and food he could find. It would be a four- or five-hour round-trip, so he needed to get going. Suddenly, it was just Bjarne and me. Two people alone at 17,000 feet, exposed on a mountain slope, waiting and waiting and . . . waiting.

A pink pastel sky kissed goodnight to the sun, and in the gathering dark, the cold slowly started to set in. Luckily for me, I was all wrapped up, but I could see that Bjarne was getting colder. To keep warm, he kept moving. By 6:00 p.m., my hopes of a rescue were dwindling; by 7:00, I accepted that we'd be spending the night. Bjarne, meanwhile, realized he should devote his energies to digging a snow cave for us to bivouac in and began excavating the snow beside me. At this elevation, it is exhausting to work hard, yet he had to keep digging — we needed that snow cave for our survival.

My thoughts ran in circles, reenacting the event, getting mad at myself for my mistake, accepting what had happened, and then starting over. I felt guilty, knowing that it had been my decision which brought us here, uncomfortable and in a tense situation. I breathed deeply to deal with the aching pain, while trying to remain relaxed to pass the time.

"Bjarne, I am sooo sorry," I said. "I was an idiot. I feel so guilty at having wrecked the day and for needing a rescue."

"Greg, shit happens. I'm just happy that you're alive — that's the main thing. Everything else we can deal with."

"I just hate that I fucked up. Obviously, I'm happy to be alive, but, well, I'm wracked with guilt at having screwed up our adventure. I absolutely hate letting the team down."

By 9:00 p.m. the stars were out, blazing brightly in a clear black sky overhead — a stirring sight, but one that also meant it would be a frigid night, with no cloud cover for insulation. By now, Bjarne had dug out the cave big enough to accommodate both of us. We put the backpacks on the floor as well as anything else that could be used for insulation. Sucking up all my pain, I crawled backward into the hole and attempted to get comfortable. Bjarne came in and we cuddled to maintain warmth. I was the small spoon.

I was shivering and unable to lie calmly, but at least I had his body heat and mine. I was starting to worry about the toes on my left foot. Because my leg had swollen inside the boot, there was a lot of pressure, and I couldn't tell how much blood flow was reaching my toes. I worried about frostbite. I kept moving my toes, hoping that would keep them warm enough. My feet were near the door, and the cold air kept cooling my feet down, increasing my worries about frostbite by the minute. I was uncomfortable, freezing, and shivering, growing ever more agitated, hoping that Daniel would return soon with sleeping bags and other creature comforts. Finally, at 10:00 p.m., I saw a headlamp and released a bit of tension. There might be some ease tonight after all!

Daniel peered into our cave. "I brought some sleeping bags, a tent, a stove, and some water," he said. "Mirghani is also following with some more stuff and a toboggan to take you down tomorrow."

Relief radiated through my body, though it didn't stop the shivering. Daniel melted snow while Bjarne helped me get a sleeping pad under my back. It felt good to not have the snow sucking the heat out of my body.

I badly wanted to take my foot out of my plastic ski boot for the night — the swelling was making it tight in there. But the brace strength of the boot was also helping hold the bones in place. I couldn't decide — it would also be super painful to try to pull my foot out, so I loosened the boot as much as possible, and then borrowed a kn⁻e to cut away at the boot to relieve the pressure. There wasn't a lot I could do, but at least I felt like I was doing something.

Because the ski poles went past my foot by a good ten inches, I realized I needed to cut off the bottom of my sleeping bag to accommodate them. I was going to stay in my boot, and therefore I needed to make my foot and boot as warm as possible. Down feathers puffed out as I cut through the bottom of my sleeping bag. Daniel guided the poles through the bottom of the bag, and soon enough I was all wrapped up in its warmth.

Although I was more comfortable, I was still shivering and moving my toes to keep them warm. Daniel and Bjarne set up a tent and used one sleeping bag to stay warm, while Mirghani joined me in the cave. The cave would be much warmer than the tent, and I felt terrible for the boys out in the Himalayan cold.

Thus began the longest night of my life. I focused on trying to sleep, but it never seemed to come. The minutes felt like hours, and each moment lasted forever. I kept checking the time, and often, it was only ten minutes between check-ins. The pressure on my foot got worse, and a few times I sat up and tried to relieve it. I kept trying to marshal the desire to pull the boot off, but I couldn't. Plus, everyone else had finally gone down for the night, and I just couldn't bother them. Already, everything that they had done was for me, because of my mistake.

I lay there with my thoughts spinning and time going nowhere. I kept coming back to the question of whether it had all been worth it. All this travel, all this effort, all this risk-taking, for what? Three turns down a slope, and then a near-miss with an avalanche, all because of my poor decision-making.

11:30 p.m., 11:38 p.m., time crept forward. I would alternate between wondering what time it was and counting backwards from 6:00 a.m., which is when I figured the rescue would resume. But the moments wore on, and so my thoughts looped in my mind. I had countless thoughts of Tracey and my kids. With the difference in time zones, they would just be getting up. Aiden's blond head would be bobbing as he munched his Cheerios and read his book. Tracey would be running around, organizing everything for the kids while she got her teaching stuff together for another day at school. Charley, likely, would still be asleep, trying to prolong her time under her duvet. I kept wondering what Charley and Aiden would think about this misadventure.

I hadn't had a painkiller in hours, and the ache was now like a heartbeat, a constant underlying throbbing punctuated by rhythmic pangs with the intensity of screams. The pain was bearable, but it required me to breathe deeply and relax. Also, I had to accept that it was what it was, and not resist. Nothing was going to change the amount of pain. The only thing that could change was my acceptance of it; if I didn't fight, I could minimize my suffering.

Breathe and believe. Breathe and believe. Use your breath to calm yourself. Believe that you will survive.

2:00 a.m. crawled in, and then 2:12 — only ten minutes, but it felt like an hour. 2:32: an entire day. Finally, it felt like I had slept . . . I checked my watch, wishing for 4:00 or 5:00 a.m., but no — it was 2:48.

More breathing and hopes for sleep. I kept wiggling my toes, reassured that they felt alive and normal.

3:15 a.m., a small nap, more shivering; then, 3:30. Oh, the relief — it was almost time to get the boys up and into action. An hour and a half wasn't that long. Finally, 4:00 a.m., more relief in that we would be moving soon. This must have been enough to relax me because I managed a thirty-minute nap. At 5:00 a.m., the boys started to move around. Oh, sweet relief. I would be doing something other than lying there shivering, breathing, and wiggling my toes.

Mirghani got up and started to get the toboggan ready. He'd cut a forty-five-gallon barrel lengthwise into two halves and then tied them together to form a canoe-shaped vessel. I would lie inside this, and then the crew would tow me via ropes anchored to the end and handles on each side. I was concerned about the toboggan's lateral stability since I knew that my left arm was not particularly strong. Mirghani assured me it would work.

The team filled the bottom of the toboggan with the sleeping mats and placed a backpack for me to lean up against. We'd situate me facing uphill so that any bumps would be on my back and bum, not on my broken leg. It meant that I would have no idea what was coming up, no way to anticipate anything, just sliding into the unknown, imagining what would happen if they accidentally let me go and I went careering down the mountain.

By 6:00 a.m., I was loaded into the sled and wrapped in my sleeping bag. The first two hundred feet were extra bumpy due to the avalanche debris. Daniel and Bjarne wore their skis with skins on, while Mirghani bootpacked behind. The only way with toboggans is to flow with the terrain. Fortunately, the first bits of terrain were mellow and allowed the boys to gain confidence with the system. I could trail my arms and provide some side-to-side stability in I started to roll over. Keeping myself upright was hard on my core, but overall I didn't feel much pain in my leg. Well, except each time Mirghani pulled up on his rope, which shortened the length of the toboggan and forced the bones in my leg together — making me howl with pain.

I kept reminding Mirghani, but he kept forgetting. For two hours, we descended through mellow morrainal terrain, but then, below, it steepened, increasing the toil and the risk. This seemed like a great place to stop and be helicoptered out — we were well under a chopper's max-altitude threshold — but Mirghani wasn't having it when I asked him to call Liver to arrange a pick-up.

"Mirghani, can we please call Liver again and find out what's happening?" I asked.

Mirghani responded, "There's nothing we can do — we need to get down to the valley before they will pick us up."

"This makes no sense. I've been heli-skiing for years and I know what helicopters can do — and they can get in here and pick me up!"

"We must get you down to the polo fields; it is the only place that they will pick you up!" Mirghani said, reiterating his point.

Finally, I forced Mirghani to give me the sat phone so I could phone Liver myself. Mirghani passed me the phone, and I immediately realized that it had been locked out — someone had punched in the wrong code three times. Mirghani acted as if he didn't understand this and couldn't figure out why it wouldn't work, which had been his go-to whenever he'd been confused or uncertain so far on the trip. Unfortunately, there was nothing we could do with the sat phone — we had to wait a certain number of hours for it to unlock itself.

We were sitting at the perfect pick-up spot, a relatively flat spot with a nice drop-away for the helicopter to float in and land, but with no way of letting them know we were ready. Thoughts of just remaining there till they came ran through my head. But Mirghani kept insisting that they could not pick us up there, and that they would not land where there was snow. He kept saying that we had to go down another 4,000 feet down to the flat polo field in the dry valley, but I couldn't see how we'd navigate the bumpy ride down in the toboggan or the team having to carry me once the snow ran out. Nonetheless, it was decided that we'd find a way to keep descending the mountain, threading the rocks on steep tongues of snow.

With Bjarne, wearing crampons and using an ice axe, serving as the anchor, and with Mirghani and Daniel in the front of the sled, they would lower me the length of the rope — twenty feet

— then Daniel would support me while Bjarne reset to belay me down again. All the while, I was hanging on hard to a rope tied around my waist, straining to keep my upper body strong. Thankfully, I could not see behind and below me, to the potential disaster that awaited were they to let go.

The first tier took at least an hour, extracting a real toll from my partners. They'd bivied at 17,000 feet the night before and barely eaten since the day before, and you could see the fatigue in their faces. Nevertheless, the team pressed on.

It seemed pointless since we could easily have been rescued from higher up, but Mirghani remained insistent that the chopper could not rescue us anywhere with snow. He kept telling me we were going to have to go to the polo grounds, which looked impossibly far away. I couldn't imagine how many times my leg was going to get tweaked on the descent. More damage to the bones would occur, for sure. Would that be enough to cripple me for life, potentially ending my career as a skier?

It was scary to be lowered backward down the slopes. I had no idea what was behind me, nor could I even look. I had to trust my crew entirely. I would watch as Bjarne held my sled stationary while the others reset, then lowered me slowly, his feet planted in the snow, the taut ropes in hand. Pitch after pitch, Bjarne lowered me off small rocks, side-hilled me across snow slopes, and maneuvered me around all sorts of obstacles. It had to have been exhausting, yet his face never betrayed a hint of doubt.

Finally, peering down the valley, I could see people in basecamp working their way up toward us. Across from us was our advanced basecamp and Ptor was heading our way, skinning over to ask if we needed any essentials from there. All I cared about was my e-book and my journals, which I asked him to grab. Fifteen minutes later, the full crew of camp folks showed up — the cook, the camp facilitator, and one of the guards.

I felt safer; some pressure had been removed, and now the rescue should get easier, with more people around to help. I had built up a lot of resolve and calmness, and it was time to let some of the worry out.

As predicted, the descent got easier thanks to our larger team and terrain that mellowed past the steeper rock moraines. We even felt relaxed enough to have our guard from camp — a policeman — document some of it for us.

Then out of nowhere, we heard buzzing. We all stopped to listen, ears tuned; we discussed whether it was a helicopter or a small plane. Most were convinced that it was a plane, but I couldn't decide. The sound faded as whatever it was flew off, up the Garol Valley.

Bummed, we continued, but then five minutes later, it became louder again. *Thwap . . . thwap . . . thwap.* It was a helicopter! Relief washed over me — wow, the ordeal was nearly over. The helicopter got closer — it was a dark-green army helicopter, doing a fly-by. I spotted snow pads on the landing skids. Maybe they could pick us up off the snow? I was still worried that perhaps this was just recon, and they would still have to pick me up off the valley, as Mirghani had insisted.

Then I noticed them looking for a place to land. I pointed seventy feet up the hill to a flat, rocky bench, but they didn't seem to like it. They tried hovering nearby and couldn't decide where to go. I am used to Canadian mountain pilots who can put their helicopters down everywhere, so I couldn't understand what these guys were doing. Then they flew away. *Please don't leave*, I thought.

Instead, the chopper flew lower down the slope and landed on the crest of a moraine, beyond which a stream of people was coming up the mountainside. I couldn't understand who these people were. They weren't the army, but they had arrived simultaneously. Suddenly, I was being rushed down to the helicopter.

One of the rescuers in our group started walking toward the helicopter, a pair of skis lashed to his back, heading right for the rotors. "Down, down!" I yelled at him. He understood immediately and backed away to take the skis off. The rest of this crew moved me beside the helicopter, and I started to untie the knots with which I'd been lashed to the toboggan. It was a bit of a frenzy with so many people around, but they managed to lift me up and into the helicopter. Before the door was closed, I made eye contact with Daniel and thanked him profusely. I continued my thanks to Bjarne and gave him a huge thumbs-up. Then the props spun faster, and we were up and into the air.

Now that the pressure was entirely off, I began sobbing and thanking the pilots between sobs. I had never doubted that I would survive, and had stayed as positive and relaxed as possible, but still, it had been twenty-three tense, pain-filled, uncomfortable hours since my accident. In that entire time, I hadn't really known if I was going to survive. I never let the doubt get past my walls, but I'd been truly concerned nevertheless about making it.

The helicopter circled to get higher, and as it did, I was able to see where I had screwed up. The enormity of the slide struck me hard. I could see where we had bivied in our snow cave and how lucky I was to be found there on the side — 100 feet farther down, the pile of debris looked deep. Between my tears, I followed my tumble down the mountainside; like an hourglass, my slide started very wide and constricted into a couloir for 400 feet before fanning out into the basin below.

Looking at the destructive size of the slide, I knew I had been incredibly lucky to tumble down that couloir and then somehow end up on top swimming. The slope I'd skied looked far more intense from this perspective, and I could now see just how susceptible it was to the winds.

I surveyed the village of Garol from far above, retracing our path up the valleys from the air. I'd screwed up and now I was going home, but I hoped that Ptor and the boys would carry on without me and realize their goal of skiing that improbable slope.

An X-ray at the hospital in Gilgit, still with my ski boot on, revealed that I had a spiral fracture, which happens when your bones break in a twisting fashion, creating a corkscrew-looking break; it had been so obvious during the slide that my foot did a 360 and snapped just below the boot top. The doctor could see that I would need surgery and told me there were orthopedic doctors in Islamabad who could fix me up. I didn't need to decide immediately, so sat with this information for a while.

Because I had no travel insurance, there was no Swiss airplane flying directly to pick me up and swoosh me back to the best surgeons in the world. In fact, nothing was happening to expedite my trip. The doctor removed my boot and gave me a back cast, which kept my bones in traction and allowed me to hobble around, as well as a much-needed prescription for morphine.

Liver, who'd arrived in Gilgit on a second rescue helicopter, delivered me to a hotel, and we started planning my exit to Islamabad or Canada. The hotel was a sad place, faded and empty; it had done well until 9/11, when most tourist activities ceased in the Muslim world.

I was helped into a room, where I started making the tough phone calls back home, riddled all the while with guilt. I began by calling Tracey, my belly filled with fear: What wife wants to receive a phone call from her broken husband, who's just narrowly escaped death, almost leaving her widowed at age thirty-eight with two young children?

There was nothing to it but to just say it. When Tracey picked up, I said, "Tracey . . . faaaack, I am sooo sorry, but I messed up. I just survived a massive avalanche — no one else was hurt; it's not Manaslu all over again. It was just me. I made a mistake and came sooo close to dying." My stomach was wound up with guilt, the right words seemingly impossible to find. "I know I promised to be as safe as possible but . . . but . . . I don't know what to say . . . My left leg is shattered, and I'm trying to figure out where to have surgery."

Hurt yet accepting, Tracey placated me: "You're alive and you'll be okay. That's all that matters."

"The good news is, I'll also be home for your birthday!" I joked, trying to bring some levity to the phone call.

I also called my good friend Dr. Paul Wright, an orthopedic surgeon back in Canada. His expertise was greatly needed. I asked him whether I should get surgery here in Pakistan or suck it up and fly home for better care. His answer was not as cut and dry as I would have liked. Surgery in Islamabad could work, although the technology lagged behind Canada's. I also risked contracting a superbug through potentially less sterile conditions. On the other hand, flying home could be hazardous, too — I could easily get compartment syndrome, which would lead to permanent muscle or nerve damage. The gamble was mine to take. Lying there in bed, half-checked out on morphine, I thought long and hard about my predicament.

Flying out of Gilgit typically is not easy, and the weather had deteriorated since our arrival. Liver, who'd helped me procure a crutch so I could hobble around the hotel, worked as hard as he could to get me out, and the best option would be in three days. Three days to sit and ponder my mistake, get mad at myself again and again, and try to determine my best course of action.

One of the first emails I opened as I convalesced was from the Association of Canadian Mountain Guides, offering me comprehensive travel insurance! Sitting there, broken, on opioids with an unknown cost for my rescue, I couldn't help but laugh at the irony. Liver had just told me how much the rescue cost, and I was still processing the $17,000 I owed him. Liver was not a wealthy man, but still he'd found a way to pay for it out of his own pocket. Due to the high elevation, they had sent in two helicopters for safety — and I had to pay for both of them. Plus, Liver needed me to pay him back ASAP. However, $17,000 is not something a passionate ski bum usually has tucked away in his mattress! Somehow, I had to figure this out. Fortunately, this was all taken care of with a quick call to my big brother Graham, who did have the wealth to reimburse Liver and whom I could figure out how to reimburse once I was home.

For three days, I sat in bed and worried about my leg, my future, my new debt, and my mistake — basically swept up in a vortex of failure. I had fucked up — again.

Eventually, a seat was arranged, and I had a flight out of Gilgit. I'd decided to fly home to Canada, risking compartment syndrome during the endless hours in the air but setting myself up for a better surgical outcome.

Six and a half days after my accident, having been spared developing compartment syndrome on my four flights home, I rolled into surgery in Banff at the Mineral Springs Hospital, where Dr. Heard, whom my friend Dr. Paul Wright had recommended, did his best to reconstruct my severely shattered leg. The operation took him and his team two-plus hours; it was human carpentry at its best. They placed a pin down the bigger bone, the tibia, essentially nailing the top and bottom of the bone together, and situating the shards of bone in the approximate right place. The hope was that the muscles and everything else would knit them in place and allow them to regrow together. The fibula, meanwhile, was put back together with a plate that screwed into the various broken pieces.

I awoke from surgery to find Tracey sitting by my bedside, worry etched in her face. In my mind, I was fine — broken but fine. I can only imagine what was in hers.

"Is there anything I can do?" Tracey asked, powerless in her inability to help me. "I'm so thankful you're alive. I can't imagine what I would have told the kids if you hadn't made it home."

I could see the struggle going on inside her, her desire to be mad at me for being an idiot and doing something mostly for the cameras balanced against her love for me.

The worst pain was yet to come, as the painkillers from the

surgery had worn off but the morphine had yet to kick in. "Keep pressing the morphine button every six minutes, and you should feel relief," the nurses told me. I felt none, and soon enough, I was sobbing in pain, I kept asking the nurse for more or to talk to my doctor, but there was no response. "It should kick in soon," they'd say. The pain increased to a far higher level than the initial break. An hour in, unbearable pain wracked my body, radiating from the site of all that aggressive human carpentry, from all that yanking, screwing, and anchoring of metal. I had never experienced pain to this level, but finally, the nurse gave me a shot of morphine that was big enough to tranquillize a horse, and just like that, the pain was gone.

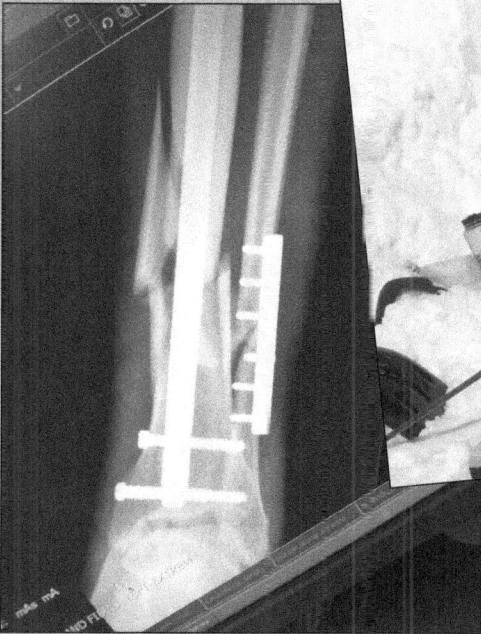

Chapter Eighteen

REWRITING THE NARRATIVE

"Be self-critical; learn through intuition to grow through your experiences, and always continue to evolve yourself."
— *Excerpt from letters to my family*

When I was sitting in the snow in Pakistan, happy to have survived, my attitude was somewhat nonchalant. I'd never seriously broken a bone before, and figured I'd need only eight weeks or so off skiing, then I could get back to it, going hard, the same as before. Optimistic, if not naïve, I had no grasp of how slow the healing or how challenging the next few years would be.

Back from the hospital, I crutched my way into our house and onto our green couch — the space that would quickly become my command center and healing HQ for the next few months.

First things first — while lying there, I worked on paying Graham back for the rescue. I didn't have 17K in the bank, so I looked into all options. Luckily for me, my two main sponsors, Arc'teryx and Salomon, split the cost. So at least I was only paying with my body and not my bank account for my error in judgment. How fortunate was I, that I had supporting sponsors to help when I had screwed up?

For the first few weeks, my mind and the pain were dulled

with Dilaudid (hydromorphone). However, I didn't enjoy the slow, heavy, foggy feeling that this synthetic morphine gave me, as well as the constipation. As quickly as I could, I weaned myself off the painkillers and switched to a THC tincture, an alcohol laced with marijuana. With that, I dulled my pain over the next six months, rehabbing, healing, obsessively playing video games, and working on the beginnings of this book.

It took six weeks before I could even bear weight on my left leg. I was open and receptive to all forms of healing, be they natural, scientific, holistic, or modern — anything that would help convince my mind and body to regenerate. Tracey got some comfrey, and we made a bone-growing poultice, a green goo with which I wrapped my leg each morning. I had an expensive electric machine that health insurance paid for. I rubbed it on my leg, and it hit a vibrational frequency that stimulated bone growth. I took supplements — calcium, vitamin D, vitamin C, iron, potassium, and lots of protein powder — and did everything possible to help the bones mesh back together.

A review of my X-rays showed that my leg was essentially a reconstruction of bones. Dr. Heard had moved the puzzle pieces back into place, making my leg look somewhat like it should, but during a follow-up visit I questioned him on what looked like misalignment. One shard looked so out of line that I worried it would pierce my skin — it really didn't look good. When I challenged him, Dr. Heard told me the theory that by being slightly away from each other, allowing space for blood flow, the bones would knit better. However, at this point, there was so much space between the shards that the leg would have collapsed if the metal nail weren't there. When I looked in the mirror, I could see that my shin had a half-inch of misalignment, my leg was no longer straight.

Dr. Heard assured me that the ankle's ball-and-socket structure would account for the oddness in angles. Looking at the rippled scar halfway up my lower leg and knowing of the metal that supported me, I seriously questioned my future as an adventurer.

While lying there healing, I'd let my mind wander, looking back on my career in the mountains. I was super proud of my achievements; I loved that I was inspiring people to live passionate, adventurous lives. My hope was that I was also an inspiration for my kids to walk their own paths and seek happiness, dig deep, and try to define themselves by their dreams, not what others wanted for them.

By the same token, I had almost died, which meant my life would have been over, all my chapters written. As cheesy as it sounds, what would have been my legacy if I'd died in that avalanche? How would I have been remembered? As an adventurer, a passionate person driven by personal challenges, sure — but what good did I actually do? Did I leave the world any better than I'd found it? Perhaps I had, by inspiring other people to search for their own truths, adventures, and potential. But what about giving back in a more tangible way?

Other than my tree-planting job, which I'd done more for the money than anything else, had I done anything for the environment? I'd led an existence in which I achieved great, selfish things yet cared little for their effects on our climate. I owned a massive diesel truck and a snowmobile. I heli-ski guided twenty-five days a year; we skied all day with a helicopter at our beck and call. Basically, I was saying, "Fuck the world — it's all about me!"

One week, I would be in Norway skiing, fly home to be a dad and husband the next week, and then be back in France skiing one week later. It was a purely selfish, albeit deeply fulfilling, life. My carbon footprint was massive, and I wasn't doing anything to reduce it. I didn't know what I could do.

In 2008, my brother Graham had co-written a book called *Ready, Set, Green: Eight Weeks to Modern Eco-Living.* Looking at my children, Charley and Aiden, I wondered what I was teaching them. Also, what I was leaving for them — a world teetering on environmental chaos? I was part of the problem but not yet willing to become part of the solution. Were there changes I could make to help the environment while also adding to my legacy?

This question kept echoing in my mind. My new lease on life offered a chance to make a profound change and become a steward for Mother Nature, who'd given me so much. How had I not prioritized defending that which I loved the most? If I, as an outdoor adventurer, wouldn't change my ways, how could I expect others to?

There is a huge, insecure part of me — going back, I'm sure, to being the tiniest kid in a pack of six children — that always wants to be self-sufficient, to be the one people can depend on, making it difficult for me to ask for help. Early in my healing,

I tried to shower; as I stood balancing on one leg, the heat of the water caused me to pass out. All I could think of as the blackness overtook me was to fall backward and protect my newly reconstructed leg. I crashed and banged my head against the tile, but protected my leg. Tracey rushed in, deep concern on her face — Man, I am such an idiot!

The physiotherapy I received at the hospital was a wake-up call as well. My leg had been shattered, and it would be a lengthy process toward recovery. I feared that I had permanently lost that which gave me so much happiness in my life — my fitness and ability to go on adventures. Instead of placating me with false hope, the physiotherapist presented me with a harsh reality: "Greg, you will never get back to what you had or be able to do what you used to do," she said. Holy shit, was that a hard one to hear!

There was no way I could accept that. I was going to stretch and work out this left leg until I could ski-tour again. That's all there was to it.

Rehab for a shattered leg like mine is a long and painfully slow process. There is no cast, since the bone is essentially a long titanium nail; I could bend my knee slightly, but the bloated and scarred lower leg couldn't do much. I couldn't really bear weight or walk, so I mostly sat on the couch and tried to heal, giving the body time to work its magic.

It was months of agonizing progress — but progress nonetheless. To get through the long, painful days, I dulled my symptoms with THC and tried to distract myself from the endless time on the couch — up to fifteen hours a day. One great pastime was the mobile strategy game Clash of Clans, a game about war and development in which you attack and loot other villages. It was Aiden who got me into it: I expanded his village and looted for his cause. He was only eight at the time and not all that into it. Soon enough, it became my cause, distracting me from where I was and from my broken body.

After two months of near constant couch-surfing, I was allowed to start bearing weight. It's astounding how quickly a leg can atrophy, and my quad was a shriveled version of its former self. My right leg wasn't much better, but at least I had used it as I crutched between the bedroom and the couch. During those months, the physio was fairly basic — just working on range of motion — and now, finally, we could start moving forward.

The muscles, nerves, ligaments, and tendons essentially have to relearn how to fire and work together to coordinate movement. So it's not only matter of rebuilding strength, but also coordination. Fortunately, our local aquatic center is great, and as soon as I was able to get there, I would crutch my way delicately across the wet tiles and ease my broken body into the water. With the buoyancy of the water, I could reteach my nerves, my synapsis, and my muscles how to move together again, without fear of injury. My left leg was so stiff and so weak that at first even lifting it was a struggle. But slowly, day after day, week after week, things got better.

I knew deep down that my future happiness relied on me working as hard as I could, so I did. One exercise had me standing balanced on my weak left leg and then closing my eyes. Initially, I would teeter back and forth, barely balancing for longer than a second, my smaller muscles weak and uncoordinated. I worked my way slowly up to three seconds then to a minute. These gains in strength and proprioception gave me hope

An important movement in everything I do is forward flexion — my knee needs to bend toward my toes. My Achilles was so tight that I could barely lean forward, with four fewer inches of range of motion in my bad leg. One exercise was forcing the shin forward, pushing against the pain and tightness that stopped the motion like a wall. Daily, I would bounce and push this wall a little farther, gaining tiny increments of motion.

In moments of despair, I would look down at my emaciated leg and know that I would never regain the 100 percent that I had then. But I knew I needed to push so that I would be happy with the new 100 percent, whatever that ended up being. I needed to be constantly stressing my leg, pushing its limits every day. Re-teaching it about all the demands I like to put on my body. Never settling for where I was but aiming for more. Pushing for more — pushing and pushing and pushing until I could get back on my skis again.

PHOTO CREDIT: BRUNO LONG

Chapter Nineteen

RELEARNING CONFIDENCE IN MY DECISION-MAKING

"There are so many quotes out there about the power of learning from failures. I didn't think much about them until I worked my way out of my own."
— *Excerpt from letters to my family*

In Pakistan, I'd made a serious judgment error, and my confidence, something I used to have a lot of, was now gone — broken and buried under the snow. Even as my body healed, my mind still felt weak, and had no idea, really, how I'd get back to where I'd been mentally.

The winter of 2014–2015 was my first season back on skis. I had lost so much strength, but I needed to slide again — my happiness, my sponsorships, and everything else relied on me skiing well again. One day that season, a group of Salomon athletes left Revelstoke Mountain Resort for a short ski tour. We barely hiked 1,500 feet, but they were two free-flowing powder runs that felt amazing. These runs went well, my muscles responded, and I was able to feel the freedom of skiing. Then we skied out the Catcher's Mitt, a bumpy, wild trail over logs, roots, and rocks, a veritable rollercoaster of a run that brought us back into the resort By now, my thighs were cooked; I had no fine muscle control and I could barely stand long enough to slide down the cat track. "Come on, you fuckers, work!" I yelled at my thighs as they rebelled against the demands. I was so tired I had to sit down on my skis and slide down on my bum — my legs couldn't handle it. My teammates both supported me and good naturedly made fun of me at the same time.

Initially, the green runs were hard, and then slowly the physical part of my skiing returned. But I still found myself full of worries out in the backcountry. When assessing slopes that never would have scared me in the past, I didn't trust my inner snow guru or mathematician who balanced all the equations to decide yes or no. How was I to guide people this winter if I didn't trust my own judgment? Everything was daunting — how could I trust myself, someone whose decisions had nearly cost me my life? This fuck-up had to prove to himself and his clients that he was up to the task of keeping them safe.

Part of my mental rehab would need to be a trip into my local mountains, to tag dream lines. For this, I wanted a group of friends with a variety of strengths, a team that would aid in my emotional comeback. A team of people I connected strongly with. I put together a wicked crew: Mark Hartley, a hardcore coffee roaster; Aaron Chance, my oldest ski partner; Derek Glowiackie, a wildman mountain guide; and Bruno Long, photographer extraordinaire. If these guys couldn't help me, no one could.

The Battle Range lies deep in the Selkirk Mountains, and is hard to access without a helicopter. In April 2015, we flew out with Arrow Helicopters early in the morning and dropped off our gear at camp near Pequod Pass, then landed at 10,000 feet near the summit of Mount Proteus (10,492 feet). I'd been here ten years earlier during an eleven-day traverse, so it was familiar territory — we had snow-caved at this exact spot. We started climbing Proteus. The last 400 feet turned out to be a bit of a struggle — a rimed-up rocky mess — but I was happy. We'd earned the summit.

The snow stability felt good, but as we still needed to feel out the snowpack, we chose the most conservative glacial line. It was an extraordinary ski, with bright-blue ice walls towering overhead and crevasses to cross — a visually dynamic ski descent.

We threaded our way back up through the blue ice and looked up at our next objective, a wild, zigzaggy couloir that had Mark all excited. We headed back up what we had just skied and climbed across a rocky ridge to stop just below the summit of Whitejacket, a minor peak between the behemoths of mounts Proteus and Moby Dick. I bootpacked to where I could stand on a rock and look down. The run was epic — it had the perfect allure. The first pitch looked confidence-inspiring and easy, and then the line rolled out of sight, haunting with its unknowns. My fear of these was too much, and my mind wasn't ready yet. Knowing I couldn't rip the first pitch, I urged Mark to shred it. And he did, pinning it down the opening ramp, slashing mad turns on his board. I then eked my way down, dropping a few jump turns but mostly just getting down lower to where I was finally in the run and could shred it up. What a feeling it was, to be back at it again.

It's hard to decipher why my fears had grown so large. Was it the fact that I now knew how close death was if I made a mistake out here? I had been so confident, so cavalier, for so long, yet that is what had gotten me into trouble, that overconfidence. How could I learn to trust myself again?

From our camp on that a sheltered bench near Pequod Pass, we looked straight at the hanging northeast glacier of Moby Dick, a line I'd long dreamt of skiing. What made this line special was how from most angles it looked like the perfect ski line, and how it ended off huge blue seracs. Massive ice walls threatened the line from all sides, and it just looked so improbable. Years before, on our traverse, I had skied past and spotted an easy way off the line. Sitting there that afternoon, I could see the way onto this easy ramp.

Meanwhile, here appeared to be only one way up the line — straight up its guts. We could traverse in a third of the way up, but from that moment on you would be over the 300-foot ice wall. If anything went wrong, even a small slide would flush us over the bench. There was nothing we could do to stop from sliding off the ice wall at the bottom.

The next morning, however, we could see snow warmed by the sun threatening the line, and decided to postpone it, instead skinning up nearby Mount Butters (10,299 feet). From here, our vantage directly onto the line revealed just how serious and wild Moby Dick would be to ski. It was tough to see the benches or safe spots — if there were any — where you could rest and regroup on your way down if anything went wrong.

That afternoon, we geared up and headed towards Moby Dick. As we got closer, the bench above the ice wall looked wider — chances were, if you fell and started sliding, you could maybe self-arrest on this ledge before plummeting off the ice cliff.

The more I unpacked it, the more I realized that the reason for my timidness in the mountains was because my fear of death was overriding my living of life. Before my accident, I'd been happy in my contract with risk; I was okay with dying because it felt like such a faint possibility. I knew then that I walked the fine line, but I felt like my decision-making, self-knowledge, and mountain sense were enough to keep death at bay. But I now knew that this was a joke — a lie I had told myself. Having survived something that should have killed me, I understood the seriousness of the Adventurer's Pact even more. And I struggled with whether I was willing to make the pact again. Death is so final — were these fleeting moments worth it? The finality of it all — how extremely close I had come to ending this magical life — was too raw and real. The only way through, really, was to cultivate acceptance: a "whatever happens, happens" mindset. I figured that if we analyzed our motives as well as the snowpack, and made the appropriate decisions, then I was ready to go for it again.

The line was also out of the sun now and beginning to cool down, the wet snow firming up and stabilizing. At the base of the face, I uncoiled the rope off my shoulders, belaying Mark while he crossed the bergschrund — the crack in the ice where the lower glacier meets the mountain. After he was safely thirty feet away, I tied in and followed him. The others got ready for their crossing.

By this point, if we were to slide uncontrollably, we would fall off the monster ice cliff, so there was no room for error. Mark held nothing back on this ascent. Plunging his axe and kicking his steps in, he stomped his way to the top, skies lashed to his backpack. For a brief 100-foot interlude, I set the track to feel the true exposure of the place. My thoughts centered on the massive difference between following a bootpack and setting one. As the second, all decisions have already been made, the hazards analyzed — it's an easier role, less worrisome. But once I stepped out in front, the massive seracs below somehow grew bigger, the slope steeper, the air thinner. Everything was more real, more frightening. Looking around, knowing the true consequences of a mistake, I froze in place, feigning crampon issues while I fought to calm myself. As I tightened the straps, I went back through all our decisions to be in this spot: it all made sense. We knew our strengths and how to offset each other's weaknesses, and we'd all agreed that we should be here.

Up near the top, we stopped to survey the final 200-foot bootpack/rock scramble — and I realized I didn't have it in me. (Now I wish I had — sometimes you only get one shot at the great lines.) Mark worked up the ridge a bit higher to get a good ski cut into the slope. By then, it was already 4:30 p.m., and we had exposed ourselves enough. We were ready for a great ski back to camp. Mark carved his first turn powerfully on the fifty-degree slope. He made it look effortless; the snow barely sloughed, and he was off, calmly carving his way down. Not having a strong jump turn, I eked my way down with some tentative turns for the first 300 feet. Then, when the slope eased back to a more comfortable 45 degrees, linked nice turns in a wild spot. The skis flowed effortlessly as we slid down Moby Dick. Many cheers followed as we gazed back up at our line — we'd never heard of anyone linking turns down this beauty, but now we all had. We thanked Mark profusely for his stairway to the top.

The next day was blue skies and perfect but getting warm, so we opted to circumnavigate Mount Pequod, a short, three-mile ski tour. It started off directly above camp with some glacial touring, a bergschrund crossing on a fifteen-foot snow bridge across the abyss, and then a steep bootpack to a high col. When we reached the bergschrund, I had it in mind to bootpack across, but Mark deemed it skinnable. The argument was that, with skis on, more weight is distributed, with less potential of falling through. That has always made sense to me, but my skins were already off and I was tied into a rope anyway.

Mark went first, followed by the rest of the gang. Darek kept the rope tight as I climbed across the bridge in my ski boots. I scampered above their skin track, and then decided to step down and use their trail. I placed one foot in their track, brought my other foot in, and weighted it. In an instant, I was falling into the bergschrund, the entire snow bridge falling with me. In no time, I had weighted the rope and was standing on the bottom, twelve feet lower than where I'd started. I walked out sheepishly, looked at the crew on the uphill side of the 'schrund above, and muttered, "All good, boys."

This moment had probably been the biggest re-learn for me. Obviously, there are hazards in the mountains and times when you have to risk it. But before those times, you must ask yourself: Have I gone through the right protocols? Do I have a good understanding of the snowpack? Are we using the appropriate tools to make this situation as safe as possible? Have I skied similar smaller lines? Is the group well balanced and in agreement? If you can answer yes to all of these, then by all means proceed — but remain cautious and follow all safety precautions, and maybe even say a little prayer to the mountain gods as you go.

Chapter Twenty

"ELECTRIC GREG" AND THE SEARCH FOR SUSTAINABILITY

"It was time to live more in tune with my values and be better."
— Excerpt from letters to my family

As you might recall, during my convalescence on the couch, I'd begun to think about how I could help the planet, instead of just using its resources to satisfy my bottomless thirst for adventure. For years — going back to my tree-planting days — I'd been having a recurring dream. This dream has taken many forms, but it always centers on the world descending into chaos. Sometimes it's a world war, sometimes zombies, and sometimes gang violence — whatever the case, the world feels like it's spinning out of control. But then in the dream, for whatever reason, I seem to know the answer to the dilemma, and I want to save as many people as possible.

Usually, this involves trying to convince everyone to follow me and that I know how escape the zombies or reach some safe location away from the gangs. I run from one alleyway to the next in rubble-strewn cities, urging people to follow me somewhere better. But it's almost always impossible to convince them. No matter how hard I try and how much my theories make sense,

I can never change the storyline. Perhaps this is a view into my insecurities around wanting to be a leader but not feeling like I'm good at it. Or maybe it's my perspective on the climate crisis and how I know we need to convince people to take action, even when they don't want to.

Change is a constant — nothing ever stays the same — yet the changes I was seeing in the mountains were beginning to feel more drastic than one would expect to see in a short human lifetime. For twenty years, I had been ski-touring up and onto the Illecillewaet Glacier in Rogers Pass. The first time I skinned up onto the glacier, I sat on a rock bluff, eating trail mix and looking up at the ice. The toe of the glacier was just feet away, and from there the ice rose steeply, blue ice peeking out of the deep crevasses that bisected the slope. The scene was intimidating. As we climbed, we would put our harnesses on and tie into ropes to err on the side of safety should we misstep over a crevasse.

The Illecillewaet is the longest-studied glacier in North America, dating back to when a brother-and-sister duo, William and Mary Vaux, began studying it in 1877. Mary was aghast at the speed of recession and began to take pictures and document the drastic change. Fast-forward to 2000, when I began skiing up the glacier, which had receded uphill by 4,000 vertical feet since measurements first began nearly 130 years earlier. This doesn't even account for the depth of glacial ice that had disappeared — as a glacier shrinks horizontally, it also shrinks vertically. I wish glaciers screamed as they shrank, because perhaps we would listen and change our ways more quickly. Instead, they drip and drip and drip away quietly.

In the sixteen years that I had been walking up and onto this glacier, those drips had pulled it farther up the slope, yet without surveying the markers it was difficult to understand the change. I just knew that when I sat on the same rock where I had eaten my trail mix, the ice no longer towered over us but just vanished up the mountain, more distant than ever.

Thinking about my legacy, it was becoming harder and harder to accept the fact that my carbon footprint was so extreme, that my flying back and forth across the globe for my professional ski career was contributing to these drastic changes visible right in front of my nose. I began to wonder how big my carbon footprint really was. Mother Nature had given me so much — the otherworldly skiing, the breathtaking sunrises from remote, snow-clad summits, the peace and harmony I got from forest bathing — and now I wanted to help her. Perhaps, just like in my dream, no one would listen Still, I needed to at least try. There was no way I could say, "Let's change policy; let's change our practices," if I wasn't doing so myself. I could only speak from an authentic place. I didn't want to be some social-media influencer boasting about his reusable water bottle all while he flew internationally to go skiing. I wanted to change my life, and to set an example for others.

In December 2016, I took the first and biggest step: I opened the University of California, Berkeley's online carbon-footprint calculator. It exposed just how carbon intensive my adventures were — you cannot change when you don't first know where your problems lie.

Each year, my house released 1.67 metric tons of CO_2, my truck off-gassed 8.7 tons, my flights totaled 9.35 tons, and my overall my footprint was 21 tons of CO_2. I would actually say it was way over 21 tons — because I could not add in the snowmobile, which blasted black fumes across the snow as it warmed up before I took it up skiing in my favorite, local giant-cedar groves. Or the helicopters I flew in while guiding heli-skiing. I'd drive my large diesel truck solo for hours to forest-bathe, all the while expelling black clouds. And then there was my jet-setting lifestyle. Massive changes needed to happen.

Looking at the calculator, I could see places where I might pick my battles — little wins that could start adding up.

In 2010, my brother Graham had spoken at a TED conference about weekday vegetarianism and its benefits for health and the planet. Weekday vegetarianism is exactly what it sounds like: you eat meat only on the weekends. With just this small change, you can decrease your carbon footprint by several tons. After Graham's talk, I loved feeding him meat on weekdays just to mess with his commitment. In any case, the commitment could be flexible. Overall, if you were 50 percent vegetarian, that was a considerable change. So, in January 2017, I committed myself and my family to weekday vegetarianism. Since I am the main chef in the house, they had no real choice!

This seemed like a little, easy change, but it ended up being more complicated than I would have wished. It is simple to substitute in tofu for meat, but who wants to eat tofu all the time? No one! Fortunately, finding vegetarian recipes online is easy, and there are endless options — I simply had to be open to new ideas, like going with certain culinary nationalities like Mexican food, which has great protein through all the beans. Meanwhile, we also had to maintain a balanced diet, ensuring the right amount of iron and other essentials. We slowly got into the flow of vegetarian weekdays, and then exciting, meat-filled weekends, no longer taking our omnivore meals for granted.

I also began to research the impacts of eating meat, learning that there is a h erarchy of meats by environmental impact. Lamb is the worst, which was fine, since to me lamb tastes and smells gross. Beef has the second-highest impact, thanks to the vast amount of land cows need to feed, the water to grow their food, and the methane emitted from their digestion. Still, I do love a nice steak, and making beef a special meal made me enjoy those tasty bites even more. Simply choosing chicken tacos instead of beef tacos was a large change we could make as well, as chicken has the smallest impact of all the meats: one-tenth the footprint of beef.

Many small changes can amount to a big impact, and simply ordering a chicken burger instead of a beef burger has an effect, as does getting two bean tacos and one beef taco, instead of three beef tacos. These small, everyday choices add up. Once I began this journey, it was easy to get down on myself when I was not following my new rules. There I was aiming to be better, a sentiment I had publicly expressed this through social media, where I wrote: "This resolution of mine is not a New Year's resolution, though it is starting now. It is a life resolution. For a long time now, I have felt guilty about my self-pleasing search for adventures. Sure, they fulfill me and challenge me in so many ways, but do they do any good for anyone else? Do they need to do any good for anyone else? Life is a selfish adventure, one that is spent in one's mind with one's opinions. But if our actions affect others, then we should recognize their effects, and, if negative, change them."

I went on to write that I'd been complacent, letting the cynic in me say it was up to the big companies and government to implement restrictions and changes. Yet, when I was enjoying a tasty burger at the ski hill on a Tuesday, it was easy to feel like a fraud. So I consoled myself with the idea that any effort at all could be part of the solution. Humans, after all, aren't perfect, and the imperfect efforts of billions can add up to a net positive.

Next, I started looking at my truck-and-sled combo. At the time, Tesla was gaining notoriety, but their cars were just for the rich. For the average person like me, there were no real options. The Nissan Leaf went about 100 miles on a charge, but that was the only other available option. Then, finally, Chevrolet came out with the Bolt, which could go 220 miles on a charge — the same distance as a Tesla. I immediately ordered one, and couldn't wait to start adventuring electrically.

As a professional adventurer, I knew I needed to please my sponsors, but was there a way I could make changes to how I travelled and skied while also honoring my contracts? I hoped so, because my body could no longer do what it once had in my younger years, meaning I needed to find new ways to create stories that inspired people. Was there enough depth in the story of me reducing my carbon footprint to keep my sponsors happy?

In April 2012, I'd given myself the goal of biking to all my summits, which meant lots of long days and local skiing around Revelstoke. With that, I'd shown that you can use carbon-friendly transport and still do adventurous things. Yet the feat was really difficult, and often my partners would drive out to meet me at the trailhead anyway, not wanting to add an extra hour of biking to an already-long day. Often there was a spare seat for me — had I wanted it. So, I knew that whatever new adventure I set out on, it had to be easy enough for the average human. We will not change unless change is easy — and relatable!

I figured I needed to prove that electric cars were not just for commuting but could also support your dream life. Thus was born the idea of "electric adventures." First, I sold my massive diesel truck for a pittance — I'd kicked the shit out of it for years, and it was probably far below Blue Book. Then, I lent my snowmobile to my sister Jesse and waited for my Bolt to arrive.

However, life doesn't always happen as planned, and the car, I was told, was delayed until July 2017. I couldn't believe it: I was ready to prove that electric cars worked, and now I couldn't even get my hands on one!

My friend and fellow backcountry skier Chris Rubens and I had been down the environmental-guilt vortex together, and we pitched Salomon on a movie about two professional skiers changing their ways and adventuring locally. Salomon was keen, and we settled on filming a local ski traverse we would access with the minimum possible carbon footprint. The traverse, however, was a total fail: I got sick at the start and spent three days in a haze of diarrhea with zero energy, never trusting a fart or being able to enjoy the skiing. Ten days later, we skied back to Revelstoke with very little footage and a weak story.

On the upside, our ideas continued to evolve, and I found a place in Vancouver where we could rent a Nissan Leaf, the E-car with the 100-mile range. We wanted to prove that electric adventures were possible; we all just had to change our mindsets. Meanwhile, there was finally a charging infrastructure down the West Coast of the United States, so we mapped out an audacious plan: we would drive along the seaboard, charging our car and attempting to ski each of the volcanoes — mounts Baker, Rainier, Hood, St. Helens, Adams, Jefferson, and Shasta, as well as a few others — as we made our way south from the Canadian border.

I rented the car from a charismatic Quebecois who was excited about our idea, though he probably didn't fully understand how far we were taking his car. Our first volcano would be Mount Baker, in Washington State. The Leaf was so silent and exciting to operate. It wasn't particularly zippy, but the quiet feeling of electric driving was new and pleasurable.

After about sixty miles, I opened an app called Plug and Share, using it to find my first car charger. Man, was it exciting! The charger wasn't some grimy gas station but instead a clean, futuristic-looking electrical unit outside a grocery store that sold locally grown fruit and vegetables.

Before the trip, I'd started accounts with various electric-car-charging companies and had some payment cards from those. BC Hydro owned this station, whose electricity was coming from the methane released by cow dung. How incredible was that! How environmentally efficient to take a waste gas and turn it into electricity! I was filled with a sense of possibility — this was better for the world! Still, the real question remained: Could I — or anyone — truly live the adventurous life out of an electric car?

We zipped across the border, fueled by cow farts. Arc'teryx was hosting a team climb and shred of Mount Baker, which was a perfect start to our trip — a new summit and the beginning of a great adventure. Although Chris was a Salomon athlete, his charisma (and my pull) allowed him to join. After summiting and skiing down Baker, Chris and I pointed the car toward Mount Rainier, using a slow charger on route that had us hanging out at a campground for five hours, testing our patience with this whole electric-vehicle thing. Throughout our trip, the app continued to direct us to chargers, and we had to trust the mileage guess-o-meter. We laughed nervously as the car's range said fifteen miles, while the charger was ten miles away. Somehow the app was always correct, and we began to trust it. At the charging stations, we'd use the downtime constructively, working, reading, relaxing, and even going for runs.

This was a major switch in mentality, from our usual way of going from point A to point B as quickly as possible. Now we had to approach travel in a more relaxed manner, driving slowly to maximize battery power and spending time relaxing at charging stations. Often life is so busy that we want to rush between places, to get shit done. Instead, Chris and I switched our mindset — we really had no choice.

A friend and Arc'teryx teammate, Michelle Parker, met us up at Paradise on Rainier, and the three of us toured up for a few hours and camped below the Fuhrer Finger, one of the more direct routes to the summit, with a long slope canted at 45 degrees — the "finger," which makes for great skiing. We awoke early and bootpacked and skinned to our second electric summit. An excellent descent followed, during which we skied 8,000 feet to the car. In the Rainier lot, I looked at the hundred or so cars parked there; I imagined them all as electric cars, and I could see the impact this would have, in the same way that weekday vegetarianism had. With the growing infrastructure, this parking lot might someday be full of EVs. We jumped into the Nissan Leaf with a minimal charge and coasted downhill, hoping for enough regeneration to get us back to that campground/charging station sixty miles away. The 5,000 feet of descent from Paradise back to sea level easily gave us the range. Watching our car slow-charge again at the campground, we decided to name it. The license plate said DA0 528 — so we called her "Dao."

After ticking Mount Hood, we had a giant leap between Oregon and California — ninety-three miles, with severe mountain passes to climb. We drove conservatively, hypermiling, going 50 mph max; where we could, we'd draft behind big transport trucks, letting their girth block the wind, eventually rolling into Shasta with a little electricity to spare.

From then on, we knew we could do this. We managed a total of six volcanoes, drove Dao deep up dirt roads, fixed punctured tires, and pushed the little car's potential. We grew so attached to her that we drove a day out of our way to show her the Pacific Ocean (slightly pointless, since she was from the oceanside city of Vancouver!). Finally, we rolled back into Vancouver, having driven 2,500 miles charge by hard-earned charge.

Thinking back to how change must be easy, this trip had definitely not been that. It worked because Chris and I got along well and enjoyed traveling in unusual ways — and didn't mind redlining it between charging stations. But I couldn't imagine the typical person enjoying what we'd done. The charging infrastructure needed to grow, and we all needed to shift our mindset away from speed and convenience. If someone's life was super busy and they needed to get to places in short order, then this wouldn't work.

In the meantime, my friend Jordan Manley had put together a film called The Curve of Time about Chris and my ski traverse and the volcano trip. The film played at the Banff Mountain Film Festival, and Chris and I had a blast showing it off and giving folks a glimpse into electric adventures, helping stimulate

Scan the QR code to see a video of Greg in action!

conversation about adventure travel and its impacts. In February 2018, Chris and I journeyed to Denver — this time via a silver Tesla Model S we rented in Calgary through Turo — to present the film to a room of 2,000 people, and we soon found ourselves also doing events with POW Canada. I also pushed my sponsors to put more thought — and tangible effort — into their actions, their gear, and their messaging to customers around climate and environmental impact. The writing was clearly on the wall for the outdoor industry, and I was happy to help catalyze a change that had come to mean so much to me.

As the time approached to get my Chevrolet Bolt, I started to develop a story idea for my sponsors. The idea was to challenge myself to do 100 different summits, all with fossil-fuel-free access — driving electrically, hiking, and/or biking — to the trailheads, proving both the merits and accessibility of carbon-friendly adventuring.

However, I knew I was also being a bit of a hypocrite — most of my clothing was made from fossil fuels, and many of the car's components were created with petrol, not to mention that the electricity for charging stations often comes from coal-fired power plants. I also knew that the lithium batteries were heavy and not super efficient (yet), plus there were the environmental impacts of lithium mining and the child labor sometimes used in cobalt mines. This solution wasn't perfect, but it was better.

However, some good news, at least in British Columbia, was that 97 percent of the electricity comes from renewable sources — primarily hydroelectricity. Perched above my house in Revelstoke is a dam that creates enough power to run 800,000 households! I could just imagine driving to the trailhead electrically, and then the snow that I skied on melting and running down the rivers to power the turbines that generated electricity for my Bolt. The loop was as closed as it could be.

I picked up my Bolt in July 2017 and was instantly in love, vibrating with excitement as I drove away from the dealership. The thing was so zippy: I could pass anyone at any time, and quietly too. My first electric summits were thrilling — I could now access the mountains cleanly and silently, leaving only tracks in the snow, not air pollution. My partners were curious about the Bolt when I'd pick them up, too, sparking conversations about how we might all help our warming planet.

Naturally, I had some haters online, people who adored pointing out the negative aspects of EVs and launching ad hominem attacks. Yet I always felt like I approached my efforts acknowledging that I was not being perfect, but simply trying to be better. It's amazing how people are so fearful of change, and I know of no other way to help people get over their fears than by showing them — most people don't know what they can do until they see it being done.

At the time, the nonprofit Protect Our Winters (POW) was crushing the outdoor scene. Started by the famous snowboarder Jeremy Jones, POW harnessed the voice of the outdoor community to advocate for policy that addresses climate change. POW was getting lots of traction in the United States and some European countries, but had no chapters in Canada. I reached out to them to see about changing this, working with a lawyer to navigate the ins and outs of running a nonprofit; however, all the red tape, political nuances of forming and running a board, and logistical tangles weren't for me. Paperwork — ugh! I have a great voice and can speak on stage and inspire people, but this was not my wheelhouse. So I was thrilled when a man named Dave Erb — to whom I gladly handed off everything I'd compiled — contacted me saying he also wanted to start Protect Our Winters Canada.

This freed up my time again to keep working on the electric summits. Some of the summits were small, easy ones, like Mount Maxwell on Salt Spring Island, just off the coast. I drove to the ocean, ran up a trail for 1.5 hours, and summitted a new electric peak.

Others were closer to home. I had never tried a summer speed ascent of Revelstoke's iconic Mount Begbie. I drove my Bolt to the trailhead and ran up the 7,100 feet of gain, with some airy climbing across a ledge and a fun ridge ramble to the top. I was climbing through a sea of smoke from all the summer fires but still managed to summit in 2:12, film a little "what's up" video, and then run back to my car in 3:35, a new fastest known time for the summer round-trip. (I still hold the winter record of 2:55 from my two-million-foot year.) It was exciting to know that I could still be on the cutting edge of adventure, even after my accident, yet also while pushing sustainability. I also pushed my little Bolt deep up a rough logging road to access the Bugaboos, Canada's iconic alpine spires, making the first "fossil-fuel-free" ascents of these technical granite peaks famed worldwide for their endless cracks and perfect stone. Well, fossil-fuel-free since the time of the first ascensionists, who in 1916 rode in on horseback and bushwhacked up into the alpine!

Eventually, I summited my first 100 summits electrically, my efforts documented in a 2019 movie called "Electric Greg," made by Anthony Bonello and Switchback Entertainment, and which I hoped would help fellow-adventurers see the potential in electric cars. I also hoped to impart some learning to my children, who watched me climb and even joined me on some of these summits. On Uto Peak (9,603 feet), where Aiden dug deep to climb its vertiginous slopes, I hoped he understood the standard I was trying to set. And as Charley joined me on Mount McCrea (5,033 feet), one of my last summits in this challenge, we hugged on top and looked out at this beautiful world, even as I hoped that she understood and would be part of the changes we need to see.

Since this is such a battle against unseen forces, it can be tough to stay focused — you never know if your actions are having any effect. But the lack of action globally is becoming more and more evident. One of my 100 summits was Mount Athabasca, in the Canadian Rockies.

As friends and I skinned our way toward this challenge on May 26, 2019, we started passing by markers. Starting from the marker for the year 1975, the glacier had receded 1.2 miles. There were many markers, but I was most interested in the ones after 1975 — the ones placed during my lifetime. At the 2006 marker, I had a big realization: that year was the last time I had been on this glacier, and I'd stood elevated on ice where now there were only glacially eroded rocks. Aiden had been born in 2006 as well, and during my son's short life so far, the ice had receded so much — 250 feet horizontally — that I almost couldn't see it. If such rapid recession had happened in the 10 years that Aiden had been alive, what would happen in the span of my children's remaining years? The thought terrified me.

Climate anxiety is growing for many of us, with summers filled with smoke, natural disasters almost a constant occurrence, and a bombardment of negative climate news rolling by on the chyron. The summer I wrote this book, 2023, British Columbia was on fire — hundreds of houses burned, and many people's lives were ruined. It is hard for me to not be scared about the future — both my children's and all of mankind's. If you dwell too long on these stories, it can become hard to breathe, the mental loop of fear overpowering hope. For me, action has always been the cure for anxiety; it's how I've overcome my personal panic and the self-questioning that began as a kid. I try to apply the same approach with climate change, and so am always exploring different ways to lighten my footprint and hence my fear. The key has been to take an approach of progress over perfection, which helps me not get mad at myself when I take a flight or get a single-use coffee cup.

During COVID, while we were all locked down, I started freaking out about food security. Our global food-supply system is quite fragile, a fact that becomes very obvious in our mountain town of Revelstoke — when the highway closes for even three days, the shelves empty out in our grocery stores. While most of us Revelstokians probably have enough food at home for a month, we aren't really prepared for more than that. Within a few days of the COVID clampdown, I drove to our hardware store and bought soil and compost to expand my gardens. Only 2 percent of the food eaten in Revelstoke is grown within a 100-mile radius, so I could only imagine what would happen if society broke down. We would be screwed. Knowing that to survive we would need to come together as a community, I started calling folks around town, trying to find solutions. Looking in my backyard at the golf course, I wanted to start tilling the entire eighteen holes of grass to grow mad amounts of food.

Chris and I built greenhouses for ourselves and also helped build a few for others. I was so stressed about food security that

I brought in 300 truckloads of soil at a group discount to help people expand their gardens. A friend and I started a Facebook growing page, to help share tips and tricks on how to best grow food in Revelstoke. I was prepping our town to be more resilient. I know it sounds paranoid, but COVID shook the foundations of society and, like so many of us, I wasn't sure what would happen next.

Luckily for us, society did not break down. Yet the whole COVID experience did make me want to be more self-sufficient. There are so many things we can do as individuals to lighten our draw. On top of working my planting beds and building a greenhouse, eating more vegetarian meals, driving electrically, and flying less, I also started to investigate the impacts of my house.

My house was built in 1974 and is a thin-walled, poorly insulated bungalow. Fortunately, Canada had created a "greener homes" grant that encouraged me to move forward on some ideas — essentially, there was $5,000 waiting for me if I made my house less energy intensive. First, an energy consultant came over and examined the insulation; she also attached a large fan to my front door and then suctioned my house to see where all the heat was escaping, and then offered tips on addressing the leakage.

Fortunately, I am handy and was able to do a lot of the grunt work involved. I spent hours crawling around my claustrophobic attic, pinned between roof and rafters, stapling cardboard to the rafters to allow air to circulate. Then I hired a company to blow insulation into the roof, where some 25 percent of our heat was leaking out via the ceilings. Finally, I replaced all my windows with triple-paned glass.

I spent a few days covered in dust peeling the stucco off my home's exterior, then I wrapped it all in three inches of spun-rock fiber, a fireproof, dampproof, and soundproof insulation that felt like wrapping my house in a nice wool sweater.

Finally, I bought $15,000 worth of solar panels and started creating my own electricity, which honestly is one of the coolest things — knowing that the sun is powering my appliances and that, some years from now, the panels will have paid for themselves and our electricity will be "free." From May through November of 2023, I created all the energy my home used. I wasn't charging my car at home because a nearby fast charger was free, and I could drive over, plug in, walk home, and then go back in an hour — free refills all summer!

I also built a chicken coop, which we used to raise five egg-laying hens. I loved the breakfasts of eggs, potatoes, onions, carrots, tomatoes, and peppers all from our yard. It was such a fulfilling meal. Yet eventually the chickens made too much noise and stank a lot, which disturbed me as well as my neighbors. I came to realize that we only ate four eggs a week but were harvesting twenty. Sadly, after two years, I gave the birds away because this was not a realistic option for us.

This stuff is neither sexy nor cool, but it's needed. I think more to the point is that we each take responsibility for our impacts, lowering them where we can and offsetting where we can't.

Climate change is a worldwide problem, but those of us in the first world, who have more means, should focus those means on reducing our impact. On Chris and my first electric adventure through the USA, we drove through lots of towns where it looked like the average person was just trying to survive, paycheck to paycheck. These people do not have the time or money to learn and care about climate change, or to be able to do much. Their struggle is real. This means that those of us who are better off need to push the needle. Our planet and its ecosystems are fragile, and the more we can do as individuals to lighten our carbon loads, the better.

In my presentations around carbon-footprint reduction, I use a cartoon to illustrate an idea. Two kids are sitting on their grandfather's lap. They all wear gas masks, with the kids peering through the glass at their grandfather. It's an idyllic, Norman Rockwell–type scene . . . except for the gas masks.

One kid asks, "Granddad, what did you do during the climate war?"

Scan the QR code to see a video of Greg in action!

I hope that someday when my grandkids ask me that question, I'll be able to give an answer I can live with. Something along the lines of: "I did the best I could, and worked toward a better future for you."

Chapter Twenty-One

THE TRUTH

"I could die at any moment . . ."
— Excerpt from letters to my family

If you are reading this, I guess I have fucked up — yet again. I've tried to not mess up, but I also have a completely uncontainable energy that sometimes clouds my judgment, as proven repeatedly during my life.

I am trying to imagine that these last words in this book will be like the last words I'll gasp before I slip away. As if I were lying in the snow, broken, the light fading from my eyes, my final moments on Earth.

Living has been the weirdest, wildest journey. From birth till now has been an absolute trip. I tried to live true to myself. I know that at times I hurt others and that I made huge mistakes, but damn, it's impossible to be perfect.

I am so terribly afraid of admitting failure and weakness that it holds me back from connecting more deeply with those I love. This emotionally removed state is beneficial in the mountains — letting me make calm, collected decisions — but down in the valley it has, I fear, kept me from making real connections with you all (Tracey and the kids). And it has, at times, driven me into obsessive, avoidant behavior, like smoking way too much weed — a lifelong vice I have yet to give up — and immersing myself to a psychotic degree in that damn Clash of Clans video game, which I eventually had to delete from my phone!

"I could die at any moment" is absolutely true of my high-risk life, but it's also true for everyone. It's really how we all should live — as if every day were our last. Living knowing that what we are doing today could be our legacy. In this way we need to live better, be better, and do better, because it's how we will be remembered if we die tomorrow.

Life is a raw, harsh, and beautiful reality. I have never been able to believe any being was sentient enough to create this wonderful world. Yet imagining that it all began as a random explosion is equally as challenging. The god particle to me is simply a magical particle that created life. Nothing really makes sense, yet what we have here — our senses, our feelings, our thoughts, the land we walk on, the mountains we play in — is full of wonder. None of this should exist, and yet it does.

There is no right or wrong path in life — life fills us all with wonder in different ways, be it music, skiing, climbing, dancing, playing games, and so on. All I know is that you should find something that leaves you in a constant state of marvel, whatever that thing is.

I look at you, Charley, and I am blown away by the incredible person you have become. The happy, confident girl who is continuously planning some scheme, whose skills and competence on the trampoline have brought many successes.

Who at age sixteen was prepared to travel solo across Europe to visit your cousin. Your demeanor is so calm and confident. Thanks for all those hugs — I love you to the end of the world and back.

Aiden, watching you grow more and more into yourself has been so fulfilling. I saw just who you were becoming as you and I climbed the final pitches of Mount Sir Donald, having passed multiple groups during our efficient day out, or the calmness and confidence I see in you as you pull through the cruxes on the steep rock climbs we've been trying together. I see the strength of character and the wildman who lives within you. I embrace every moment we've had together and love you to the depths of my soul.

Both of you, always be a little wary of every situation — the world is beautiful, but it's also harsh. In the mountains and in life there are dark sides: look out for them and be prepared.

Tracey, thank you for your incredible support over the years — I don't believe I deserved someone like you. I apologize for being so wild and unconstrained. I hope all the benefits of hanging out with me have outweighed my mistakes and the worry I've surely shouldered you with. I am sorry I wasn't always as warm or open as I could have been; sadly, one major reason was I worried that if we got too tight and then I died, the loss would be harder on you. It's also possible that my addiction to weed kept a barrier between us. I am so sorry for all of that. Regardless, you are the only woman I have ever said "I love you" to, and I cherish all our years together.

To the rest of you, family, friends, acquaintances, I hope you know that I support you in everything you do and hope that the moments we had together were worthwhile for both of us. Continue to be awesome — and get off your phones and get outside!

Know that for me, it was all worth it — every moment, from the deep breaths of cold mountain air to my heart hammering against my rib cage on an especially strenuous skin up, to the sun heating my face and calming my mind on an exposed ridgeline. In my most efficient moments, everything entered a flow state and life was simple — I was at my very happiest, without anxiety, without regret.

So, Tracey, Charley, and Aiden, let's end back where we began: "I am sorry, absolutely heart-stoppingly sorry." My death — as all of ours someday will be — was inevitable, and we need to accept this fact and free ourselves to live life as it comes and as it most fulfills us. The end scares me more than anything — I love this life, but I also understand that it can't go on forever. Nothing ever does, even — or especially — a life as singular and wild as my own.

Appendix

TIMELINE AND LIFE ACHIEVEMENTS

1975: Born December 19, 1975

1995: Started backcountry skiing

2003: Pioneered the Northern Monashee Ski Traverse, a 21-day, 21-summit adventure

2004: Backcountry-skied 30,000 feet in 15 hours

2005: Backcountry-skied 40,000 feet in 20 hours

Climbed and skied 1 million feet in a single season

2006: Set a record of 50,000 feet ski-toured in 24 hours

2010: Climbed and skied 2 million vertical feet in North America and South America, summiting 71 different mountains

2012: Attempted Mount Manaslu (8,163 meters), the eighth-highest mountain in the world

First responder on avalanche that buried 30 people, 11 of whom perished

2014: Climbed and skied 330,000 vertical feet in a month

Survived an avalanche in Pakistan

2017: Started on a quest to adventure sustainably

2021: FKT Rogers Pass to Bugaboos — 140-kilometer ski traverse in 52.25 hours

2022: Spearhead Traverse — 16 summits in 19 hours

2024: Finally finished this book!

Scan the QR code to access ALL of Greg's videos!

ACKNOWLEDGEMENTS

First off, let me apologize.

I am sorry if you didn't make my story; it doesn't mean you were not important to me. Throughout our lives, we are developed by the multitude of different people we meet along the way. I couldn't include everyone in my memoir because my focus was on risks and my reasons for taking these risks. So many other relationships were important in developing me into who I am, and I appreciate all of those.

If I included you and you were not happy with the way I depicted you, or if you feel like I misrepresented you, then I am sorry. There are at least three sides to every story: life through my lens, life through your lens, and the story untainted by our perspectives.

I want to thank everyone for being a part of this wild journey. We are incredibly lucky to live and breathe and share experiences, positive or negative. It was great to know all of you.

Lastly, thank you to everyone at Di Angelo Publications; this could not have happened without every single one of you. Thank you for helping me craft my story, and for publishing it in the best possible way.

About the Author

GREG HILL

The pro skier, filmmaker, and ski guide Greg Hill found ski mountaineering as a teenager; he was hooked and hasn't stopped since. A father to two teenagers and a husband to his amazing wife, Tracey, Greg lives with his family in the small mountain community of Revelstoke, deep in the mountains of British Columbia, Canada. Backcountry skiing is where Greg found his passion and wonder, which drove him to summit more than 200 mountains around the world. Greg has pioneered hundreds of first descents and set records like climbing and skiing over 2 million feet in less than a year, and 50,000 feet in 24 hours. But Greg's biggest recent objectives are found in his everyday quest to adventure in a more sustainable fashion. Fueled by fortitude rather than recognition and fame, Greg challenges himself and us all to leave the planet in better shape than we found it.

About the Publisher

DAP BOOKS
DI ANGELO PUBLICATIONS

CATHARSIS

Di Angelo Publications was founded in 2008 by Sequoia Schmidt—at the age of seventeen. The modernized publishing firm's creative headquarters is in Los Angeles, California, with its distribution center located in Twin Falls, Idaho. In 2020, Di Angelo Publications made a conscious decision to move all printing and production for domestic distribution of its books to the United States. The firm is comprised of eleven imprints, and the featured imprint, Catharsis, was inspired by Schmidt's love of extreme sports, travel, and adventure stories.

Printed in the USA
CPSIA information can be obtained
at www.ICGtesting.com
JSHW080327310824
69094JS00001B/1

9 781955 690591